Thinking about Thinking

VERITAS
Series Introduction

"... the truth will set you free" (John 8:32)

In much contemporary discourse, Pilate's question has been taken to mark the absolute boundary of human thought. Beyond this boundary, it is often suggested, is an intellectual hinterland into which we must not venture. This terrain is an agnosticism of thought: because truth cannot be possessed, it must not be spoken. Thus, it is argued that the defenders of "truth" in our day are often traffickers in ideology, merchants of counterfeits, or anti-liberal. They are, because it is somewhat taken for granted that Nietzsche's word is final: truth is the domain of tyranny.

Is this indeed the case, or might another vision of truth offer itself? The ancient Greeks named the love of wisdom as *philia*, or friendship. The one who would become wise, they argued, would be a "friend of truth." For both philosophy and theology might be conceived as schools in the friendship of truth, as a kind of relation. For like friendship, truth is as much discovered as it is made. If truth is then so elusive, if its domain is *terra incognita*, perhaps this is because it arrives to us—unannounced—as gift, as a person, and not some thing.

The aim of the Veritas book series is to publish incisive and original current scholarly work that inhabits "the between" and "the beyond" of theology and philosophy. These volumes will all share a common aspiration to transcend the institutional divorce in which these two disciplines often find themselves, and to engage questions of pressing concern to both philosophers and theologians in such a way as to reinvigorate both disciplines with a kind of interdisciplinary desire, often so absent in contemporary academe. In a word, these volumes represent collective efforts in the befriending of truth, doing so beyond the simulacra of pretend tolerance, the violent, yet insipid reasoning of liberalism that asks with Pilate, "What is truth?"—expecting a consensus of non-commitment; one that encourages the commodification of the mind, now sedated by the civil service of career, ministered by the frightened patrons of position.

The series will therefore consist of two "wings": (1) original monographs; and (2) essay collections on a range of topics in theology and philosophy. The latter will principally be the products of the annual conferences of the Centre of Theology and Philosophy (www.theologyphilosophycentre .co.uk).

Conor Cunningham and Eric Austin Lee, *Series editors*

Thinking about Thinking

Mind and Meaning in the Era
of Techno-Nihilism

JAMES D. MADDEN

CASCADE *Books* · Eugene, Oregon

THINKING ABOUT THINKING
Mind and Meaning in the Era of Techno-Nihilism

Veritas Series

Cascade Books
An Imprint of Wipf and Stock Publishers
199 W. 8th Ave., Suite 3
Eugene, OR 97401

www.wipfandstock.com

PAPERBACK ISBN: 978-1-6667-5418-6
HARDCOVER ISBN: 978-1-6667-5419-3
EBOOK ISBN: 978-1-6667-5420-9

Cataloguing-in-Publication data:

Names: Madden, James D., author.
Title: Thinking about thinking : mind and meaning in the era of techno-nihilism / Author Name.
Description: Eugene, OR : Cascade Books, 2023 | Series: Veritas | Includes bibliographical references and index.
Identifiers: ISBN 978-1-6667-5418-6 (paperback) | ISBN 978-1-6667-5419-3 (hardcover) | ISBN 978-1-6667-5420-9 (ebook)
Subjects: LCSH: Technology—Philosophy. | Human-machine systems—Philosophy | Nihilism (Philosophy). | Philosophy of mind. | Philosophy of mind—History.
Classification: BF38 .M35 2023 (print) | BF311 .M35 2023 (ebook)

For Paul F. Johnson, who remains my best teacher. For good or ill you got me into this, and for that I am grateful.

Philosophy . . . can breathe only when it rejects the infinitely infinite thought in order to see the world in its strangeness.

—MAURICE MERLEAU-PONTY, "MAN AND ADVERSITY"

Contents

Preface ix

Introduction: The Darkness of This Time
    and Worldly Philosophy of Mind 1

Chapter 1: Thinking Isn't Any-Thing 21

1. Can Minds Be Pictured? 21

2. Thinking beyond Picture Thinking 27

3. Mind-Brain Dualism? 41

Chapter 2: The Mind as Participation in the Spaces of Reasons,
    Embodiment, and Skills 53

1. Participation in the Space of Reasons and Material Commitment 58

2. Inheritance and Responsibility 67

3. Embodiment 71

4. The Practical Space of Skills 80

Chapter 3: Freedom, Tragedy, and Retrospection 87

1. The "Free Will" Debate 88

2. The Neuroskeptical Case against Free Will 91

3. What Are Ethically Significant Actions? 96

4. Freedom as Threefold Responsibility 104

5. The Tragic Threat to Human Freedom 110

6. Self-Consciousness and Evolutionary Psychology 116

Chapter 4: The Anxiety of Not Being a Machine 125

    1. Why Would Anyone Think Machines Can Think? 129

    2. What about Meaning? Syntax vs. Semantics 134

    3. The Chinese Room Objection 139

    4. Relevance, Care, and Authenticity 142

Chapter 5: Dignity and Meaning in the Face of Techno-Nihilism 157

    1. The Happy Paradox of Technology 163

    2. The Unhappy Paradox of Technology 172

    3. Nietzsche and Techno-Nihilism 180

    4. Shall We "Go Gently into That Good Night?" 185

Epilogue: Thinking about Eternal Thinking 191

Bibliography 197

Index 207

Preface

THIS BOOK EXISTS IN between many things and in various ways. The origin of a good bit of the material to follow was in lectures I gave to undergraduate or otherwise non-specialist audiences, while equally as much of what you are about to read draws on some technically sophisticated sources intended for academic specialists. Moreover, this book is a mélange of disparate influences that have held me under their spell at various moments over the last thirty or so years. As an undergraduate I was quite taken by Nietzsche and existential phenomenology, but then began my graduate work by writing a master's thesis on Sellars and Wittgenstein. My doctoral dissertation focused on Aristotle and Leibniz, and my first book was a treatise on Thomism and contemporary analytic philosophy of mind. As you are about see, all these figures speak out in the dialogue I conduct in this book. I realize that there is some risk incurred by producing a work of this nature, as it is likely to leave many typical readers dissatisfied while giving the impression of eclectic superficiality. Those who approach the text looking for technical philosophical arguments may find my attempts at broader cultural relevance to be distracting, just as their counterparts who are focused on the much bigger picture might be put-off by some of these technicalities. Readers who prefer their philosophizing to come from the Continent may be bored with the austerity of the analytic philosophy that will be crucial at certain junctures, while others who are more amenable with the philosophizing typical on the other side of the English Channel may be impatient with the phenomenological jargon. No doubt, many Aristotelians and Thomists will be puzzled by the proposal that they find common cause with Hegel and even Nietzsche. Academic specialists in all these areas may well find my efforts unfair to the rich peculiarities of their rightly cherished objects of meticulous scholarly concern.

Of course, I am indulging in caricatures already, but I emphasize these "risks" as they are not accidentally related to one of the central themes of this book. I am going to paint a picture of the human mind not as a substance (physical or non-physical), but as a kind of tension, between dependence and independence, passive acceptance and active responsibility, practice and theory, worldliness and transcendence; and our failure to see ourselves in this light contributes mightily to our various crises of meaning. One should not be surprised that articulating a way of *being-in-tension* requires one to draw on sources that are not entirely free of mutual unease. That being said, I believe that the incompatibility among many of these approaches and authors is often exaggerated, and I hope this book can play a role in smoothing out the landscape without distorting the essential claims of its motley cast of characters. I am willing to take the risk of appearing superficial or conveniently selective in order to gather the diverse tools necessary to provide a glimpse of ourselves in the full breadth and complexity of the proverbial "30,000-foot view." Moreover, if a few of my readers are opened to different avenues of thought they previously dismissed, then one of the aims of this book will have been met.

There is a common argumentative thread throughout the book, but the chapters can be taken on their own with relative ease. Those of you primarily interested in the philosophy of mind (the mind-body problem in particular), can get much of what you want from the first two chapters. The third chapter takes up the free-will debate (such as it is) and provides a generalized account of the requirements for responsible agency that is amenable to the findings of both neuroscience and evolutionary psychology. Readers particularly concerned about the prospects of artificial intelligence and its implications for our self-understanding might want to skip to the fourth chapter, and those who have come looking to confront Nietzsche and the nihilistic churnings of modern technological civilization will find plenty to keep themselves busy in the final chapter. In any event, one does best to take the chapters in order.

As always there are many people I need to thank, but the fallibility of memory assures that I will neglect some of them, and for that I apologize. I appreciate the vigor with which the students in my Modern European Philosophy course discussed these issues with me in the spring of 2021, and I have benefited from questions and comments from the audiences at many Thomistic Institute lectures. I have also profited by opportunities to think through these issues aloud on various podcasts, and I am especially grateful to Patrick Flynn and I. J. Makan in this regard. My colleagues Matthew Ramage, Francis Petrucelli, Andrew Salzman, and Andrew Jaeger have done yeoman's work in discussing this material with me over the last several years. Michael Ferguson is a sturdy source of encouragement who also keeps me from underestimating what can be known. Thanks are owed to McKenzie Kilkawley, who endured proofreading an early draft of the entire manuscript at a time of great inconvenience to her growing family. My wife, Jennifer Madden, has been my most valuable conversation partner throughout this process, and her insights as a psychologist and a skilled denizen of the real world have taught me more than can be contained in a thousand books. I am thankful to our children for what I have learned by watching their initiation into the fellowship of mind and for their willingness to endure my distraction by this project during the waning years of their childhood. Encountering them as equals in the space of reasons has become one of the great joys of my life. Finally, I am grateful to my friends and teammates at St. Joseph Brazilian Jiu Jitsu and Mixed Martial Arts for being in the world with me through some trying years of many of our lives. "A man alone is a beast or a god."

Introduction

The Darkness of This Time
and Worldly Philosophy of Mind

Since I know what will be
in all its particulars, no pain can surprise me.
I must bear my fate as lightly as I can;
the strength of necessity can't be contested.
Still I can neither keep silent nor speak out
about what happened. The gift I gave to mortals
has yoked me in these sad necessities:
I hunted down fire's stolen spring and hid it
in a fennel stalk, revealing it to mortals
as teacher of all arts, a great resource.
And that's the crime for which I pay the cost,
pinned here in chains beneath the open sky.

—AESCHYLUS, *PROMETHEUS BOUND*[1]

L UDWIG WITTGENSTEIN PREFACES HIS posthumously published *Philosophical Investigations* with a notorious bit of pessimism regarding the likelihood of its being understood very widely at all. Referring to the inquires to follow, Wittgenstein admits that "I make them public with misgivings. It is not impossible that it should fall to the lot of this work, in its poverty and in *the darkness of this time*, to bring light into one brain or

---

1. Aeschylus, *Prometheus Bound*, lines 106–18 (7).

1

another—but, of course, it is not likely."[2] Wittgenstein presented his youthful *Tractatus Logico-Philosophicus* with the expectation that "this book will perhaps only be understood by those who have themselves already thought the thoughts which are expressed in it—or similar thoughts,"[3] but in that earlier work the source of the author's worry is the idiosyncratic nature of the ideas he is attempting to articulate. Wittgenstein does not attribute the obscurity of the *Tractatus* to the darkness of the times during which it is to be published. When introducing the *Philosophical Investigations*, Wittgenstein again cites the "poverty" of the work itself as an obscuring factor, but, as I have emphasized, he additionally raises the specter of "the darkness of this time" as grounds for his glum expectation that the treatise to follow will fall mostly on deaf ears. Curiously, one of the canonical works of twentieth-century philosophy, if not all modern philosophy, is presumed by its very author likely to be mostly misunderstood, because the conditions of modernity, or at least modernity in its particularly twentieth-century manifestation, will somehow prevent its readers from a transparent view of what he is trying to say.

Wittgenstein does nothing in his preface explicitly to clue us in on the nature or source of this obscuring darkness, but no doubt the international affairs of the interwar and wartime years during which he wrote the notes eventually published as the *Philosophical Investigations* made fertile grounds for gloomy expectations. Nevertheless, it is hard to see why the economic desperation and international belligerence of those times would make it unlikely that even a highly educated readership would understand a philosophical treatise. The obscuring elements Wittgenstein despairs over must, therefore, not be the dire events abroad during his generation, but something more like the cultural conditions of modernity in the twentieth century itself, and we might expect these same fundamental circumstances still to frame the experience of readers of the *Philosophical Investigations* today. I am doubtful that Wittgenstein would identify our times as any better illuminated than his own. In what sense, then, does Wittgenstein believe that we are in a renewed Dark Age?

The following remarks from some of Wittgenstein's other writings provide hints as to the motives behind his pessimistic preface.

> The truly apocalyptic view of the world is that things do *not* repeat themselves. It isn't absurd, e.g., to believe that the scientific and technological age is the beginning of the end for humanity;

2. Wittgenstein, *Philosophical Investigations*, 4. Emphasis added.

3. Wittgenstein, *Tractatus Logico-Philosophicus*, 27.

that the idea of Great Progress is a bedazzlement, along with
the idea that the truth will ultimately be known; that there is
nothing good or desirable about scientific knowledge and that
humanity, in seeking it, is falling into a trap. It is by no means
obvious that this is not how things are.[4]

Men have judged that a king can make rain; we say this contradicts all experience. Today they judge that aeroplanes and the
radio, etc. are means for closer contact of peoples and the spread
of culture [and this contradicts all of my experience].[5]

These remarks, taken from *Culture and Value* and *On Certainty* respec-
tively, suggest that a sort of quiet, cultural apocalypse has gone on behind
the scenes of modernity; a bedazzlement by a simulacrum of truth has
warped our sense of what would count as authentic solidarity in much
the same way as a tyrant's primitive subjects might become so deluded by
wishful thinking as to believe that their naked emperor can control the
weather by royal fiat, contrary to all of their most obvious experiences.
In short, Wittgenstein fears that we have lost contact with the world un-
awares. Without even knowing it, we have mislaid the ability to see our
hand before our face, and he identifies the culprit as our "technological
age" that has promised us the "Great Progress." Wittgenstein's point is not
to reject technological progress or scientific knowledge as such. Rather,
he believes that our fixation on a particular conception of ourselves that
comes part and parcel with technological and scientific development
amounts to a spiritual cataclysm. In his view, the apocalypse has already
come to pass (or, at least, we are no longer in position to notice the difference), so any invitation to an inquiry availing itself of a richer self-
understanding will only fall on deaf ears. While the recovery of a more
robust or humane relationship to the world is exactly the sort of project
that Wittgenstein undertakes in the *Philosophical Investigations*, he is
convinced that those of us left behind after this technological rapture,
as it were, are quite unlikely to have a clue as to what he is even trying to
achieve, because our way of thinking is structured by the technological
mentality in its most fundamental assumptions. As Wittgenstein claims
in these remarks, our most basic primordial and grounding experiences,
for which he is attempting to assemble reminders, have been rendered
opaque by technological bedazzlement.

4. Wittgenstein, *Culture and Value*, 64.
5. Wittgenstein, *On Certainty*, 19 (§132).

Wittgenstein is not alone among twentieth-century luminaries in his dire diagnosis of our shared obsession with the Great Technological Progress, and it is not only philosophers who have voiced these reservations. Max Weber famously characterizes modernity in terms of a sort of technological disenchantment of the world:

> It means that in principle, then, we are not ruled by mysterious, unpredictable forces, but on the contrary, we can in principle control everything by means of calculation. That in turn means the disenchantment of the world. Unlike the savage for whom such forces existed, we need no longer have recourse to magic in order to control spirits or pray to them. Instead, technology and calculation achieve our ends. This is the primary meaning of the process of intellectualization.[6]

Of course, Weber is not one to rue the rise of modernity and its rationalization of our institutions, and indeed it is hard to take seriously anyone who claims to regret our ability to control more things "by means of calculation" with a straight face (at least not while on the way to visit the dentist's office, or as I write a book on a laptop). Weber, nevertheless, does not deny that technological progress has come at a great cost. With disenchantment comes a sense of homelessness and aimlessness.

Using the example of the application of medical technology for the preservation and enhancement of life, Weber worries that scientifically engineered technique has given us great power to control a newly disenchanted nature, but it cannot tell us to what *end* we should do so:

> All natural scientists provide us with answers to the question: what should we do *if* we wish to *make use of technology* to control life? But whether we wish, or ought to control it through technology, and whether it ultimately makes any sense to do so, is something that we prefer to leave open or else take as given.[7]

In other words, the coupling of the disenchanted stance and technological progress have delivered into our hands an ever-increasing power while at the same time proportionally obscuring our sense of having an objectively determined end toward which to aim it. By this very process of "rationalization" we have disabused ourselves of the notion that nature stands as a normative corrective to our whims as we find them. That is, as nature has become disenchanted for us, and thereby more pliable to

6. Weber, "Science as Vocation," 13.

7. Weber, "Science as Vocation," 18. Author's emphasis.

our interests, it has been lost to us as a guide to how things *ought to be*. Instead, nature is lately taken merely as how things *happen to be*, even if these happenings can now be predicted with high degrees of certainty and to good effect. All we can direct ourselves to, worries Weber, is an empty notion of progress for its own sake. One, however, cannot help but ask: "Progress towards what?" To that question, Weber broods, there can be no *rational* answer. For him, once nature has been disenchanted, reason is only an instrument that mediates between given ends and proposed means, but it can do nothing to determine those ends on rational grounds. We are left to fall back onto our subjective "values" and look to the sheer power of expertise and mechanistic effectiveness. Once again, one cannot help but ask: "Effectiveness toward what?" As Alasdair MacIntyre puts it, for Weber, "no type of authority can appeal to rational criteria to vindicate itself except that type of bureaucratic authority which appeals precisely to its own effectiveness. And what this appeal reveals is that bureaucratic authority is nothing other than successful power."[8] Progress without some ultimate teleological aim, dictated to us by nature (or maybe super-nature), does not seem very much like progress at all. Moving toward *nothing* in particular on the authority of whim and arbitrary power is not advancement. As Weber worries, "senseless 'progressivity'" renders both life and death pointless, because our pretensions to mastery of the world leave us clueless as to how we ought to master it. Inevitably, "civilized life" in the technological age condemns itself to meaninglessness.[9] We are then trapped in a sort of "iron cage" that bars us from seeing things as they really are, or at least in a way that allows us to see them as meaningful, and locks us into self-destructive practices.[10] MacIntyre, reminiscent of the apocalyptic themes in Wittgenstein we discussed above, characterizes this entrapment by techno-bureaucratic authoritarianism as a "new dark ages which are already upon us."[11]

---

8. MacIntyre, *After Virtue*, 26.

9. Weber, "Science as Vocation," 13.

10. The nihilistic consequences of the disenchantment and disengagement originally diagnosed by Weber are thoroughly thought through by Charles Taylor throughout his mature work. For his most concise reflections in direct conversation with Weber along these lines, see Taylor, *The Ethics of Authenticity*.

11. MacIntyre, *After Virtue*, 263. See also MacIntyre's "Disquieting Suggestion," *After Virtue*, 1–5.

Weber is not alone among cultural critics of the last century who have a gloomy estimate regarding the obscuring possibilities of our technological era. Aleksandr Solzhenitsyn claims that:

> Yet it turns out that from this spasmodic pace of technological Progress, from the oceans of superficial information and cheap spectacles, the human soul does not grow, but instead grows more shallow, and spiritual life is only reduced. Our culture, accordingly, grows poorer and dimmer, no matter how it tries to drown out its decline with the din of empty novelties. As creature comforts improve for the average person, so spiritual development grows stagnant. Surfeit brings with it a nagging sadness of heart, as we sense that the whirlpool of pleasures does not bring satisfaction, and that, before long, it may suffocate us.[12]

Here, again like Wittgenstein, Solzhenitsyn raises the dimming and obfuscating possibilities of technological progress. On his view, we are distracted and stunted by a milieu of "superficial information and cheap spectacles" that threatens to "suffocate us" from the real air that we need to breathe. I take it that Solzhenitsyn partly has in mind that we have lost contact with a meaningful world, and that before long we will, because of our palliative distractions, cease even to have a sense of what has been lost, much like Wittgenstein's quiet apocalypse. We are alienated and disengaged because we are distracted and manipulated by the productions of technological "progress." This leads to a sort of spiritual vacuity by tempting us with empty self-understandings based on the shallow fantasies of popular culture and manipulative brand identities.[13] Just as Wittgenstein worries that we are seduced into fantasies such that "aeroplanes and the radio, etc. are means for closer contact" between peoples and cultures, Solzhenitsyn claims we are spiritually reduced by distancing and distraction from what should be most intimate to us by a "whirlpool" of technologically delivered pseudo-culture and *faux* satisfactions.[14] In other words, the modern technological era promises us satisfaction and

12. Solzhenitsyn, "We Have Ceased to See the Purpose," 595.

13. For a recent piece of cultural criticism emphasizing the obscuring effects of technologically promulgated "pseudo-events," see Hedges, *Empire of Illusion*. See also Guy Debord's classic in this vein, *Society of Spectacle*.

14. Herbert Marcuse's opening chapters of *One-Dimensional Man* provide a similar critique of the obscuring and distracting effects of modern technologically driven media and consumerism, however different his positive social vision may be from Solzhenitsyn's.

fulfillment, but in the end renders us alienated nomads, because it obscures our vision of the real world in which we can make our home.

My mention of alienated homelessness brought on by the obscuring effects of the modern technological era cannot but hint at the name of Wittgenstein's rival for the position as the most important philosopher of the twentieth century.[15] Martin Heidegger plays on this same notion of being distracted from what truly is the closest to us by what is actually quite far from us in his own cautionary pleas regarding technology:

> Hourly and daily they are chained to radio and television. Week after week the movies carry them off into uncommon, but often merely common, realms of imagination, and give the illusion of a world that is no world. Picture magazines are everywhere available. All that with which modern techniques of communication stimulate, assail, and drive man—all that is already much closer to man today than his fields around his farmstead, closer than the sky over the earth, closer than the change from night to day, closer than the conventions and customs of his village, than the traditions of his native world.[16]

> Russia and America, when viewed metaphysically, are both the same: the same hopeless frenzy of unchained technology and of the groundless organization of the average man. When the farthest corner of the globe has been technically conquered and can be economically exploited; when any incident you like, in any place you like, at any time you like, becomes accessible as fast as you like; when you can simultaneously "experience" an assassination attempt against a king in France and a symphony concert in Tokyo; when time is nothing but speed, instantaneity, and simultaneity, and time as history has vanished from the Dasein of all peoples; when a boxer counts as the great man of a people; when tallies of millions at mass meetings are a triumph; then, yes, there still looms a specter over all this uproar the question: what for?—where to?—what then?[17]

15. There are many worthy discussions of the symmetries between Wittgenstein's and Heidegger's thought available, but for an illuminating comparative treatment of these thinkers on the issues I am raising in this introduction, see Cahill, *The Fate of Wonder.* Anthony Rudd offers an excellent overview of the intersection between Wittgenstein and Heidegger on the issues in philosophy of mind that I will discuss in the following chapters in *Expressing the World.*

16. Heidegger, "The Memorial Address," 48.

17. Heidegger, *Introduction to Metaphysics*, 40.

Heidegger, like Weber, fears that we have become alienated and disengaged from a meaningful nature and culture that can give us a non-arbitrary direction in which to point our newfound powers ("what for?—where to?—what then?"). Like Wittgenstein and Solzhenitsyn, he believes we have been distracted by a pseudo reality and false promises of satisfaction and security by frenzied productions and organization wrought by modern innovation. For Heidegger, it is not that the object of our distraction is some sort of systematic illusion (what technology reveals is "really there"), but that it gives us the false sense of a closeness to what is actually remote (what technology reveals as "here" is really a distant "there"), which in turn causes us to miss what is right before our eyes.[18] Technological media has brought us to think of ourselves on a global or mass scale ("any place you like . . . becomes accessible"), which obscures the actual grounding for meaning and action in our immediate surroundings, both literally in our natural environment ("the sky above the earth") and culturally ("the traditions of his native world").

Heidegger understood presciently that in his lifetime this process of technological de-worlding was only getting started: "What we know as the technology of film and television . . . of news reporting . . . is only a crude start" and eventually "in all areas of his existence, man will be encircled ever more tightly by the forces of technology," which will "everywhere and every minute claim, enchain, drag along, press and impose upon man under the form of some technical contrivance or other."[19] Heidegger would not have been at all shocked to see us addicted to poking at images of distant and ultimately existentially insignificant events on our own private pocket televisions, nor any of the myriad other ways communication technology has restructured our lives root and branch in order to draw our attention away from where we really are. We now (or soon will) occupy, according to Heidegger, a nearly collapsed space, one without significant distances, and therefore lacking of any meaningful depth ("Everything gets lumped together into uniform distancelessness"[20]), and hence, "The world's night is spreading its darkness."[21] Heidegger, once again like Wittgenstein, became doubtful that those living in this Dark Age will be likely to understand his diagnosis before reaching the very

18. Once again, notice the similarity to Wittgenstein's "this contradicts all of my experience."

19. Heidegger, "Memorial Address," 51..

20. Heidegger, "The Thing," 164.

21. Heidegger, "What Are Poets For?" 89.

depth of alienation.²² Curiously, both leading figures of twentieth-century philosophy called our attention to nihilism and obscurity as salient features of the modern technological era, while worrying that the very crisis they tried to diagnose might block us from understanding their prophetic philosophical announcements. The apocalypse they fear goes on without being noticed, as it veils itself as progress and blocks our vision of any alternative possibility.

What is it that the technological age has occluded? Is this incipient nihilism our destiny or can it be averted? For both Wittgenstein and Heidegger, technology has caused us to misunderstand ourselves by leading us to misunderstand our relationship to nature (broadly construed), and the saving hope is to recover a self-understanding that does not fall prey to these confusions. Notice that in the "Memorial Address," from which I quoted above, Heidegger's counterproposal to the oncoming technological domination is to recover a "meditative thinking" grounded in an organic relationship with the world we are thrown into. This recovery of *thinking* is one of the central themes of Heidegger's later thought and, I

22. Since Heidegger will be a major contributor to our discussion in the following chapters, I should note up front, along with John Haugeland, that "Heidegger was born; he was a Nazi; he died," *Dasein Disclosed*, 85. That is to say, we should recognize that Heidegger's legacy is far more than a matter of academic philosophical concern and far less than admirable, while likewise admitting that many profound insights can be excised from his hideous political commitments and his troubling reticence about those dealings after the fact. Teasing out the historical lacuna necessary to make that case is not part of what follows, and I will help myself to the safely pragmatist version of Heidegger presented by Haugeland and Hubert Dreyfus (see *Being-in-the-World*). Of course, whether Heidegger can be so easily domesticated is a controversial matter. Simon Critchley is not convinced and offers a different reading of Heidegger's philosophy that serves as a very good introduction to recent scholarship on *Being and Time* in his contribution to Critchley and Schurmann, *On Heidegger's Being and Time*. For a subtle and illuminating reading and ultimate rejection of Heidegger's broader views because of their political and theological implications, see McGrath, *Heidegger*. For a recent and far less subtle (and I might go so far as to say unfair in terms of what can be reasonably salvaged from Heidegger's work) rejection of Heidegger on political grounds, see Beiner, *Dangerous Minds*. Michael Millerman situates Heidegger's thought among both liberal and conservative views in his controversial, though enlightening, *Beginning with Heidegger*. I am not willing to make the effort to enter this scholarly fray; I am happy to concede that the figure I am dealing with is possibly better named "Haugelandegger" or "Heidreyfus" than "Heidegger." Also note that I am not claiming that the pragmatist interpretation of Heidegger is the most faithful or the most philosophically fruitful for all issues. I only find this approach is helpful for issues in philosophy of mind in particular, whatever its other strengths and liabilities. For an incisive critique of "Heidreyfus," see Harman, *Tool Being*, 114–27.

believe, can be found implicitly in his early work, though in quite different ways. As we shall see, much of what Heidegger has to offer in *Being and Time* is a redescription of our "thinking" as grounded in a *being-in-the-world*. Likewise, Wittgenstein follows his pessimistic preface with an extended dialectical meditation on the worldly conditions for the possibility of language and discursive thought—thinking. Wittgenstein famously guides us to see that our thinking (as a form of speaking) can only come online embedded in a "form of life" or in the "stream of life." That is, both Heidegger and Wittgenstein attempt to "let the fly out of the bottle"—to adopt Wittgenstein's famous metaphor—by asking us to rethink how we think about thinking.[23] Our technological attitude has caused us to lose a sense of what we really are as thinking beings, i.e., embodied and embedded participants in a world of practices, normative commitments, and inherited meaning. They both came to see the very opposition between mind and world as a symptom of the same virus that was driving our incipient nihilism, and they sought to overcome this problem by first addressing the manifestation of the illness by developing a thoroughly *worldly philosophy of mind* (though neither of them would much care for that phrase as a characterization of their work). The disease itself is to be managed, even if never cured, by Wittgenstein's and Heidegger's suggestions that we return to the practices that allow minded beings like us to be at home in the world. This talk of a *worldly* philosophy of mind is not at all to suggest that either Wittgenstein or Heidegger is some sort of reductive materialist or philosophical naturalist. Rather, as is well known, both thinkers are dismissive of the dualism-materialism dichotomy as symptomatic of the very demon they are trying to exorcise. In short, Wittgenstein and Heidegger ask us to rethink our thinking under better, and they would say more *primordial*, assumptions so that we can recover our place in a meaningful world.

Wittgenstein and Heidegger are hardly alone in their attempt to redirect us to a self-conception elucidated in terms of a world-bound

---

23. Heidegger does claim as he initiates one of his later inquiries into thinking that "we shall not think about what thinking is" (*What Is Called Thinking?* 21), but that is not to say he refuses any thinking about thinking. What Heidegger refuses is to take thinking as an object of thought in its own right, in precision from "what is most thought-provoking." Rather, thinking can only be thought in relation to what gives it significance, what it inclines toward, and, more importantly for Heidegger, what inclines toward it. This is exactly the sort of worldly philosophy of mind (an outside-in as opposed to an inside-out framing of the issue) I am setting out after in the following chapters.

mindedness. Even Hegel, himself a great critic and champion of modernity, took "relational states of individual mindedness and common
like-mindedness . . . as constitutive of freedom," and these shared commitments to the world as we find it are "indispensable elements of a
rationally sufficient and therewith free life."[24] That is, for Hegel, the
modern ideal of self-determining freedom is always parasitic on a prior
"ethical life" of given meanings and ends, a shared world of culture and
tradition, that gives content to what would otherwise be an empty act of
pure will (which Hegel denies as a practical possibility in his critique of
Kant's disengaged reckoning of moral freedom). Much work in recent decades by philosophers such Charles Taylor and Robert Pippen has been
dedicated to understanding the delicate balance between transcendental
freedom and world-boundedness highlighted by Hegel, along with its
possible consequences for our social, political, and cultural institutions.
The epistemological and cognitive implications of the distinctively Hegelian (or otherwise neo-Kantian) version of worldly philosophy of mind
have been drawn out in great depth by philosophers in the Pittsburgh
School, such as Robert Brandom, John McDowell, and more recently
by their fellow-traveler Markus Gabriel. Moreover, the idea that mind is
not strictly "in the head" is a common mantra among many externalist
analytic philosophers (originating with the work of Saul Kripke and Hilary Putnam), who argue that without taking the content of thought as
intrinsically connected to the world, the prospects for accounts of meaning and knowledge are all but lost. Contemporary Aristotelian-Thomists,
most notably Alasdair MacIntyre (who no doubt is also influenced by
Wittgenstein and Hegel), have likewise emphasized the precarious social,
emotional, and biological conditions under which human mind and action can realize its potential, and have stressed the life-long dependence
of these capacities on embodiment and cultural embeddedness. There is
also a well-established movement afoot in cognitive science, originating
with work by Andy Clark and David Chalmers, which takes as its point
of departure the *extended-mind thesis*, i.e., the view that what is most
distinctive about human cognitive powers is our ability to "off load" our
cognitive labors into an environment we structure for ourselves by creating shared symbolic representations, social organization, cultural institutions, etc. Thus, human mindedness is not located exclusively in the brain
(or mind or soul), nor even the human body. Rather, the human mind

24. Pippen, *Hegel's Practical Philosophy*, 7.

is spread out in a shared environment that we have rigged for ourselves. Once again, mind *is* an involvement in the world. Similar insights into the worldliness of mind have been uncovered recently by the work of enactive phenomenologists and the development of neurophenomenology by such thinkers as Evan Thompson, who is applying insights from the phenomenological and Eastern philosophical traditions.[25]

The task of this book is to think about thinking as a contribution to restored *meaning* by advancing this project of a worldly philosophy of mind. Much as George Lakoff and Mark Johnson endeavored to rethink philosophy of language in light of "what people find *meaningful* in their lives" and to "address questions of the meaningfulness of our everyday experience,"[26] I want to approach the philosophy of mind as it might help remind us of the conditions for a meaningful form of life that have been obscured by the technological mentality.[27] I do not claim to do anything as groundbreaking for the philosophy of mind as Lakoff and Johnson did for philosophy of language and linguistics. Indeed, I will hardly advance an original thesis of my own. Though there are moments when I will go my own way, the main task is to gather the strands of the disparate sources of worldly thinking about thinking that I have mentioned above. If my efforts are successful, I will weave these Wittgensteinian, Heideggerian, Hegelian, Aristotelian-Thomistic, analytic externalist, phenomenological, and cognitive scientific fibers, along with an even broader cast of characters we will pick up along the way, into a coherent fabric. These are not threads of philosophical discourse one typically expects to compose into a seamless garment; e.g., "Heidegger, Hegel, and Aristotle" is not exactly a *prima facie* tension-free conjunction, so the synthetic task will be no small feat, even without worrying too much about adding to the initial cacophony with my own attempts at novelty.

I begin in chapter 1 by considering mind-brain identity theories and their metaphysical descendants, strong supervenience accounts, extant in contemporary analytic philosophy of mind. These materialist theories come in many "shapes and sizes," but they all minimally claim that certain physiological states (though there may be no universal definition

---

25. For an integration of many of these varied versions of the notion of an extended mind, see Rowlands, *The New Science of the Mind*.

26. Lakoff and Johnson, *Metaphors We Live By*, xi–xii.

27. For a very different, though complementary, critique of our technological society stemming from considerations in the philosophy of mind, see Tartaglia, *Philosophy in a Technological World*.

identifying these state-types) are strictly sufficient for the occurrence of certain mental states (I will be primarily concerned with thoughts). The sense of "sufficiency" in play here is very strict, i.e., the mental states supposedly *just are* or *are nothing more than* the occurrence of their underlying physiological correlates. I use thought experiments taken from and inspired by Wittgenstein to show that these sorts of materialism (even if non-reductive) are easily undermined. The upshot is that, without doubting that activities within the nervous system are necessary conditions for thinking (I do not call into question any "If thought, then brain" thesis), it is clear that no occurrence within an organism is sufficient in this strong sense for the occurrence of a thought (I am calling into question the "If brain, then thought" thesis). Note carefully, however, that I do not see these considerations as advancing the case for a metaphysical dualism understood as the neat contrary to these versions of metaphysical materialism. Indeed, I will argue that the thought experiments tell equally well against standard versions of metaphysical dualism as they do against metaphysical materialism. The problem is not, I hope to show, determining what kind of discrete entity with which we should identify the mind, whether that be the brain or some mental substance distinct from its associated organism, but the very notion that the mind is something that can be identified with any sort of discrete entity at all. The considerations in chapter 1 are aimed to "de-ontologize" our concerns in the philosophy of mind and to suggest that the mind is not a discrete entity but a participation in a natural history and a historically conditioned culture. For these reasons, I adopt the Hegelian technique of speaking of mind as *Geist*, and I will refer to the world in which it is necessarily a participant as its *Lebenswelt* ("life world") as construed by later phenomenological and hermeneutical thinkers. Our mindedness is a participation in *Geist*, which is itself a relation to an open-ended *Lebenswelt*. Since the history giving rise to our mindedness is not over, aspirations to deliver a final accounting of mindedness by some idealized scientific account of the physical universe as a whole are just as misguided as any attempt to identify "mind" with an internal state or constituent of an organism or ghostly mental substance.

With that de-ontologized, world-bound notion of mindedness as *Geist* in hand, I turn in chapter 2 to consider what exactly is necessary to constitute a *Lebenswelt* in which creatures like *us* can participate. Certainly, *Geist* is a rational way of being, and I account for this in terms of our residence in a "logical space of reasons," as that notion has been developed by neo-Kantiona/Hegelian thinkers in the Pittsburg School (Sellars, McDowell, and Brandom). Minded beings can give reasons for their sayings and doings; our utterances are not merely *caused* like ordinary natural occurrences, but also *justified* by logical relations to normatively sufficient reasons (at least, we hope, some of the time). That is, we participants in *Geist* are expected to take normative responsibility for our judgments (both practical and theoretical). Notice, however, that normative responsibility for any judgment always demands commitments to other judgments. If I judge *that P*, then, as a denizen of the logical space of reasons, I am committed to denying any other judgment that entails *that not-P*, and I am also committed to affirming any other judgment itself entailed by *that P*. For example, if I judge *that today is Friday*, then I am likewise committed to the judgments *that today is not Thursday* and *that tomorrow is Saturday*. One can only make a rational judgment involving the concept "Friday" inasmuch as she also has the concepts of "Thursday" and "Saturday" in her cognitive toolbox. In other words, as we shall see, any judgment in the logical space of reasons presupposes a broad network of concepts, and since life in the logical space of reasons is not a frictionless spinning of linguistic trivialities, it presupposes that our conceptual framework is sensitive to empirical "push-back."

All of this is to say that participation in *Geist* presupposes a "world" of interrelated and empirically grounded conceptual contents that we can only inherit from more senior residents of the space of reasons. Though *Geist* is initially an inheritance of a vast network of empirical and normative commitments, with its own long-tested history of surviving push-back from the world that must be taken for granted in the beginning, our participation in mindedness is not ultimately passive. Mature residents in the space of reasons are its guardians, i.e., they take responsibility for the good order of their neighborhood. That is, participants in *Geist* are obliged to endure collective self-scrutiny, always with an eye to assuring as best as possible that their space of reasons has not lost touch with reality. Thus, *Geist* is perennially subject to self-revision by the next generation of its inheritors, and this is partly why a final scientific reconning of mindedness is forever beyond the pale.

I will add to these neo-Kantian/Hegelian conditions for mindedness further considerations drawn from phenomenological and psychological insights to highlight that our manner of worldliness is not only a matter of conceptual contents and rational self-scrutiny, and this may be seen as a transition from Hegelian to later phenomenological motifs drawn from

Heidegger and Merleau-Ponty. There is a great deal of evidence suggesting that human beings can only develop the ability to operate in something like the logical space of reasons in a context involving attachments to and interactions with other human beings with whom they share emotionally significant bonds. We primarily learn our first language, it might be said, at our mother's knee, and without such original attachments, we are forever prone to miss something in our experience. It also seems to be the case that our cognitive abilities are beholden to these emotional involvements long after our initial linguistic tutelage, probably for our entire lives. Even supposedly irreducible qualitative awareness (the notorious *qualia* of recent analytic philosophy of mind), so I will argue, are unintelligible apart from these background emotional involvements and framings, at least for beings like us who participate in *Geist*. Moreover, we will discuss the great degree to which our higher cognitive abilities are tied to certain very nitty-gritty practical skills required to deal with a world that can stand as a source of *bona fide* material content for our judgments. Connection to a world we can reason about explicitly presupposes a great deal of implicit knowing-how. The central point throughout this chapter is to introduce *Geist* as arising through a tension between rational responsibility and emotional dependence, transcendent theory and grounded practice, explicit conceptual determinacy and implicit precognitive skill, spontaneity and intuition. This irony at the heart of our mindedness will be the centerpiece of all the following chapters. Ours, as Wittgenstein so aptly puts it, is a "complicated form of life."

Seeing mindedness as stretched between poles of independence and dependence will be particularly crucial as we turn in chapter 3 to ponder the relation between participation in *Geist* and the prospects for human freedom. We will arrive at a deeper reiteration of the irony of mindedness that reveals freedom as both our greatest dignity and the occasion for our greatest *tragic* vulnerability. Of course, the mysterious double-edged sword of human freedom has probably not been news since St. Paul said "I do not understand my own actions. For, I do not do what I want, but I do the very thing I hate,"[28] but I hope to shed just a little light on this perennial mystery by showing its relationship to the irony of mindedness and its connection to the sort of tragedy that the Greek dramatists bring to our attention as an inherent possibility for the human condition. Rethinking our thinking in worldly terms will help us likewise to rethink freedom and the tragic possibility fruitfully.

28. Romans 7:15.

Before all that, however, I will perform another bit of *de-ontologizing* like what I did for the mind-brain problem, but this time aimed at the "problem of free will" in its most recent manifestation. That debate is often catalyzed by the infamous Libet experiments that seem to show that our sense of willful control of our actions is illusory, as events in the nervous system are already on their way to causing the downstream effects leading to our actions before our consciousness of an act of will occurs. I do not dispute that Libet's experiments show exactly what the "neuroskeptics" regarding "free will" claim they do. That is no bother, as I think ethically significant actions have very little, if anything, to do with whether they are subject to prior causal conditions. Rather, ethically significant actions are doings subject to reasons explanations and not just causality, i.e., actions performed by denizens of the space of reasons. These actions are significant *as actions*, because of their relation to reasons *as such*, but they are *ethically* significant actions because of their relationship to a special kind of reasons. Ethically significant actions are justified by the agent's commitment to a certain conception of the good life (or an agent's commitment to this sort of action entails a further commitment to a certain conception of the good life), and it is here that I will begin to draw Aristotelian themes into the conversation. Reasons explanations of that sort do not require a prior, conscious act of will, as I will argue, because many of our most ethically significant actions are doings for which we can only make our reasons explicit well after the fact. Here, following Brandom and MacIntyre, I will try to show that much of our most significant reasons-giving is done retrospectively, and as such many of our most important decisions are made while we are "piggy-backing" on our *Lebenswelt*.

Participants in *Geist*, however, are not only passive recipients, but also take responsibility, so there is a distinctive sense of freedom that takes us beyond our off-loading of the burden of practical rationality onto the wisdom of our form of life. I will argue that freedom should be re-thought as a three-fold responsibility: an accountability *to our form of life*, an accountability *to reality*, and an accountability *to ourselves*. That is, freedom should be understood as explicitly taking up the question of our fidelity to what we have been given as our *Lebenswelt*, whether that form of life is actually good, and whether we are authentic adherents to this form of life, as opposed to being motivated by other subterranean and less flattering ends. I then offer Sophocles's Oedipus as a paradigmatic example of someone failing to satisfy the final authenticity condition for freedom, and who thereby suffers the gravest of tragic consequences. The point is that the Fate that threatens our freedom is not a sub-personal causal determination discovered by the neurosciences, but our own failure to make our reasons for acting explicit in full clear-eyed honesty. Freedom requires us to ask ourselves hard questions about our form of life, its relationship to reality, and our relationship to it. The anxiety that comes with entertaining possibly dark answers to those questions is the cost of our dignity as free beings, but that is the only route to avoiding Oedipus's tragic fate. I then employ the insights earned in the first three chapters to suggest that evolutionary biology and psychology, far from threatening out self-understanding as free beings, make crucial contributions to the self-consciousness necessary for ethically significant agency.

The anxiety that comes part and parcel with the dignity of human freedom, which is a consequence of the irony of *Geist* as a tension between independence and dependence, is the cornerstone concept of the final two chapters. In chapter 4, I take up artificial intelligence as another potential threat to our understanding of ourselves as participants in *Geist*, and here it should be obvious that we also begin to return to the grave concerns about the occlusion of mindedness in a technological age that occasion this inquiry. As a stipulation, I do not question artificial *intelligence* as a possibility, but instead concede it as a fact. That is, on a standard notion of intelligence as it is understood in mainstream psychology and cognitive science, i.e., the ability to learn, solve formalized problems, maneuver environments, etc. it is obvious that we already have artificial beings among us that are so enabled. One wonders whether the AI debate is a rigged game in the sense that the accepted definition of intelligence among cognitive scientists so happens to be about what we would expect we could make a machine do, but I will not digress on that issue. Be that as it may, that notion of intelligence, however, is a far cry from what I mean by *Geist*, and the question of whether there are machines currently minded in that sense or whether there ever could be such machines is most certainly an open question. I suggest then that, instead of investigating the possibility of artificial intelligence, we pursue the question of *artificial rationality*. I begin by unfolding a greatly simplified story as to why someone might take very seriously the proposal that a machine could indeed take up residence with us in the logical space of reasons. As is standard in these discussions, I consider the proposal that a machine that could pass a Turing test, i.e., show linguistic competence indiscernible from human discourse, would have to be given the benefit of the doubt as being "one of us." Though I have in the past defended arguments against the Turing test as a measure of *bona fide* rationality, I argue that counter-considerations such as Searle's "Chinese Room" thought experiment do not manage to shift the burden of proof against the proponent of artificial rationality.

That is all well and good, but I go on to argue that whatever else might be the case for a machine passing a Turing test, much more would have to be shown in order for us to conclude that it is a participant in *our* form of life. At that point I will draw extensively from the Heideggarian resources that Haugeland and Dreyfus have deployed in their own critiques of artificial rationality. In any given situation there are indefinitely, maybe infinitely, many semantically significant utterances that can be made (there is always another true statement one could voice). We sort out that otherwise intractable cacophony of truths by limiting the options based on pragmatic relevance. I could bring up the bonding properties holding together the molecules composing my shoes in the middle of a business meeting, and in doing so I might even say something true. I would not, however, make such a statement (and my business partners would find it exceptionally odd, if I were to do so) because that is not *what we are doing* at the moment. There are, no doubt, any number of pragmatic possibilities that could frame any situation, but those options are winnowed down by what we *care* about or are *concerned* with. That is, human sense-making, reason-giving, truth-telling, etc., are framed by *care*. We talk about something in particular (and not all the other things we could have spoken about), because there is something that we care about, and in our most important, ethically significant conversations, these concerns are for ultimate things: the good life, death, love, pride, honor, fear, and all the other "cares in the world" one might have. I have no argument showing that it is impossible, but I believe it strains credulity to claim that we have the slightest inkling as to what it would even mean for a machine to have these existential concerns as its ultimate means of pragmatic sorting.

Remember also the three-fold responsibility that I introduced above, which I propose as the central source of human dignity. *Geist* puts itself into question; it cares about whether or not it measures up to the world and whether it measures up to itself. *Our* rationality, whatever else a machine might have, entails self-scrutiny of a distinctive *concernful* kind. A participant in *Geist* puts its most self-definitive and cherished practices and commitments to question, which requires her to be open to the possibility of dark answers. Once again, I will give no proof that a machine cannot have an existential crisis, but I find it hard to take the possibility seriously. The anxiety that inevitably follows therewith is no doubt a high price to pay, but, as Haugeland memorably puts it, that is the cost of "giving a damn," which is itself the mark of not being a machine.

I circle back completely to the problem of nihilism in the technological age in chapter 5. I am not concerned in this discussion with how specific devices (smart phones, social media, armed robots, nuclear weapons, etc.) threaten our well-being (though I have little doubt about the gravity of those threats). Rather, I focus on how the modern technological attitude occludes our participation in *Geist*. It is the consequences of the modern technological attitude for our stance toward the world and toward ourselves (and if I am correct in the foregoing, these two stances cannot be separated) that I see as the "greatest danger." That phrase comes from Heidegger's canonical critique of the modern technological attitude, "The Question Concerning Technology." This text has its role in my discussion, but it will not be my primary source for a critique of technology. Rather, I will focus on an essay by Keiji Nishitani, who comes to much the same conclusions as Heidegger, but along the way he constructs a fascinating natural-philosophical history according to which the development of machine technology is both the perfection and downfall of humanity and the entire universe. In particular he sees the development of the distinctively human rationality that enables technological development as the manifestation of the rational principles of the universe in a higher, more explicit form than their implicit occurrence in an un-cognized natural world. These ideas dovetail interestingly with principles from Thomistic epistemology and psychology, and their role in Nishitani's critique of technology gives us a considerable clue as to how adherents to the scholastic tradition should approach the question of modern technology. What we will see is that Nishitani (along with Heidegger, and I suggest Aristotelian-Thomists, though in different ways) concludes that the modern technological attitude instrumentalizes the natural world and humanity alike, because it hides our status as *Geist* by anesthetizing the very anxiety that is the sign of our highest dignity. The more we depend on our machines, the more we will see ourselves as mere extensions of them or fuel for their consumption. That process of dehumanization relieves us of our existential angst, though at the price of our dignity.

Not everyone will see the exchange of *Geist* for the relief of anxiety as a net loss. Nietzsche, at least in some very interesting, yet little discussed, moments in *Will to Power*, suggests that the *Ubermensch* will finally be a completely mechanized post-humanity. In short, Nietzsche is the history of philosophy's most influential transhumanist. Once the human being has been fully incorporated into a universal "economy" of machine control, she will be relieved of the anxiety of living up to what Nietzsche sees as the impossible normative standards of *Geist*, and thereby liberated from the requisite anxieties of responsibility. The entire tale of human mindedness, so Nietzsche famously argues, was nothing more than a lie produced as a stopgap measure against the intractably tragic character of existence, i.e., an inert pressure valve that allows us to communicate our otherwise unrelieved suffering. With mechanization comes dehumanization and a return to a sort of sub-consciousness, which liberates us from the need for pragmatic lies. Nietzsche, in the end, sees that final dissolution of *Geist*, the mechanization of humanity, as the ultimate move beyond *all-too-humanity* to an uninterpreted expression of power for its own sake. In reply to Nietzsche, I motivate the inevitability of the normative stance, and thus the unavoidability of our self-consciousness as *Geist*. Nietzsche's position, so I will argue, is a willful ignorance of (a renewed forgetting of) what is truly closest to us, and it, despite all his claims about a manly courage in the face of ugly truths about life after the Death of God, is a cowardly evasion of the responsibilities and anxieties that are intrinsic to the space of reasons.

It would seem that I leave the reader with dignity, but at the cost of anxiety. The picture of *Geist* I have painted has no End of History, at least none that we can see, that serves as a resting point. *Geist* seems to be an ever moving target because our world (both cultural and natural) is on the move, and our mindedness is worldly. We are seemingly forever subject to self-criticism, revision, and return to our contingent attachments, and all of these processes are time-bound and open-ended. We can hedge against the tragedy of Oedipus through honest scrutiny of ourselves and our form of life, but it appears that this dignity may be no better than Sisyphus' proud, yet absurd, struggle. Does our becoming ever arrive at being? Do we avert tragedy only to face absurdity? I close the book in a brief epilogue in which I take up these questions with Aristotle, and here I will finally indulge in just a bit of metaphysical speculation, or maybe just an attempt at recollection.

1

Thinking Isn't Any-Thing

We see the things themselves, the world is what we see: formulae of this
kind express a faith common to the natural man and the philosopher—
the moment he opens his eyes; they refer to a deep-seated set of mute
"opinions" implicated in our lives. But what is strange about this faith
is that if we seek to articulate it not into theses or statements, if we ask
ourselves what is this <u>we</u>, what is <u>seeing</u>, and what <u>thing</u> or <u>world</u> is, we
enter into a labyrinth of difficulties and contradictions.

—MAURICE, MERLEAU-PONTY, *THE VISIBLE AND THE INVISIBLE*[1]

. . . we can use the world as its own best model . . .

—ANDY CLARK (PARAPHRASING RODNEY BROOKS),
BEING THERE[2]

1. Can Minds Be Pictured?

A RECENT EDITION OF a very popular introductory psychology
textbook refers to a set of images produced by various brain-scanning

---

1. Merleau-Ponty, *The Visible and the Invisible*, 3. Author's emphasis.
2. Clark, *Being There*, 29.

technologies as "Windows on the Mind," and this caption appears within a section under the title "Windows on the Brain."[3] The implicit idea here seems to be that these images are windows on the mind because the mind and the brain are the very same object. This supposed picture of the mind is also a picture of a brain, so the caption that glosses it entails that taking a picture of a mind is the same as taking a picture of a certain organ engaged in a certain activity, in this case an active human brain. In other words, a mind is the sort of thing that can be captured in a discrete image (what we will call a picture), because minds *are* brains, and we can certainly take pictures of brains.

Of course, the authors of this textbook are just innocently trying to write an introduction to basic issues and methods in psychology, not necessarily to contribute to debates in the philosophy of mind. Nevertheless, I want to use this caption as something of a foil, as I believe that answering the question of whether a mind is the sort of thing that can be pictured, in the same way one might produce an image of a bodily organ, raises a nest of important philosophical issues around which much unclarity loiters. The point is not to criticize these psychologists, but to get some of the philosophical issues in this vicinity out in the open where we can consider them explicitly. That being said, I do believe that these remarks by the authors are representative of a certain knee-jerk identification of minds with brains that goes without much critical scrutiny outside of philosophical circles, and not entirely rarely among philosophers too.[4]

In fairness to the authors, they do not explicitly identify the mind and the brain in the text. They never say anything like "The mind *is* the brain in the same way that water *is* H2O," though I suspect that sort of mind-brain identity thesis is likely how the students reading the book will interpret the captions. In any event, what the authors actually do claim is wrought with ambiguity. For example, they write earlier in the text that "modern biological psychologists have rejoined mind and body . . . and now view *the mind as the product of the brain*."[5] Talk like "the mind is a product of the brain" and "the mind is based in the brain"

3. Zimbardo, Johnson, and McCann, *Psychology*, 63. I am referring to the 7th edition of this text, and it should be noted that this episode does not appear in the subsequent edition.

4. I offer a critical treatment of sophisticated versions of mind-brain identity theories in *Mind, Matter, and Nature*, 102–13.

5. Zimbardo, Johnson, and McCann, *Psychology*, 12. My emphasis.

is a common parlance in these discussions, but it is crucially ambiguous.[6] Notice that "is a product of" and "is based on" are not the same as "is identical to" or "is the very same thing as." One can consistently affirm that the mind is not identical to the brain or not the very same thing as the brain, while also affirming that the mind is *based on* or *the product of* the brain. Being the basis of something is not necessarily *being the very same thing as* something. CO_2 is the product of carbon and oxygen, but it is not the *very same thing as* carbon and oxygen. There certainly can be carbon and oxygen without the occurrence of CO_2. A wall is the product of a pile of bricks, but the pile of bricks is not the very same thing as the wall. The existence of the bricks predates the existence of the wall and taking a picture of a pile of bricks is not necessarily to take a picture of a wall. What is this "rejoining" of mind and body that modern biological psychologists have supposedly pulled off?[7] Is it an identification of mind and brain (minds and brains are the very same things), or is it an insight into how the brain provides a basis for the mind (the brain is a cause of the mind)?

Notice another ambiguity. Does the caption mean that every case of taking a picture of a mind is a case of taking a picture of an active brain; or does it mean that every case of taking a picture of an active brain (at least in the activity pictured in the textbook) is likewise taking a picture of a mind? In other words, is the claim that all brains are minds, or that all minds are brains? Maybe the claim is even stronger: all brains are minds *and* all minds are brains. Obviously, every case of taking a picture of a

6. For examples of typical talk of how neurophysiological activities and structures "underlie," "mediate," "correlate" with, and are "involved" in thinking, see Yang and Shadlen, "Probabilistic Reasoning by Neurons," 1075; Senior et al., "Organizational Cognitive Science," 812; and Fletcher and Carruthers, "Metacognition and Reasoning," 1366. My point is not to accuse any of these authors of intentional ambiguity. The meanings of their claims are perfectly clear in the narrow contexts for which they are intended, and I have no reason to doubt that their research supports these claims. My point is merely that these sorts of results lend themselves to crucial ambiguities when we move to philosophical considerations about the mind-brain relationship. Thanks to Marcus Otte, who pointed these references out to me.

7. One wonders how much "rejoining" of mind and brain was really done by modern biological psychologists. Surely, the fact that a sharp blow to the head does much to hamper one's cognitive powers, as does ingesting great quantities of alcohol or other intoxicating substances, would not be news to our pre-scientific forebearers. The highly specified mind-brain identification implicitly pushed in this passage is, no doubt, something new under the sun in recent decades, but the fact that the mind is something closely linked with organic human life is old news.

brick wall is a case of taking a picture of a collection of bricks, but not every case of taking a picture of a collection of bricks is taking a picture of a brick wall. All brick walls are collections of bricks, but not all collections of bricks are brick walls. A photograph of a pile of bricks in the alley behind my house is not a picture of a brick wall. Thus, how one answers any one of these questions about "picturing" a mind by picturing a brain is independent from how one answers the others. One could consistently say that any case of picturing a mind is a case of picturing a brain, while denying that every case of picturing a brain is picturing a mind, and so forth.

I am not quite sure how to sort all these ambiguities out for the authors (along with the legions of others trading in these unclarities), so let's operate under the following modest and charitable supposition: the caption claims that taking a picture of an active brain (of a certain sort) is *sufficient* for taking a picture of a mind. I take it that this supposition entails the further claim: *being an active brain* (of a certain sort) is *sufficient* for *being a mind*. All there need be for there to be minds is that there are certain sorts of brains engaged in certain sorts of activities. There is no hint that the authors are claiming that by showing us a mind, they are likewise showing us a brain; they do not begin by showing a picture of a mind that they claim to be "A Window on the Brain." Indeed, it is difficult to fathom what such an exercise would even be like, a fact that is relevant to the argument to follow below. They are, however, clearly saying that by showing us a brain (involved in a certain activity) they are showing us a mind (involved in a certain activity). Maybe there are minds that are not brains, but, so the story goes, any brain that is operating in a certain way *is* a mind. If we have a complete story about the operations of a brain, then we likewise have a complete story about any associated minds.

That is fair as far as it goes, and we are thus not ascribing to the caption any stronger thesis about the relationship between minds and brains than is absolutely necessary. For future reference, we need to tighten things up a bit with some examples. Let's suppose that the state of the mind supposedly in the picture is *thinking-about-Paris*. Let's further suppose that the state of the brain in the picture is, just to give it a name, *Zeta*. Of course, what I'm calling *Zeta* (the state of the brain in the fMRI) in reality may have nothing whatsoever to do with *thinking-about-Paris*, but let's just roll with this example. Thus, I am so far taking the authors' claim to be that a brain's being in *Zeta* is sufficient condition for a mind's being in a state of *thinking-about-Paris*. Well, actually, the caption might say something a bit stronger than that. Notice that the caption does not seem to say that "This is a state of a mind," but that "This is a mind." The title of the caption is "Windows on the Mind," not "Windows on a state of the mind." It is one thing to say certain brain activities, e.g., *Zeta*, are sufficient for certain mental states, e.g., *thinking-about-Paris*, but quite another to say that the existence of a certain brain is sufficient for the existence of a certain mind. On the one hand, we have the thesis that every state of a mind has an activity of a brain as its sufficient condition. On the other hand, we have the thesis that every mind has a brain as its sufficient condition. Those are distinct claims, and generally claims about the *conditions for the state of something* do not necessarily entail *claims about the conditions for that thing itself*. Nevertheless, this possible ambiguity need not worry us very much. If something is sufficient for being a chameleon, in the relevantly strong sense of "sufficient" that I will discuss below, then picturing that thing's activity is sufficient for picturing a chameleon's activity. That is, if a properly arranged, living set of chameleon organs is sufficient for a chameleon, then the act of hunting by a properly arranged, living set of chameleon organs should be sufficient for an act of hunting by a chameleon, and likewise picturing the former would be picturing the latter. Moreover, picturing a chameleon hunting entails picturing a chameleon. In this light, if the activities of brains are sufficient for activities of minds, then picturing the activities of a brain is picturing a mind. At the very least, I am willing to operate under this modest assumption. Thus, I take it that if the brain is sufficient for the mind, then picturing *Zeta* should be sufficient for picturing *thinking-about-Paris*.

If it turns out, then, that *Zeta* is insufficient for *thinking-about-Paris*, i.e., having a picture of *Zeta* does not suffice for having a picture of *thinking-about-Paris*, then the mind that has this mental state does not have the brain that is undergoing *Zeta* as its sufficient condition. In other words, if it turns out that no brain being in *Zeta* is alone enough for there to be a mind in a state of *thinking-about-Paris*, then the mind that so thinks is not pictured by picturing any brain (supposing *Zeta* is the only brain state significantly correlated with *thinking-about-Paris*). There is nothing special in these respects about *thinking-about-Paris*; it is just an arbitrarily chosen example of a mental state. If it is shown that this mental state, simply by virtue of its being a mental state, cannot be pictured by picturing *Zeta*, then it will follow that mental states in general cannot be pictured by picturing their correlated brain states, and furthermore minds in general will not have brains as sufficient conditions.

In what follows in this chapter, I will argue that *Zeta* is indeed insufficient for *thinking-about-Paris*. Notice, however, that none of this calls into question the fairly obvious fact that *Zeta* is a *necessary condition* for *thinking-about-Paris*, nor does it question that having a brain is a *necessary condition* for having a mind, or at least a human mind. In other words, nothing in what follows supports the claim that you could think about Paris without having a brain, though I will show that the activity of your brain is not all on its own sufficient for you to have a thought about Paris.

Before we get down to that argument, one more clarification is necessary: What do we mean by all this talk of *sufficient condition*? I am sure you know what "sufficient" means in common English, i.e., *X* is sufficient for *Y* means that *X* alone is enough for *Y* occur. For example, if the syllabus for a course states, "A score of a 'C' on the final examination is sufficient to pass the course," that would mean that all that one need to do in order to pass is to get a "C" on the final examination. Notice, however, that one could claim that the brain is sufficient for the mind without likewise claiming that the brain and the mind are one and the same thing. One could actually claim that minds are, at some point in their histories, caused by brains to come to be in the first place, but, at later points in their histories, minds exist without any brains at all. On such a view, a properly functioning brain is sufficient to bring about the initial existence of a mind, but that is not to say that such a mind cannot exist without its brain. Certain activities of my wife and I are, in this sense, sufficient for the initial coming to be of our children, but now they are up and running on their own (to various degrees). Though we are sufficient for our children's origination, they are not the very same things as us. If a similar relation obtains between the brain and the mind, then taking a picture of a brain is not at all to take a picture of the mind, even though minds depend on brains originally (any more than taking a picture of my wife and I is likewise to take a picture of our children). Thus, this is not at all the notion of sufficient condition that we need to explore.[8]

Recent philosophers dealing with this issue have introduced a much stronger notion of sufficient condition, typically called *supervenience*: if *X* supervenes on *Y*, then sufficient for something's *being X* is that it *is Y*. In other words, every case of something *being-Y* is necessarily a case of that thing *being-X*. Maybe there are *X*s that are not *Y*s, but there cannot be a

8. For examples of influential versions of such views, see Hasker, *The Emergent Self* and Swinburne, *The Evolution of Soul*.

case of *Y*s that are not *X*s. Notice that where *X* supervenes on *Y*, we are not saying that *Y* causes *X* in the sense that my wife and I are the cause of our children, but that *Y* and *X* are the *same* thing. *Y* and *X* are not identical, because supervenience allows that *X* could have something other than *Y* as its sufficient condition, but as things actually stand *X* is the same thing as *Y* in some looser sense. That looser sense of "same" (short of identical) is often supposed as a *constitutive* relation between the supervenience base and the supervening entity. For example, the parts (wood, screws, metal screening, etc.) that compose my chameleon's cage are constitutive of the cage. All that is needed for there to be such a cage is for those parts to be arranged appropriately. We cannot identify the cage with its parts, since that cage could have different parts (maybe we will eventually need to replace the screening, etc.), and such cages could be made out of entirely different kinds of parts (someone could make a chameleon cage out of stainless steel and plastic mesh instead of wood and metal mesh). Through a process of incremental replacement, *this* cage could be composed of very different kinds of materials from those that currently compose it. Nevertheless, it is not as though the chameleon's cage is something in addition to or independent from its parts, it *just is* those parts in their arrangement. We might say that *being-a-chameleon-cage* supervenes on *being-this-configuration-of-parts* as things stand right now. Notice that since the chameleon cage supervenes on this configuration of parts, taking a picture of those parts in this configuration is likewise to take a picture of the chameleon cage.[9] To return, then, to our main question: Does *thinking-about-Paris* supervene on *Zeta*? Is the relationship between *Zeta* and *thinking-about-Paris* analogous to the relationship between the configured parts of the chameleon cage and the cage itself?

2. Thinking beyond Picture Thinking

Before making my case for a negative answer to these questions, let's stop for a moment to consider why someone might answer them affirmatively. Of course, there is no lack of trendy, *faux*-sophisticated materialism available, but philosophers who claim that mental states are the same as brain states (in any one of a number of senses of "same" extant

---

9. Non-controversial examples of supervenience are notoriously hard to come by, and supervenience is itself a controversial notion in the philosophy of mind. For a more detailed discussion of supervenience and its difficulties, see my *Mind, Matter, and Nature*, 114–21, and "Thomistic Theories of Intentionality and Physicalism."

in the contemporary literature) do not do so merely due to a knee-jerk, materialist bias. The most common motivation for strong versions of supervenience (along with other proposals in this vicinity) by academic philosophers is a respect for established scientific results and theoretical simplicity. Through the use of neuropathology, lesion mapping, direct stimulation, fMRI and other imaging technologies, neuroscientists have identified structures in the central nervous systems of higher animals that *somehow* account for the phenomena of consciousness, along with the behaviors following on such conscious phenomena. At the very least, we are now aware of many structures and networks of activity correlated with vast swaths of our mental lives. Certainly, neuroscientists are far from constructing a complete geography of mental life out of the topography of networks in the central nervous system, but it is equally clear that much progress along these lines has been made. The degree to which our mental lives have been "mapped onto" the activities of our central nervous systems has been overstated in popular discussions, though the extent of progress in the neurosciences is impressive. So much so that one is unwise to bet the prospects of her metaphysics of mind on a future failure of the neurosciences to discover a neurophysiological correlate for some mental activity in particular.

For our purposes, I will suppose (once again optimistically, and quite possibly naïvely) that there will, someday, be such a complete mapping, i.e., all conscious phenomena will be shown to have a neurophysiological correlate. Of course, this talk of "mapping" is just the correlation of mental states with structures and networks of activity in the central nervous system, and correlation is famously not causation, let alone identification or strong supervenience. Just showing that whenever Cormac is in *Zeta* he also reports some thought about Paris, is not alone enough to show that *Zeta* is the very same thing as *thinking-about-Paris*. True enough, but correlation is only part of the case for mind-brain supervenience, and one should ask just how much can be reasonably demanded of someone trying to support such a thesis. Absolute proof of the *very sameness* of two entities would be a curious maneuver indeed! It seems that the best that can be done would be to appeal to the outstanding reliability of the correlations so far and the overall theoretical simplicity and fecundity of the supervenience position. It is fair for the proponent of mind-brain supervenience to point out that we do have (or very soon will have) the mind-brain correlations, and something like strong supervenience provides a metaphysics of the mind that fits in well with the overall scientific picture of the world while averting some of the major puzzles that trouble philosophers. So long as this position leaves nothing out that cries for an explanation, it would seem that nothing more is needed.

There are a great many proposals for what even sophisticated supervenience theories leave unexplained, but I do not plan to wade into all of those issues here.[10] Instead, I am going to focus on concerns inspired by remarks Ludwig Wittgenstein made in his later writings. Recent philosophers working in the broadly Wittgensteinian tradition have diagnosed the line of materialist reasoning I have outlined above as a case of the *mereological fallacy*.[11] Their point is that identifying conscious phenomena with their neurophysiological correlates is a hasty bit of invalid, part-whole reasoning. Maxwell Bennett and Peter Hacker are moved by Wittgenstein's claim that "only of a human being and what resembles (behaves like) a living human being can one say: it has sensations; it sees, is blind; hears, is deaf; is conscious or unconscious."[12] The point here is that our concepts covering conscious life only have applications in situations involving organisms involved with an environment, e.g., it only makes sense to talk of "seeing" when we can say something like "Cormac sees the bear approaching." To attempt to apply these concepts to a discrete part of an organism (physical or non-physical), divorced entirely from that organism's environmental situation and subsequent behaviors, is a deep confusion. Brains do not *see*; only certain conscious organisms *see*. Thus, neatly identifying feeling, willing, thinking, etc., with the activities of discrete neurophysiological parts of an organism is quite literally nonsense. Consciousness is had by the whole organism, not any discrete part of such an organism.[13] Thus, Maxwell and Hacker, for these Wittgensteinian reasons, would conclude that taking a picture of a brain in *Zeta* is not at all the same thing as producing an image of a thought about Paris. What follows is an attempt to extend the "whole" on which thinking depends beyond that to which Maxwell and Hacker appeal by developing a different argument introduced by Wittgenstein.

Wittgenstein pretty clearly claims that we should not understand *thinking-about-Paris* as supervening on *Zeta*: "No supposition seems to me more natural than that there is no process in the brain correlated

10. For my treatment of these issues, see *Mind, Matter, and Nature*, 133–70.

11. See Bennett and Hacker, *Philosophical Foundations of Neuroscience*, 68–80.

12. Wittgenstein, *Philosophical Investigations*, 103 (§281).

13. See Anscombe, "The Immortality of the Soul," and Geach, *God and the Soul*.

with associating or thinking; so that it would be impossible to read off the thought process from the brain processes."[14] Don't be too hasty to conclude that he means to unhinge thinking from brain processes, as Wittgenstein is not denying an empirical correlation between expressions of thought and processes in the brain. He says that there is no thought-to-brain correlation only in the sense that there is no process from which one can "read off" the content of the thought, e.g., there is nothing about *Zeta* that allows us to see that its subject is thinking about Paris. Although Wittgenstein does not believe that brain processes can be used as pictures of thought, he is perfectly happy to admit that "if I talk or write there is, I assume, a system of impulses going out from my brain and correlated with the my spoken or written thoughts."[15] Wittgenstein does not doubt (and in fact he assumes) that any expression of *thinking-about-Paris*, e.g., Cormac's saying or writing "Paris is the capital of the Fifth French Republic," will be correlated with an occurrence of *Zeta*. Even supposedly "inner" thoughts that go unexpressed could be so correlated retrospectively, consistent with Wittgenstein's claims. For example, if we saw that Patrick's brain was in *Zeta* two minutes ago, when we ask him what he was thinking a couple minutes back, we should expect him to say that "I was thinking about Paris."

Nevertheless, Wittgenstein maintains that it is impossible to "read off" *thinking-about-Paris* from *Zeta*. He motivates this claim, as is typical for Wittgenstein, by offering a rather odd thought experiment:

> The case would be like the following—certain kinds of plants multiply by seed, so that a seed always produces a plant of the same kind as that from which it was produced—but nothing in the seed corresponds to the plant which comes from it; so that it is impossible to infer the properties or structure of the plant from those of the seed that it comes out of—this can only be done by the history of seed. So an organism might come into being even out of something quite amorphous, as it were causelessly; and there is no reason why this should not hold for our thoughts, and hence for our thinking and writing.[16]

Wittgenstein's proposal is strange, but intelligible. He supposes that we might be aware of a curious relationship between a certain type of plant

14. Wittgenstein, *The Wittgenstein Reader*, 209–10.

15. Wittgenstein, *The Wittgenstein Reader*, 210

16. Wittgenstein, *The Wittgenstein Reader*, 210. Wittgenstein makes a similar point using a different thought experiment in *The Blue and Brown Books*, 5–10.

and a certain type of seed, such that any case in which such a seed is appropriately nourished, we would expect that type of plant to occur. Thus, there is a sense in which the seed is a sufficient condition for the plant, i.e., the proper occurrence of the seed is *predictively sufficient* for the occurrence of the plant. All we would have to know about the world in order to predict that such a plant will show up is that such a seed is appropriately situated. In Wittgenstein's example, however, there is nothing about the properties or structure of the seed that sheds any light on the properties or structures of the plant. It is simply an explanatory surd that these seeds regularly precede these plants. There is nothing about the intrinsic nature of the seed leading us to connect it with the plant. We make that connection only based on what we know about the history of such seeds and plants. All we have ever needed to do to get such plants to grow is to plant such seeds, and we know the prior history of each of these plants involves one of this kind of seed as its origin. There is, however, nothing about the seeds that sheds light on why they give rise to such plants. That is why Wittgenstein claims that the plant comes about "causelessly," even though the seed is a predictively sufficient condition for it. The seed *predicts* the occurrence of the plant (given a reasonable induction over past occurrences), but it does not *explain* the structure and properties of the plant. Thus, even though the seed is a predictively sufficient condition for the plant, the plant does not supervene on the seed; this plant is not *just* this seed, as there are properties that the plant has that the seed lacks and there is no intrinsic connection between those properties and any properties in the seed. Taking a picture of a seed would not be the very same act as taking a picture of a corresponding plant, even though we might know that all you need to bring about such a plant is such a seed.

Of course, this is just a thought experiment invented by Wittgenstein. There are no seeds and plants so mysteriously related (at least of which I am aware), but such a predictive, though non-explanatory relation, seems perfectly coherent. Wittgenstein connects this thought experiment to our current concern regarding the mind-brain supervenience thesis: "It is thus perfectly possible that certain psychological phenomena cannot be investigated physiologically, because physiologically nothing corresponds to them."[17] Following Wittgenstein's analogy, something like *Zeta* is an analogue to the seed, and *thinking-about-Paris* is an analogue to the plant. Nobody doubts that *Zeta* is predictively sufficient for an

17. Wittgenstein, *The Wittgenstein Reader*, 210.

occurrence of *thinking-about-Paris*. It is perfectly plausible that the neurosciences have revealed that if Cormac is in *Zeta*, then it is highly probable that he is thinking about Paris. Nevertheless "nothing corresponds," in Wittgenstein's sense, between *Zeta* and *thinking-about-Paris*. Given the history of *Zeta-type* states, we might be able to say that knowing that *Zeta* occurs is alone enough to expect that *thinking-about-Paris* is occurring, but nothing in the intrinsic character of *Zeta* is at all connected to the content or information contained in an occurrence of *thinking-about-Paris*. Ultimately, *Zeta* is just an intersection of electrical impulses moving along highly structured networks of membranes, and none of that has any bearing on the content of *thinking-about-Paris*. One might say that *Zeta* occurs in regions of the brain associated with this sort of thinking, but that seems to beg the question against Wittgenstein's point. The only reason we know to correlate those regions with those kinds of thinking is based on their history not their internal character. *Zeta* is just chemical impulses moving along membranes that have nothing whatsoever to do with the content of a thought about Paris.

Fair enough, but an obvious objection looms. Certainly, we might have only a non-explanatory correlation from certain seed-types to certain plant-types, but that could just be reflective of our currently limited understanding of seeds and plants and not an ontologically significant difference between the two. Maybe, with further investigation, we will come to understand that there is indeed an intrinsic connection between the structures and properties of these seeds and plants, such that we can say there is something like a supervenience relation (or some sort of strongly explanatory causation) in play here, e.g., the plants and seeds are the very same things at different stages of phylogenesis.

I agree that Wittgenstein's example is weak in this way; there is always the possibility that what *appears* as an unbridgeable ontological gap will be closed by future discoveries. Its weakness is considerably mitigated when we consider the *Zeta* and *thinking-about-Paris* case in particular. Even if we do not know what connects the seeds and plants yet, it is perfectly plausible that we will eventually make such a discovery. At least we can conceive of what such a discovery might look like based on other cases of botanical progress in the past. There is already much in common between seeds and plants, such that it pays to hold out for an answer. What, however, would it even be like to discover the nature of an intrinsic connection between *Zeta* and *thinking-about-Paris*? What could chemical impulses moving across membranes (or even systems of such impulses across membranes or systems of such systems, etc.) have to do with the content of a thought? When it comes to *Zeta* and *thinking-about-Paris*, it seems we have arrived at the ultimate apples vs. oranges comparison. Betting on the possibility of some sort of scientific revolution, the nature of which goes beyond anything currently in our ken, is not a good way to motivate a position. Certainly, we should be wary of a "mind of the gaps" argument in the way that one does well not to appeal to a god of the gaps, but we should be equally wary of how much latitude we give to "promissory note" materialism. As Thomas Nagel puts it, bridging the difference between thinking (or consciousness more generally) and the activities of the brain would "require a major conceptual revolution at least as radical as relativity theory, the introduction of electromagnetic fields into physics—or the original scientific revolution itself."[18] Refusing to hinge one's theory of mind on a currently unfathomable, future theoretical revolution is not an appeal to ignorance, but being realistic about what we can reasonably expect in terms of scientific progress.[19]

There is much traction to this reply, but we can do more to motivate Wittgenstein's position. The following thought experiment makes a much stronger case. Like any thought experiment, it's a piece of just-so science fiction built entirely on conjecture about things that have never actually happened (and probably never will), but it is plausible enough to reveal our most reasonable intuitions in this area. Suppose a brain scientist cloned a living, adult human brain. This need not be a direct copy of any existing adult brain, but just a clone made using some future technology to cultivate an organ from stem cell lines. Further suppose that our brain scientist stimulates this brain directly such that it exhibits an occurrence of *Zeta*. The brain is not embedded in an organism that has traveled to Paris, seen a picture of Paris, read a book about Paris, etc. Our scientist just directly "fertilizes" the "seed" by electromagnetic stimulation to bring about *Zeta*. Does that brain thereby have an occurrence of *thinking-about-Paris*? I find it hard to believe someone can seriously answer this question affirmatively. There is no intrinsic connection between *Zeta* as brought about in the cloned brain and the actual city Paris. If one allows that *Zeta* in the cloned and isolated brain is sufficient to have a thought about Paris, then one must likewise grant that had Paris never existed,

18. Nagel, *Mind and Cosmos*, 42.

19. There is also an interesting question regarding whether it is technologically possible to settle this issue, given the plausible limitations of our imaging methods. See Gidon, "Does Brain Activity Cause Consciousness."

an occurrence of *Zeta* would, nevertheless, leave a brain thinking about Paris. That seems pretty odd. Are we to believe that evolution has left an intrinsic connection between *Zeta* and an eternal essence of a city that may or may not exist in the concrete? Are we to suppose that a caveman who accidentally had an occurrence of *Zeta*, say by a fortuitous blow to the head, would have had a thought about Paris before Paris even existed? Even if we admit (and I am not at all prepared to concede this point) that the caveman would have something like the phenomenology associated with our *thinking-about-Paris*, that gives us no reason to conclude that he is thinking about Paris as opposed to some nearly similar city. It isn't the phenomenal qualities we associate with that thought that refers our thinking to Paris; those qualities could refer to infinitely many qualitatively similar cities. Rather, we manage to refer to Paris by being related to *that* actual city, however remotely so. Surely, people could have had dreams or fantasies including such images, but those images need not be images *of Paris* unless they are in some sort of relation *with Paris*. I could keep piling on, but suffice it to say, it is hard to take seriously the suggestion that the occurrence of *Zeta* really is strictly sufficient for an occurrence of *thinking-about-Paris*.

Maybe I'm being too simplistic. Talk of singular brains states like *Zeta* is a philosopher's invention. Brain states are not nice and neat, discrete events like states of a digital computer. They are always mixed with the myriad of other goings on simultaneously in the brain, as they are also always consequent to prior global goings-on that affect them. Maybe our neuroscientist also stimulates the cloned brain to have corresponding occurrences of brain processes associated with memory traces of reading *The Count of Monte Cristo*, seeing photos of the Eiffel Tower or the Louvre. All of these so-called brain states were forged together, and together they may be what constitutes thinking about Paris. Might we not then say that an occurrence of *Zeta* in the cloned brain is eligible to be an instance of *thinking-about-Paris* because it is couched in a network of other brain states relevantly associated with such a thought? Not really, because this proposal just kicks the can down the proverbial road. Would a caveman who accidentally had the set of brain processes associated in our brains with having read *The Count of Monte Cristo* then have inklings of the foibles of Edmund Dantes millennia before Dumas even conceived of this character? Once again, even if we grant that the caveman would have something like the qualitative aspects of such a thought (and I am, once again, not prepared to make that concession), that seems extravagant.

There is no intrinsic connection between any set of neurophysiological states and any specific cognitive content. In short, *Zeta* is associated
with *thinking-about-Paris* because it was forged by the interaction of the
human organism with Paris, even if the interaction has been mediated
culturally by long causal chains. Without occurring in that context, there
is nothing about *Zeta* that gives it anything like a relation to Paris.[20]

There is, however, an important insight behind this objection that
will be crucially important for what follows: Whether we are talking
about the cloned brain or the fortuitously injured caveman, *neither of
these supposed thinkers learned to use the concept of Paris in the same way
we do.* We did so by reading, say the *Count of Monte Cristo*, talking to
people who had traveled there, finding our way around the actual city,
learning to locate it on the map, etc. As I have mentioned, contrary to
the hypothetical objector, the brain states formed by taking up these activities do not suffice to identify *thinking-about-Paris* any more than does
our now-fabled *Zeta*. We can appeal to as many goings on in the brain as
we like, but we do not get the content of a thought about Paris until we
go outside the head and into an engagement with the city. The suggestion
that *Zeta* follows on other practically gained neurophysiological developments, however, does bring to light the connection between *dealing* with
Paris and *thinking-about-Paris*. We learned how to use "Paris," and the
concept we express by the word, by working with Paris, even if remotely
and indirectly. Come what may, we gain cognitive access to Paris (we
gather the concept of Paris or learn to think about Paris) by doing things
"out there" in the world. Moreover, *Thinking-about-Paris* only comes
up in the first place in the context of other thinkings and doings, and
the notion that this resulting battery of concepts can be sharply excised
from either each other or the practically accessible world whose demands
they were originally formed to meet is at best highly questionable. Thus,
our initial thinking about Paris was not done in some internal theater of
consciousness exclusively caused by or otherwise realized in a brain, but
"outside" in much the say way that we learned to think about arithmetic
using a pen and paper (or more recently poking an electronic tablet),

20. I am bordering on issues germane to the debate over descriptivism in the
philosophy of language, i.e., the question of whether descriptions (qualitative or otherwise) are necessary or even sufficient to fix the reference of a word. The kind of
externalist position I am staking out here certainly has kinship with anti-descriptivists
in the philosophy of language, e.g., Kripke, but I do not believe that it entails any
definite commitment in those thorny debates. See Soames, *Reference and Description*,
for a comprehensive treatment of the debate in the philosophy of language.

and it likewise continues to depend on this broader context, however remotely, in perpetuity.[21]

For this reason, Wittgenstein argues that in cases like observing the correlation between *Zeta* and our reports of *thinking-about-Paris*, we are indeed

> observing a correlation of two phenomenon. One of them [the scientific observer] calls the *thought*. This may consist of the train of images, organic sensations, or on the other hand of a train of various visual, tactual and muscular experiences which he has in writing or thinking or speaking a sentence.—The other . . . seeing [the] brain work. Both these phenomena could correctly be called "expressions of thought"; and the question "where is the thought itself?" had better, in order to prevent confusion, be rejected as nonsensical.[22]

In other words, neither a supposed inner experience (sensation or image) or a brain state is a plausible candidate for being the very same thing as a thought. An inner process, whether neurophysiological or mental, is alone insufficient to constitute thinking about something. Thinking for us is initially done by learning to speak or write *about something*; which is to say that thinking is not something that can be located in any such straightforward sense, and it definitely cannot be located in the head (or isolated mind). Anything that can be discretely "located," e.g., a neuro-physiological event or mental episode, does not by itself reach out to an object of thought. For Wittgenstein, *thinking-about-Paris* is neither a brain state nor inner mental event, but a practically mediated relation to an actual city. In short, thought in many ways begins just as much outside-in as inside-out.

It then seems Wittgenstein is correct: an occurrence of *Zeta* is insufficient for the occurrence of *thinking-about-Paris*. Indeed, if we take our thought experiment seriously, we might even say that *Zeta* isn't even predictively sufficient for *thinking-about-Paris* under all conditions. We supposed that the brain scientist was able to produce an occurrence of *Zeta* without producing an occurrence of *thinking-about-Paris*, and that, for the reasons I have given above, seems quite plausible. Thus, *thinking-about-Paris* does not supervene on *Zeta* even in some weaker (causal as

21. See Kording and Lillicrap, "What Does It Mean," for a neuroscientific case that the conditions under which we learn to engage a certain cognition has bearing on our understanding of what such a cognition is.

22. Wittgenstein, *The Blue and Brown Books*, 8. Wittgenstein's emphasis.

opposed to "sameness") sense. Since, as we discussed earlier, we would say that one can picture *thinking-about-Paris* by picturing *Zeta*, only if *thinking-about-Paris* supervenes on *Zeta*, we should now conclude that we cannot picture *thinking-about-Paris* by picturing *Zeta*, and therefore picturing a brain is not the same as picturing a mind. All of that is just to say that whatever *thinking-about-Paris* is, it is not the very same thing as *Zeta*, and, therefore, brains are not the very same things as minds. We will have much more to discuss about all of that in the following sections of this chapter and its sequel.

There are, of course, no small number of extant thought experiments in contemporary philosophy of mind purporting to show that the operation of the brain is alone sufficient for the full menu of perceptive and cognitive phenomena. For example, we are often supposed to see the intuitive obviousness that a human brain floating in a vat of properly fortified, life-supporting fluids would have the complete compliment of mental processes as you and I enjoy, if only it were stimulated properly. John Searle prominently argues that such "brain in a vat" scenarios are plausible, because it is obvious that this is simply how things actually operate in human cognition:

> The brain is all we have for the purpose of representing the world to ourselves and everything we can use must be inside the brain. Each of our beliefs must be possible for a being who is a brain in a vat because each of us is precisely a brain in a vat; the vat is the skull and the "messages" coming in are coming in by way of impacts on the nervous system.[23]

Here Searle speaks along with what many thinkers in the mainstream of Anglo-American philosophy of mind and seemingly ubiquitous speculation in popular culture take as an unquestioned given: our intuitions show us that all that is necessary for our mental lives is a stimulated brain, whether or not it floats in a skull or a vat. We do know from certain well-verified experimental results and clinical presentations (phantom limbs, etc.) that direct stimulations of brains, in lieu of the mediation between the body and the external world, can result in various conscious experiences, even if limited and episodic. Thus, we cannot say that the intuitions behind the brain-in-a-vat scenario (and similarly aimed thought experiments going back to Descartes' dream hypothesis) are utterly unfounded empirically.

23. Searle, *Intentionality*, 230.

Be that as it may, I take it that these empirical suggestions are a far cry from sufficiently motivating the claim that activity internal to the brain is sufficient for what I have been calling *thought*. First there are prominent arguments against the very coherence of the brain in a vat scenario. For example, Hilary Putnam argues that if we were brains in a vat, the hypothesis of our being brains in a vat would be nothing we could take seriously, since it would require of us some sort of access (a causal connection) beyond the vat as it were. The content of our thoughts would have to be grounded in states of affairs in the world, i.e., there is nothing cognitive "in here" unless there is some grounding "out there." Putnam's argument to this effect is famously technical, complicated, and controversial, but his central thesis is essentially that the words or representations occurrent to the hapless brain in the vat can only gain their meaning via causal contact external to its contrived experience. Thus, to deny that our thinking connects us beyond "the vat" is to undermine the very meaning of the terms in which this hypothesis is expressed, i.e., the brain in a vat scenario is semantically self-defeating.[24] I will not wade into those treacherous waters here, though there are very prominent thinkers who do not take the brain-in-a-vat scenario as unassailably plausible.

In any event, all of these sorts of scenarios purporting to prove the supposed plausibility (or maybe just possibility) that "it's all just in our heads or minds" share a conceptual difficulty that can be readily shown.[25] When I'm dreaming, it is not a dream that I am dreaming and the realization would put me in contact with reality beyond my dream. *That I am dreaming* is not an illusion of the dream; a lucid dream gets its status as a dream objectively correct. In other words, it is never just a dream that I am dreaming. These considerations undermine the various "simulation hypotheses" currently abroad in both academic philosophy and popular culture. *The fact that I am in a simulation* is not a fact merely in the simulation (an illusion) but an extra-simulation fact, i.e., *that I am*

24. This is an extremely quick treatment of a very technical argument that has inspired a great deal of debate. See Putnam, *Reason, Truth, and History*; Wright, "On Putnam's Proof," 216–41; and Putnam, "Reply to Wright," in *Reading Putnam*, 242–95.

25. In the spirit of the ontological neutrality I am trying to maintain in this chapter, the following should not be taken as a defense of realism over idealism. The point is not to argue about the ontological character of the world, but to claim that for there to be thinking inside me, there must be a world beyond me with which I am involved. The argument of this chapter is anti-solipsistic (in the vein of the later Wittgenstein), without commitment *per se* to the materiality or immateriality (whatever we might mean by those fraught terms) of the world.

in a simulation would not be merely an illusion of the simulation. If I can claim that I am in a simulation with epistemic warrant, then there is at least one extra-simulation fact to which I am privy, i.e., *that I am in a simulation*. Thus, if I could know that I'm in a simulation, then I am not in a simulation in the fullest sense. In other words, the simulation hypothesis cannot be coherently asserted with rational justification (if we take the simulation to be utterly complete, i.e., there is nothing I am aware of that is not merely simulated). In short, the fact that we can ponder whether we are in a simulation (or dreaming our whole lives) and can come to some reasoned conclusion on the matter implies that we are not trapped in a simulation. We have some, however slight and tenuous, hold on a world outside the simulation. The brain in a vat scenario is akin to these other skeptical hypotheses about the external world inasmuch as it is similarly self-defeating, If we are really brains in vats, that fact (the fact that we are brains in a vat) is not merely an illusion of a brain in a vat. In that scenario, our being brains in vats would not merely be "in our heads," but really "out there." Any reason, empirical or conceptual, that could then be given to support that we are brains in a vat would then be self-refuting; every reason to think we are brains in a vat ultimately presupposes that we are not just brains in a vat but have some access beyond the proverbial veil of illusions. Thus, we cannot claim with any sort of rational justification that we are brains in a vat.

Leaving aside those semantic and conceptual concerns, it is far from clear that the empirical evidence supports the plausibility of anything remotely close to the brain in a vat scenario. Evan Thompson makes this point quite well:

> The proposal [the brain-in-a-vat as sufficient for thinking thesis], however, depends on empirical considerations that are far from settled. We simply do not yet know the minimal biological requirements for the instantiation or realization of consciousness. It is one thing for neural activity to be the minimal sufficient condition for the instantiation of a fleeting, episodic moment of phenomenal consciousness. It is quite another thing for neural activity to be the minimal sufficient condition for the instantiation of consciousness in the sense of coherent and temporally extended intentional experience of the world . . . such consciousness might require nothing less than a living body engaged with the world.[26]

26. Thompson, *Mind in Life*, 241.

That is, even if we have good reason to think that fleeting episodes of consciousness can be produced by stimulating a brain in a vat, that does very little to motivate the notion that something like Cormac's *thinking-about-Paris* can be so produced. Thoughts, of that sort any way, are not fleeting moments of consciousness, but long-term commitments to the materially grounded (empirically falsifiable) inferential consequences of a certain claim. Even if a pure qualitative subjectivity or episodic memory can be produced by direct stimulation, atomistic mental events are insufficient to account for the contents of our thinking. Moreover, suppose that in the future we were able to produce inferentially situated and phenomenologically rich experiences by direct brain stimulation in experimental subjects. Even so, as long as those subjects have been formed by a prior human practical engagement with the world, such experiments would not prove the plausibility of brain-in-a-vat scenarios at all. It seems those subjects would still be drawing on prior thinking out beyond the head. If one supposed we could in principle clone a brain and appropriately stimulate it to bring about fully human experience or thought, she would only beg the question against the thought experiments I have raised above.[27]

Using Wittgensteinian thought experiments I have attempted to motivate the conclusion that our thoughts have contents that reach beyond our skulls (or vats) into a world and history, and this shows us that our minds are not discrete entities behind our skulls. To understand our thinking, we must appeal to more than brains, or anything else that can be neatly pictured. Once again, with Thompson, it is not an organ, i.e., the brain or even an individuated soul, that thinks, but an "organism, animal, or person that has conscious access to the world. As conscious subjects we are not brains in cranial vats; we are neurally enlivened beings in the world."[28] It seems then that Wittgenstein is correct: an occurrence of *Zeta* is insufficient for the occurrence of *thinking-about-Paris*. Indeed, if we take the foregoing line of argument seriously, we might even say that *Zeta* isn't even predictively sufficient for *thinking-about-Paris*. In our thought experiment, the brain scientist was able to produce an occurrence of *Zeta* without producing an occurrence of *thinking-about-Paris*. Thus,

27. The claims of this paragraph will be discussed and defended in detail in the following chapter. For a phenomenological critique of much of the empirical motivation for the brain-in-a-vat intuitions, see Merleau-Ponty's masterful treatment of the phantom limb and other similar pathologies in *Phenomenology of Perception*, 78–89.

28. Thompson, *Mind in Life*, 242.

thinking-about-Paris does not supervene on *Zeta* even in some weaker sense. Since, as we discussed earlier, we would say that one can picture *thinking-about-Paris* by picturing *Zeta*, only if *thinking-about-Paris* supervenes on *Zeta*, we should now conclude that we cannot picture *thinking-about-Paris* by picturing *Zeta*. Thus, taking a picture of a brain in action is not taking a picture of a mind in action. In the following section, I will show why this conclusion does more than highlight a gaff by innocent textbook authors but holds far-reaching consequences for how we think about our thinking.

3. Mind-Brain Dualism?

Be cautious against common tendencies to make too much of the conclusions reached by these arguments against strict mind-brain supervenience. We have shown that minds are not supervenient on brains, and maybe even the latter are not even predictively sufficient for the former, i.e., *Zeta* alone is not enough to predict *thinking-about-Paris* in a brain that has not been relevantly situated in a world. That, however, is not to say that certain brain states are not necessary conditions for correlated mental states, nor that brains are not necessary conditions for minds. In short, one can accept all that we have argued thus far while granting an "If no brain, no mind" thesis with perfect consistency. Indeed, much of what we know about the world, both through science and common sense, should encourage us to accept such a thesis. I have only attempted to cast doubt on an "If brain, then mind" thesis. Furthermore, nothing I have argued so far casts doubt on the possibility that thoughts *emerge* from situations involving living organisms (including their brains) that are *properly situated in a world*. In fact, in the following section I will try to make this claim plausible, though what I count for "being situated in a world" will be a fairly complicated matter that will not be fully detailed until chapter 2.

Nothing in the foregoing argument has given us any reason to conclude that mental states should be identified with non-physical processes internal to a mind, which is itself identified as an immaterial organ or substance that parallels the brain. Wittgenstein himself is very quick to point out that, although thought is not a material process internal to the individual thinker (a process in the brain), that does not imply that a thought is therefore an immaterial process internal to the thinker (a process internal to an immaterial organ, a mind taken as an immaterial substance).[29] In this spirit, Elizabeth Anscombe grants that "thought and understanding are immaterial, since no act of a bodily organ is [a mental state]," but she denies that from this premise it follows that "thought and understanding are the acts of an immaterial part."[30] Thought cannot be identified with the activity of any single physical organ, but that is not because there is need of "an additional element existing along side by side" the physical processes in some "immaterial, or spiritual, substance."[31] The premise "thought is not a physical event" implies "thought is an immaterial occurrence in a separate, immaterial mind," only if we operate under the assumption that "thought must occur internal to some individual substance." That, however, is the very assumption the Wittgensteinians are calling into question, as it has caused philosophers nothing but confusion and frustration. As Peter Hacker puts it, whether the mind is identical to a brain (or any other kind of substantial entity, such as a disembodied soul) "becomes transparently absurd, since the mind is not the kind of entity that might be identical to anything."[32]

In fact, the identification of thoughts with discrete, immaterial events (like invisible finger snaps or some such) or the mind with an immaterial substance (a ghostly thinker) would be subject to the very same line of criticism raised by the thought experiment I have leveled against the mind-brain supervenience thesis. It would be quite odd to claim that an immaterial, substantial mind that acts as the ground for an instance of *thinking-about-Paris* could have such a thought even though Paris had never existed, etc. Would an immaterial mind, existing in a possible world where Paris never has and never will exist be capable of having thoughts about Paris? Maybe such a ghost could have imaginings about a beautiful city, known for an impressive steel tower, and that was also once conquered by a chauvinistically Teutonic dictator with a little mustache (though I believe these sorts of speculations mostly go beyond our ken). In any event, those would not be thoughts about Paris, but merely a

---

29. See Wittgenstein, *Philosophical Investigations*, 63–66 (§146–54), 108–9 (§304–6).

30. Anscombe, "The Immateriality of the Soul," 69.

31. Anscombe, "The Immateriality of the Soul," 69–70. In this article, Anscombe does not deny that the soul survives death in some sense, though she claims not to be able to make any sense of it as a separate substance. For another account of the nonsubstantial survival of death, see Johnston, *Saving God*, 174–86, and *Surviving Death*.

32. Hacker, *Human Nature*, 251.

general description that can be satisfied by infinitely many possible cities. There is nothing *internal* to those imaginings sufficient to make them *about* Paris in particular, and this content can arise only if the subject is in some relationship to Paris itself. Moreover, it is no less absurd to say an immaterial substance has *thinking-about-Paris* as an essential feature than it is to say as much about a brain. Whether something thinks about Paris is contingent on its bearing a certain relationship to that particular city, the existence of which is itself contingent. A thought is then not a process strictly *internal* to the thinker, whether we conceive of thinkers as material or immaterial substances, but always something that extends beyond the discrete boundaries of any discrete individual.

Whether it is taken to occur in a material or immaterial thinking substance, to have a thought about Paris requires that the thinker be related to Paris in some very definite way, and the relation will require much more than factors *internal* to the thinker. Thus, no "picture" of anything internal to a thinker is a picture of a thought, nor is a picture of any solitary, individual object a picture of a mind. That is not to say at all that there are no such things as minds, nor is it to deny that there are such occurrences as thoughts. The claim is that minds and their thoughts are quite real, but they are *categorically* different from events like finger snaps and entities like brains, or even ghosts. That is not to say that minds are physical things, nor is it to say that minds are non-physical things, in the typical substantial sense of "thing."[33] Brains (and their processes) and ghosts (and their processes) are (or would be in the latter case) discretely individuated entities, whereas minds (and their processes) are not. Thus, inferences about the latter modeled on the kinds of inferences we can make about the former are suspect. These ways of thinking about thinking and thinkers are wrought with tempting invalidities, against which Wittgenstein and his students have so strenuously tried to caution us since the middle of the last century.[34]

33. Except in Anscombe's sense of immaterial as not being identifiable with any discrete material entity. Remember, however, that does not imply something immaterial in that sense can therefore be identified with any discrete immaterial entity.

34. The most famous accusation of a category mistake at the heart of modern philosophy of mind is Gilbert Ryle's famous attack on Descartes' substance dualism in *The Concept of Mind*. A common misreading of Ryle is that he is out to defend a materialist version of behaviorism. Whatever the excesses of his attack on dualism might be, Ryle's position is equally damaging to materialist attempts at identifying the mind as some sort of discrete object internal to individual thinkers. David Braine is superb on this point in *The Human Person*, 19–68.

Heidegger, like Wittgenstein, eschews any neat identification of thinking with discretely individuated entities, physical or non-physical. For example, when thinking about or even directly perceiving some actual tree, Heidegger asks "Does it by any chance take place in our heads? Of course, many things take place in our brain when we stand in a meadow and have standing before us a blossoming tree in all its radiance and fragrance—we perceive it," but these "brain currents" are not the tree we perceive, nor are they the content of a thought about a tree.[35] Nevertheless, Heidegger does not thereby leap to identify the perception or thought of the tree with some immaterial event within consciousness (as opposed to a brain):

> When ideas are formed in this way, a variety of things happen presumably also in what is described as the sphere of consciousness and regarded as pertaining to the soul. But does that tree stand "in our consciousness," or does it stand in the meadow? Does the meadow lie in the soul, as an experience, or does it spread out there on earth? Is the earth in our head? Or do we stand on the earth?[36]

The thinking or perceiving of a tree only occurs inasmuch as the thinker or perceiver is, in some sense, *with* the tree in the meadow. That is, thinking is not something that occurs internal to the subject of thought, like a process in an organ. Rather thinking is a *being-related-to* something, or really a whole world of somethings (the tree is in the meadow, and the meadow is "spread out on the earth"). The thought of a tree, like Cormac's *thinking-about-Paris*, cannot be pinpointed as any single event in an organism or disembodied ghost. Thinking is a sort of involvement with a *world*.

All of this is to say that thoughts and the minds that have them, though real, are not discrete entities, neatly individuated spatially or temporally in the manner of tables, chairs, molecules, changes in velocity, and ghosts (should there be a way of neatly individuating ghosts). Mental entities (minds and their thoughts) are beings, but not the same kinds of beings as the objects we can capture in our scientific understandings. As Aristotle so famously claimed, "Something is said to be in many ways."[37] The discourse by which we capture truths about brains is incommensurable

---

35. Heidegger, *What Is Called Thinking?*, 48.
36. Heidegger, *What Is Called Thinking?*, 43.
37. Aristotle, *Metaphysics*, 1003b33 (48).

with the discourse by which we capture truths about minds. Paul Ricoeur captures this stance well in his notion of a *semantic dualism*:

> I proceed, then, from a semantic dualism that expresses a duality of perspectives. The tendency to slip from a dualism of discourses to a dualism of substances is encouraged by the fact that each field of study tends to define itself in terms of what may be called a final referent, something to which appeal can be made as a last resort. But this referent is final only in its respective field, and comes to be defined at the same time as the field itself is defined. It is therefore necessary to refrain from transforming a dualism of referents into a dualism of substances.[38]

In other words, what is at stake is not a plurality of substances, even though the world turns out to be ontologically richer than what can be articulated in scientific discourse.[39] Rather, as Markus Gabriel puts it, "There exist different fields of sense [ways of being] which are accessible in different ways and capable of being interpreted in various ways."[40] All that the Wittgensteinian arguments (and their equivalents proffered by philosophers like Ricoeur writing on the other side of the English Channel) secure is that scientific methods, vocabularies, descriptions, resources for explanation, etc., do not constitute the only veridical discourse about human nature.[41] Even if the complete story about the brain were told, there would still be more left to be said about thinking. Since Ricoeur casts his stance as a semantic *dualism*, I take it that he does not think there is any theoretical link by which the discourse of human physiology and the discourse of the human mind can ultimately

38. Ricoeur, *What Makes Us Think*, 14.

39. This might be taken to mean that Ricoeur's *semantic dualism* is not apropos to what I am up to, as I am claiming that minds and thoughts add to an austere ontology of brains and neurological events (or ghosts and ghostly events). Fair enough, but I take it that most parties to these debates are primarily concerned with whether the fact that there are beings with minds requires us to add to our inventory of individual, discretely demarcated substances, and in that sense the position I am developing is a *de-ontologized* philosophy of mind. If it helps, think of it as more-subtly-ontologized philosophy of mind or simply bracket the ontological question for present purposes.

40. Gabriel, *Why the World Does Not Exist*, 142. Grabriel's book provides a sustained and convincing defense of the sort of ontological pluralism (as opposed to dualism) I am suggesting in this chapter that is conversant with both the analytic and Continental traditions.

41. For a very helpful interpretation of Wittgenstein's defense of the aspectual character of discourses, which I find dovetails with the point expressed by Ricoeur (and other authors on the Continent we will discuss below), see Verdi, *Fat Wednesday*.

be merged. There is no one-to-one translation of the one discourse into the other. There are two distinct, both legitimate, ways of conceptualizing and explaining the world. These two discourses are not in competition, because they are performing completely unrelated explanatory tasks. The discourse to which talk of *Zeta* belongs and the discourse to which *thinking-about-Paris* belongs are not entirely unrelated (the former in all probability refers to a necessary condition for the latter), but the content of the thought is completely *sui generous* with respect to the underlying neurophysiology. The neuroscientific story about *Zeta* may tell us some of the conditions under which thought about Paris can occur, but it does not provide an explanation of what *thinking-about-Paris* really is. That sort of question opens us to a much broader discourse than what can be captured in any narrowly scientific discourse.

Roger Scruton, himself drawing on the nineteenth-century tradition of *Geisteswissenschaften* (human sciences), makes much the same point when he introduces the notion of "*cognitive dualism*, according to which the world can be understood in two incommensurable ways, the way of science and the way of interpersonal understanding."[42] Scruton agrees with Wilfrid Sellars's famous dictum, "in the dimension of describing and explaining the world, science is the measure of all things, of what is that it is, and what is not that it is not."[43] Nevertheless, again like Sellars, Scruton argues that in addition to the world revealed by scientific description, there is also a discursively distinct world that is

> known in another way, through the practice of *Verstehen*. The world known in this other way will be an "emergent" world, represented in the cognitive apparatus of the perceiver, but emerging from the physical reality, as the face emerges from the pigments on the canvas, or the melody from the sequence of pitched sounds.[44]

42. Scruton, *The Soul of the World*, 34. My emphasis.

43. Sellars, "Empiricism and the Philosophy of Mind," 173. Note that I do not share Scruton's endorsement of the "science is the measure" dictum for reasons that will become apparent in the following chapter. At times it is unclear how serious Scruton takes Sellars' scientific realism, rather than operating within something of a neo-Kantian pluralism more akin to the position I mention above as developed by Gabriel. At the very least, there is a deep tension between Scruton's endorsement of Sellars's dictum and his invocation of the Husserlian notion of the autonomous *Lebenswelt* that I will discuss below.

44. Scruton, *The Soul of the World*, 36. For Sellars's seminal treatment of the distinction between the "scientific image of man" and the "manifest image of man," see "Philosophy and the Scientific Image of Man," 1–40.

Scruton is playing here on a distinction between scientific explanation and interpretive understanding, *Verstehen*. The former is the discourse of the causes of things, whereas the latter is the discourse of their meaning or significance. Scruton is happy to grant a kind of ontological priority of the scientific image over the discourse of *Verstehen*, in the sense that the scientific approach governs our account of what exists in a narrow sense, i.e., "what there is" among individuated entities. The inventory of discrete individuals occupying mathematically specifiable positions in space-time is not increased by the discourse of *Verstehen* over what is counted by the scientific image. Be that as it may, *Verstehen* discloses an emergent realm of meaning and significance that cannot, to return to Wittgenstein's phrase, be "read off" the entities inhabiting the world of the scientific image.

This *Lebenswelt* (lifeworld) is irreducible, as "we understand and relate to it using concepts of agency and accountability that have no place in the physical sciences."[45] The scientific image enjoys a sort of ontological priority in the sense that we are not calling into question the "If no brains, then no minds" thesis. The domain of meaning and significance in which we "live and move and have our being" can only come to be on the foundations of the physical world, including, of course, human neurophysiology (at least that is how Scruton takes it). The *Lebenswelt*, nevertheless, is not supervenient, but *emergent*. Even though "neuroscience describes one aspect of people," it does so "in language that cannot capture what we mean when we describe thinking, feeling, or intending."[46] Once it is up and running, the *Lebenswelt* has a sort of explanatory autonomy from its preconditions in the physical world. When the neuroscientist discovers *Zeta* as a rudiment of a certain thought, she has not shed any light at all on what it *means* to have a thought about Paris.

To use Scruton's favorite case, having a mind is an emergent phenomenon in much the way music emerges from the physical dynamics of acoustics. A sonata is irreducible to its constituent sounds and the laws governing their interactions, not because it is a separate, parallel process over and above the relevant physical processes, but because it expresses

45. Scruton, *The Soul of the World*, 36. Once again, I am not entirely in line with Scruton regarding the ontological ordering priority between the *Lebenswelt* and the natural sciences, for reasons that will become apparent in the following chapter. For something more akin to the view I will develop, see Michel Henry's treatment of Husserl's original notion of the *Lebenswelt* in *Barbarism*, 23–38.

46. Scruton, *The Soul of the World*, 67.

an aesthetic meaning or significance that is wholly absent among those constituent physical processes. If, by some fluke, that same acoustical phenomena were to occur (say on some uninhabited planet) without any meaningful context to which they were related, they would not constitute a sonata any more than *Zeta* in the caveman's brain makes for *thinking-about-Paris*. Certainly, sonatas are not separate substantial entities from their acoustical expressions, but neither are they the same thing as their composing sounds. To relate yourself in the same way to a sonata as you would to the underlying physical principles of the acoustics involved is at best a truncated understanding of what is really going on. Likewise, with the emergence of mind a "new order of understanding, in which reasons and meanings, rather than causes, are sought in answer to the question 'why?'" comes to be.[47] Appeal to the physical laws of acoustics is misplaced in explaining why a composer made certain decisions in the composition of a sonata.[48] Likewise, understanding the brain is not the same thing as understanding the mind, even if the being of the former is a necessary condition of the being of the latter, because our *Lebenswelt* is the domain of *Verstehen* and not scientific understanding.[49]

47. Scruton, *The Soul of the World*, 67.

48. None of this is to say that a physicalist, evolutionary account of why we experience visual or auditory patterns as pleasurable is impossible. That is all well and good. Scruton, however, has in mind that we not only find these visual and auditory patterns pleasurable, but, when in the right meaningful context, these experiences provide the grounds for *judgments* that purport to universal assent. That is, there is a sort of quasi-rational content to aesthetic experience that is wholly missing from any reductive story. Scruton takes up this point throughout *Soul of the World*, and of course Kant's *Critique of Judgment* is the canonical source for this line of thought. See also Scruton, *The Face of God*, 51–72.

49. Obviously, this approach to the mind has its origins in nineteenth-century German philosophy, but there are adherents of a such an approach in the heyday of analytic philosophy. Classic presentations of this sort of view in the analytic tradition (in addition to the works by Sellars I have cited above) are Donald Davidson's "Mental Events" and Strawson, *Individuals*. See also Hilary Putnam's *The Many Faces of Realism* and *The Threefold Cord: Mind, Body, and World*. For a magisterial attempt at a synthesis between these two traditions (including treatments of Davidson and Strawson in their Hegelian and Kantian aspects), and a significant contribution to our understanding of Hegel, see Brandom, *A Spirit of Trust*. Though Scruton draws primarily on German critical and hermeneutical resources in *The Soul of the World*, he treads much of the same ground from an Anglo-American empiricist angle in *Art and Imagination*. Markus Gabriel pulls many of these strands together in *I Am Not a Brain* and *The Meaning of Thought*. For another superb account of this intersection, see Braver, *Groundless Grounds*.

Thus, *thinking-about-Paris* is not only a neurophysiological event, but an act of *Geist*, mind or spirit, where by "spirit" we do not mean something merely "mental or subjective; rather, it signifies the meaning dimension of human understanding."[50] The mention of mind as *Geist* evokes the Hegelian origins of many of these ideas. In a famous moment of the *Phenomenology of Spirit* [*Geist*], following an extended debunking of daffy pseudo-sciences of mind abroad in his day (physiognomy and phrenology), Hegel then considers the now more familiar and empirically legitimate proposal to regard "the being of Spirit" as "brain fibers." Hegel is no less critical of the dogmatic confidence of mind-brain reductionism than he is of physiognomy and phrenology. As he puts it, "brain fibers" when separated from the meaningful context of a living human organism occupying a place in history

> are dead objects, and then no longer pass for the being of Spirit . . . the Notion underlying this idea is that Reason takes itself to be *all thinghood*, even *purely objective* thinghood itself; but it is this only in the Notion, or only the Notion is the truth of this idea; and the purer the Notion itself is, the sillier an idea it becomes when its content is in the form, not the Notion, but of picture thinking. . . .[51]

Like just about any randomly chosen sentence from Hegel's writings, there is a lot going on in even these brief remarks, which are themselves taken from one of the opaquest sections of a very long work noted for its frustrating opacity.[52] Even so, what Hegel is up to here should be familiar to us. By "Reason" in this passage Hegel means *observing reason*, which is an attitude that seeks to account for everything in the world in terms of empirically verifiable laws, including its *own* mindedness. That is, Reason is the attempt by self-consciousness to subject itself to scientific explanation, in the same terms as it would explain nonrational beings. Taking

50. Gabriel, *Why the World Does Not Exist*, 142.

51. Hegel, *The Phenomenology of Spirit*, §346. For a discussion of Hegel's remarks in the context of the neuroscientific reductionism of his day and ours, along with some earthy and hilarious comparisons with arguments Hegel goes on to make in this section of the *Phenomenology*, see Gabriel, *I Am Not a Brain*, 141–44. He aptly calls this section of his chapter "Puberty-reductionism and The Toilet Theory," though I will leave it to the reader to encounter Gabriel's witty treatment firsthand.

52. Peter Kalkavage provides an extremely helpful commentary on this section of the *Phenomenology* in *The Logic of Desire*, 157–234. Kalkavage's book is highly recommend as a road map to reading the *Phenomenology*, likely the best entry point into the densely populated world of commentaries on Hegel.

any physical description (whether phrenological or neurophysiological) as the final description of mind (identifying "brain fibers" as the "being of Spirit") is to assume the universal hegemony of a single type of discourse (identifying the domain of science as the discourse of "all thinghood"). This is a category mistake on a grand scale, whether it is made on the evidence provided by pseudo-sciences (physiognomy and phrenology) or legitimate modes of investigation (neuroscience). All of these forms of reductionism, despite the varying scientific legitimacy of the physiology to which they appeal, are myopic attempts to fit everything into the same categorical framework. We are led to this category mistake by simplistic picture thinking: the insistence that we can only admit into our ontology what can literally be pictured (say on an fMRI), or at least find a place in an abstract model.

Hegel sees these tendencies as an expression of a self-deprecating narcissism, a kind of adolescent conformism. Observing reason tries to see itself everywhere by interpreting itself in the same manner as everything else. Reason so badly desires to see its own reflection in the world that it forfeits its distinctiveness in order to maintain a *faux* sense of harmony with nature. Observing reason (or the mind-brain reductivist of today) finds a relief from its well-placed anxieties (fear of the extravagances of Cartesian dualism, the torture of frustrated otherworldly pretensions, and the like) in a contrived conformity with the natural world. To relieve the rupture between itself (Spirit) and the other (Nature), this immature mode of self-consciousness finds its place in the world by effacing its own *otherness*. Observing reason surrenders its distinctive dignity, so that it can be spared the anxiety brought on by its obvious contrasts with the rest of nature. Anxiety is the expense of the dignity of *Geist*, and we are perennially tempted to deny this unique status to circumvent its costs. (This tendency to forfeit our *Geist* will be a recurring theme in what follows.) Hegel is quite happy to steer well clear of the excess of Cartesian substance dualism, but he is likewise wary of throwing the baby out with the bathwater in an adolescent insistence on a bland, all-too-easy monism that can leave no room for the realities of *Geist*.

Alasdair MacIntyre summarizes Hegel's basic argument against the universal hegemony of observing reason:

> There is thus a difference between seeing a set of physical features and seeing that set as a face with a particular expression, just as there is a difference between seeing a string of physical shapes and seeing that string as an English sentence and as a

sentence with a meaning. To learn how to read a face or a sentence is not to follow rules justified by observation that embody
a correlation between two sets of items, one of which is the
physical features or shapes.[53]

Any attempt to *see* mind in some discrete material object or event, i.e.,
picturing mind, will always leave something out, in the same way as
attempting to account for the meaning of a sentence solely in terms of
the shapes of the letters (or the sounds of the speaking) will fall short.
Meaningful entities are always meaningful in contexts broader than anything squarely within the domain of a discourse limited to objects neatly
individuated in time and space. That discourse, i.e., natural science, may
treat the necessary grounds of these vast emergent worlds, but that is not,
once again, to deny their distinctness. The defender of the autonomy of
Geist does not ask observing reason to abdicate the ontological priority
(in a sense) of the scientific image. On the contrary, the fact that observing reason can arrive at such a critically self-aware image (the scientific
image) of the world is part of what makes human mindedness so distinctive; that we can take the scientific perspective only underlines the fact
that there is more to us than can be captured in the scientific perspective. Unless observing reason admits that there are "more things under
heaven and Earth" than appear in its philosophy, the scientific image is
itself in peril. The scientist implicitly shows herself as a participant in
Geist (someone offering justifications, concerned with meanings, etc.),
unless the scientific project itself should become self-defeating.

If we stand on the hegemony of observing reason, i.e., claim that the
scientific image is the only legitimate discourse, while admitting what I
hope is now the obvious fact that such observing reason cannot account
for the meaning of thought, then the scientist will be forced to admit the
meaninglessness of her very endeavor as observing reason.[54] For Hegel,
the fact that we can go "behind the back of consciousness," i.e., we can
ask of our various discourses whether they are true, meaningful, justified,

53. MacIntyre, "Hegel on Faces and Skulls," 75.

54. These sorts of self-defeat arguments against scientistic versions of naturalism
or materialism are common in recent philosophical literature, even if highly controversial. Particularly influential in analytic circles are Alvin Plantinga's *Where the
Conflict Really Lies*, 307–50; and Nagel, *Mind and Cosmos*, 71–96. I treat many of these
issues in *Mind, Matter, and Nature*, 210–21. Duane Armitage provides an excellent
treatment of self-defeating scientism, brilliantly pulling together Nagel, Nietzsche, and
Heidegger, in *Heidegger and the Death of God*. Ian Markham connects this issue to
medieval and scholastic arguments in *Truth and the Reality of God*.

semantically significant etc., is all the "proof" we could ask for to show that we occupy a higher order, self-conscious perspective, which cannot coherently be denied, however despairingly difficult it is to fit that perspective into an overall account of the world.[55] The denial that we occupy a "space of reasons" from which we can ask "But what does this all mean?" is incoherent because such a denial would require one to assume that very perspective, a stance one must take in the very act of comprehending this paragraph. I will motivate many of these claims in the following chapters as I elaborate what it means to achieve *Geist* in terms of our *dependency on* and *responsibility for a world.*

---

55. Hegel, *Phenomenology of Spirit*, §87. The perspective of the "phenomenological observer," the view of someone capable of holding her own consciousness at arms-length in order to put it to critical scrutiny, is the only way the *Phenomenology* can be coherently read. For Hegel, this means that we readers of the *Phenomenology*, by our very act of reading, are implicitly placing ourselves in the realm of Spirit. The "way of despair" that one follows in reading the *Phenomenology* is Hegel's attempt to make our being as Spirit explicit, what Hegel calls "Absolute Knowing." Kalkavage has an excellent discussion of the perspective of the "phenomenological observer" in *The Logic of Desire*, 18–25. See also Brandom's *A Spirit of Trust*, 101–6.

2

The Mind as Participation in the Spaces of Reasons, Embodiment, and Skills

None of the notions philosophy had elaborated—cause, effect, means, end, matter, form—suffices for thinking about the body's relationships to life as a whole, about the way it meshes into personal life or personal life meshes into it. The body is enigmatic: a part of the world, but offered in a bizarre way, as dwelling, to an absolute desire to draw near the other person and meet him in his body too, animated and animating, the natural face of mind.

—MAURICE MERLEAU-PONTY, "MAN AND ADVERSITY"[1]

Both views, the materialistic as well as the spiritualistic, are metaphysical prejudices. It accords better with experience to suppose that living matter has a psychic aspect, and the psyche a physical aspect.

—CARL JUNG, *FLYING SAUCERS: A MODERN MYTH OF THINGS SEEN IN THE SKIES*[2]

1. Merleau-Ponty, "Man and Adversity," 193.
2. Jung, *Flying Saucers*, 105.

IN THE PREVIOUS CHAPTER I used Wittgensteinian thought experiments and Hegelian phenomenological analysis (along with other techniques) to motivate a redescription of mindedness in terms of *Geist*. The central concern of the foregoing was *de-ontological* in the sense of motivating the abandonment of the assumption that the mind is a discrete, substantial entity. At the very least, we should bracket the metaphysical questions about the materiality/immateriality or subsistence/insubsistence of the mind until we have actually come to terms with what it means to have a mind in the first place. Subsequently, we should not concern ourselves with categorizing the mind as a type of substance in virtue of its possession of certain fundamental properties, i.e., arguing whether the mind is properly placed on our list of physical entities or non-physical things or our list of things that exist on their own or do not exist on their own. Those questions may arise, but I suggested that having a mind is not foremost to have a special organ or property (whether physical or non-physical), but to be an organism participating in a natural and cultural history; what we have called a *Lebenswelt* or *lifeworld*. Having a mind, on this view, is not to possess something (either a substance or property), but to be involved with or a participant in, as it has been famously put, a "form of life." Supposing I have plausibly incentivized this de-ontologized understanding of mind (or I have managed to get you to set aside the standard metaphysical worries), I now want to move the discussion more explicitly towards questions about the *worldly* conditions of our being minded and what is distinctive about our human form of life such that it has this dignity of participating in *Geist*. There are forms of life that do not amount to *Geist*, and there may be ways of being *Geist* that are not *our* forms of life. We shall see that our *geistig* way of being involves a tension between transcendence and dependence, emotional attachment and critical reflection, responsibility and creativity, practical and theoretical rationality. I will leave aside the question of whether this balancing act is necessary for all minded beings until a later discussion, but suffice it to say that *our* way of *Geist* is so entangled wherever we actually find it.

What I have advanced thus far is akin to a well-worn, even if controversial, position in cognitive science associated variously with the "extended theory of mind" and the "embedded mind thesis."[3] Whatever our stance on the mind-brain relation, there is no doubt that somehow mindedness for us involves the transference of "inscriptions" in the

3. The canonical defense of this sort of approach in cognitive science is Clark, *Being There*.

neuro-networks of the brain into cognitions with rational standing. So, at some level, Cormac's judgment about Paris involves his "reading off" information in his brain, though that is a metaphor we should now find far from completely satisfying (if not downright distorting). Now, consider a case in which Cormac writes notes about Paris while attending a lecture for a World Civilization course, and later refers to those inscriptions to prepare for an examination. It seems that there is no difference, in principle, between Cormac accessing inscriptions in his brain or inscriptions in his notebook, so long as that information bears the appropriate relationship to Paris. "Dry notes" on paper and "wet notes" between the ears play the same role, and the cognitive agent seems to have the same relationship to them, so presumably the cognitive act is essentially the same, even though it is executed through different media. Where, then, does Cormac's thinking about Paris occur? In his head, as it were? In his notebook? Well, it looks like we have to say in some cases thinking extends beyond the head and into artifacts such as notebooks, and certainly we should add computers, cell phones, etc.[4] These pieces of technology are extensions of our mindedness into the world beyond our heads.[5]

Not only does this thesis hold stark implications for the metaphysics and ontology of mind (Where is the mind? It's not exhaustively *in* the head!), but also for our self-understanding. Human beings are master "off-loaders" of our cognitive labors onto our environment and community. Cormac can put the burden of memory and belief into his notebook, a hard-copy encyclopedia, a study partner, and today even Google, all of which greatly expand the amount of information he can call "to mind." Since memory is a necessary condition for all of our most important cognitive acts, e.g., belief, judgment, and volition, our mental lives are off-loadable or already off-loaded to a great extent. Our ability to share our cognitive labor with devices, social institutions, works of art, other people, i.e., to extend mind out beyond the confines of the cranium (or immaterial substance), is partly why shared symbolic representation has been such an evolutionary boon for our species; we can avail ourselves of more than what can be cognized by one solitary individual. As Andy Clark puts it, "advanced cognition depends crucially on our ability to dissipate reasoning: to diffuse achieved knowledge and practical wisdom

4. See Clark and Chalmers, "The Extended Mind."

5. This remark invokes the title of Matthew Crawford's excellent treatment of the extended-mind thesis and many of its implications in *The World Beyond Your Head*, to which I am greatly indebted.

through complex structures, and to reduce the loads on individual brains by locating those brains in complex webs of linguistic, social, political and institutional constraints."[6] Distinctively human cognition (so far as we know) is then marked partly by its diffusion among communities of human cognizers through our structuring of our environment to carry the cognitive load and to communicate that information to our fellows. This off-loading onto a technologically structured, meaningful environment not only relieves each individual of much of her cognitive burden, but further allows for greater social interaction and organization, while steeply increasing the sophistication of cognitive tasks beyond what could be done by a solitary agent. Clark sees us as "parasitizing environmental resources" in our cognitive problem-solving to such a degree that we should doubt "the traditional boundaries between mind and the world themselves,"[7] which suggests our ideas and attitudes "are determined and explained by the intimate, complex, continued interplay between brain, body, and world."[8]

The extended-mind thesis invokes the central concern of this book, i.e., the relationship between humanity and technology and its consequences for the meaningfulness of our lives. From the beginning of their advocacy for the extended mind, Clark and Chalmers saw that it suggests that human development (both as a species and as an individual) cannot be separated from technological development:

> Moreover, it may be that the biological brain has in fact evolved and matured in ways which factor in the reliable presence of a manipulable external environment. It certainly seems that evolution has favored onboard capacities which are especially geared to parasitizing the local environment so as to reduce memory load, and even to transform the nature of the computational problems themselves. . . . Perhaps there are other cases where evolution has found it advantageous to exploit the possibility of the environment being in the cognitive loop. If so, then external coupling is part of the truly basic package of cognitive resources that we bring to bear on the world. . . . Once we recognize the crucial role of the environment in constraining the evolution and development of cognition, we see that extended cognition is a core cognitive process, not an add-on extra.[9]

6. Clark, *Being There*, 180.
7. Clark, *Being There*, 62.
8. Clark, *Being There*, 217.
9. Chalmers and Clark, "The Extended Mind," 31–32.

We humans, to a degree utterly distinctive among animals, rig our environment so as to make it bear our cognitive burdens to such an extent that "the chicken or the egg" question regarding the priority of human intelligence viz. technological development is likely unanswerable. The development of technology, especially information technology, has always been in a feedback loop with our cognitive evolution. The emergence of distinctively human cognition is not a distinct process from our history of technological innovation. If we come to see language and social organization as technological developments for the sake of cognitive off-loading (which Clark and Chalmers correctly suggest above), then this point is obvious. Technology is then something of a destiny for humanity, as our standing as thinking beings is inextricably and symbiotically correlated with our artificially constructed environment. Any attempt to reject technology as such is not only performatively silly (nobody, however far off the grid they may live, is not to some degree dependent on modern technology), but also a rejection of the rudiments of human cognition itself. The question of technology is then whether our technological destiny will continue as a mutually beneficial symbiosis. Is our technological destiny finally a tragic fate or an ultimate fulfillment? As we discussed in the introduction, there are many thinkers who have worried that we face the former.[10] Be that as it may (and this is a central theme we will confront in the latter chapters of this book), inasmuch as we are masterful cognitive off-loaders, we cannot deny that technology is baked into the human cake, as it were.

Leaving those broader concerns aside for now, we can see that the extended-mind thesis is complementary to my more immediate task of redescribing mind as *Geist*. If advanced, possibly distinctively human, cognition requires that thinkers be able to off-load the burden of thinking into an extended world of symbolic meaning and technological gerrymandering, we are certainly well-away from thinking of a mind as anything that can be neatly reduced to either a disembodied ghost or a brain in a vat. I do, however, note that the position that I am staking is subtly more robust than the standard extended-mind thesis. For Clark, "human reasoners are truly distributed cognitive engines," and we should spread the "*epistemic credit*" beyond the boundaries of the skull.[11] I very much agree, but I emphasize further that mind is not extended merely into an

10. Though Chalmers seems more than a little enthusiastic about our technological destiny. See Chalmers, *Reality+*, 311–66.

11. Clark, *Being There*, 69. Author's emphasis.

informationally constructed environment (though it certainly is), but a *Lebenswelt*. This shared form of life in which our minds are cultivated is not only a technological-informational extension of our nervous system, but likewise essentially involves normative self-criticism, emotional attachment, and practical involvement. Consider the following remarks from Hubert Dreyfus, as he cautions us against "confusing the human world with some sort of physical universe":

> My personal plans and my memories are inscribed in the things around me just as are the public goals of men in general. My memories are stored in the familiar look of a chair or the threatening air of a street corner where I was once hurt. My plans and fears are already built into my experience of some objects as attractive and others as to be avoided. The "data" concerning social tasks and purposes which are built into objects and spaces around me are overlaid with these personal "data" which are no less a part of my world. After all, personal threats and attractions are no more subjective than general human purposes.[12]

That is, the individual mind does not extend into and incorporate an otherwise neutral world of bald physical facts. Rather, we are always "already there" in a world of rational, practical, and emotional *meaning*. Again with Dreyfus: "A normal person experiences the objects of the world as already interrelated and full of meaning. There is no justification for the assumption that we first experience isolated facts . . . and then give them meaning."[13] That *being-there-already* in a world of *significance* is a necessary condition for human-mindedness, or, as I prefer to put it, participation in our *Geist*. At least that is what I shall attempt to show in what follows. None of that, however, should be taken as a criticism of something along the lines of Clark's view, but merely an enrichment of that basic stance. In short, I want to offer an account of the sort of world in which *Geist*, our mindedness, can dwell.

1. Participation in the Space of Reasons and Material Commitment

Do not confuse *Geist* with consciousness. There are plenty of conscious organisms that are not participants in *Geist*. Robert Brandom draws the

12. Dreyfus, *What Computers Still Can't Do*, 266.
13. Dreyfus, *What Computers Still Can't Do*, 270.

distinction between *Geist* and bald consciousness by contrasting *sentience* and *sapience*: "We are *sentient* beings, and we are *sapient* beings—we *feel*, and we *think*."[14] Merely sentient beings have sensations, see colors, feel pains, hear sounds, etc. How that sort of qualitative awareness is possible for material beings in the first place is, to understate the matter, no small mystery. Nevertheless, puzzling as this famed hard problem of consciousness is, mere consciousness is nothing distinctive in human beings, but something we find at least among our mammalian brethren. Our sapience, however, marks the threshold beyond which mind emerges.

> Sapience is *conceptual awareness*—a kind of mindedness that is tied to *understanding* rather than *sensing*. Paradigmatic sapient states are thinking or believing that things are thus-and-so (or desiring or intending that they be thus-and-so)—*that* Vienna is the capital of Austria, *that* the Washington Monument is 555 feet high, *that* freedom is better than slavery. In order to be in these sapient states one must grasp the *concepts* that articulate their content. The content of sapient states is accordingly something that at least in principle can be *said*.[15]

Sapient beings are capable of judgment. We make claims about the world that can be either true or false, and we take responsibility for where they fall between the two. Brandom is amplifying Wilfrid Sellars's famous dictum that having a human mind is the ability to place oneself in "the logical space of reasons, the space of justifying and being able to justify what one says."[16] In other words, to have a thought is to make a judgment, and to make a judgment is to take a certain kind of responsibility, i.e., an obligatory preparedness to put your judgment under rational scrutiny.

Thinkers are able to give answers to the question "Why do you think *that*?" or "How can you believe *that*?" and their answers are not merely *causes*, but *reasons*. One might come to believe in a multiverse cosmology

14. Brandom, *Reason in Philosophy*, 135. Brandom's emphasis. See also Brandom's *Articulating Reasons*, 80.

15. Brandom, *Reason in Philosophy*, 135.

16. Sellars, "Empiricism and the Philosophy of Mind," §36. For an introduction to the general orientation of the Pittsburg School, whose origin is traced to Sellars, see Maher, *The Pittsburg School of Philosophy*. James K. A. Smith provides a good introduction to the Pittsburg School (in particular Brandom's inferentialism) in *Who's Afraid of Relativism*, 115–50. I should note that in this chapter I have somewhat artificially treated the Pittsburg School monolithically, though there are plenty of internecine disagreements to be found even among its major figures. Maher's book does a fine job of mapping these disputes.

by drinking too much cough syrup or by making an inference from the body of evidence provided by astrophysics. The former case is merely a causal process, and it says nothing in favor of the rational credentials of the resulting judgment, i.e., it tells us nothing as to whether one *ought* or *ought not* to believe in the multiverse. The truth or falsity of the belief is irrelevant to whether it has been caused by drinking too much cough syrup, and the conceptual contents of the judgement (if we can really call it a judgment) have no role in the account of why Smitty arrived at it. If I say "Smitty believes that there are infinitely many universes, *because* he has been drinking cough syrup all morning," the veridical and conceptual standing of Smitty's judgment is accidental to the explanation. Nobody is saying that Smitty's reckless consumption of cough syrup in anyway recommends there actually are infinitely many universes, even if that explanation is sufficient to explain why Smitty thinks this to be the case. Such a statement is not an *endorsement* of Smitty's judgment, but merely a *description* of how Smitty ended up making it. In the case of a belief in the multiverse based on the evidence of astrophysics, however, there is a different kind of explanation in play. If I say "I believe in the multiverse *because* of the evidence of astrophysics," I am claiming that the multiverse hypothesis is true, and I am citing a certain body of evidence as implying as much, i.e., there is an appropriate connection between the conceptual contents of the evidence and my judgment. This is not a claim about what causes a certain judgment, but what one *ought* to judge in relation to a body of evidence. In this case I offer an endorsement of the belief, I relate it to other propositional states that credential this endorsement, and thereby I have moved from the space of causes to the space of reasons.[17]

17. This is not to deny that acquaintance with the evidence is sufficient to cause a judgment. Rather, the point is that the judgment based on an inference from evidence is subject to a *reasons explanation* that is irreducible to any accompanying causal explanation. There may be more than one, non-competing explanation as to why Smitty believes in the multiverse. Of course, this glosses over the problem posed by the *prima facie* tension between reasons and causes. That is, if we can explain Smitty's belief causally, that often seems to debunk or undermine any reasons he can cite: "Smitty says he believes in the multiverse because . . . but we know he's been at the cough syrup again." I will leave this worry aside for now, but note that in the following sections I will find that both the space of reasons and the space of causes are consequent to our residence in a prior space of agency and commitment (*Lebenswelt*) wherein such worries do not arise. That is, whatever the tensions between causes and reasons, we are first in a world in which we are the subjects of meaningful actions.

The Sellarsian story about the logical space of reasons is therefore a "*normative characterization* of the mental," according to which sapient creatures are not distinguished *ontologically* by a special immaterial process, but *performatively* or *pragmatically* by the distinctive way that they hold themselves responsible for their judgements; they explain their judgments not by causes but by rational credentials, and being in the space of reasons requires knowing how to do as much. As Brandom puts it, "Judging and acting involve *commitments*. They are endorsements, exercises in *authority*. *Responsibility, commitment, endorsement, authority*—these are all normative notions."[18] Having a mind is knowing how to find one's way around in the logical space of reasons and understanding how to explain judgments based on what one ought to believe in the wake of other judgments to which one is committed. Notice that this always entails a potential to provide such justifications to others who are likewise involved in the space of reasons.

Brandom cites this *ability* to bind ourselves to our judgments by the reasons we can give for them as what distinguishes participants in *Geist* from "merely natural creatures,"[19] and John McDowell implores us to "sharply distinguish natural scientific intelligibility from the kind of intelligibility something acquires when we situate it in the logical space of reasons."[20] Neither Brandom nor McDowell is positing a separate, nonphysical process to account for thinking. They are not looking for causes (physical, non-physical, or whatever). Rather, their point is that certain activities of human beings are subject to a kind of explanation "in the *sui generis* logical space of reasons" that is absent at the level of scientific explanation, and the shared mistake of substance dualists and reductive materialists alike is "to forget that nature includes second nature. Human beings acquire a second nature in part by being initiated into conceptual capacities, whose interrelations belong in the logical space of reasons."[21] Our achievement of a critical stance toward our judgments is the emergence of mind. Even though mind has the "merely natural" as a necessary precondition, it is nevertheless explanatorily autonomous from those grounds. Asking for my reasons for a certain judgment or whether I can tolerate (on pain of inconsistency) the consequences of holding such a

18. Brandom, *Reason in Philosophy*, 32–33. Author's emphasis.
19. Brandom, *Reason in Philosophy*, 62.
20. McDowell, *Mind and World*, xix.
21. McDowell, *Mind and World*, xx.

position for other commitments to which I am obligated is an entirely different sort of query from wondering what sort of process (whether in a brain or a disembodied mental substance) might have caused that judgment.[22]

The normative nature of our life in the space of reasons means that we are always citizens of a community of fellow reasoners. As Brandom puts it, "we sapients are discursive scorekeepers . . . that requires being able to move back and forth across different perspectives occupied by those who undertake commitments and those who attribute them."[23] Notice that our existence in the space of reasons is partially constituted by our preparedness to give reasons for assertions, but giving reasons is always something that can in principle be done in response to the demand for justification from another participant in the space of reasons. That power, however, presupposes that we can adopt the perspective of others. Giving *reasons* assumes that the justifications that I offer are just as binding on anyone as they are on me. In order for *my* reasons to be reasons (as opposed to, for example, mere appeals to force or verbal trickery), they must be *anybody's* reasons. As Sellars famously makes the point: "there is no thinking apart from common standards of correctness and relevance, which relate what I *do* think to what *anyone ought* to think. The contrast between 'I' and 'anyone' is essential to rational thought."[24] This move from "I" to "anyone" is the very move from causality to normativity that we discussed above as the very mark of the emergence of the space of reasons. Thus, my giving reasons, even if they are only part of my internal dialogue, is always at least potentially a practice I share with another (anyone). Life in the space of reasons is, in principle, a cooperative affair. That is, being in the space of reasons is being with others (actually or

---

22. I want to be careful here not to commit myself to too sharp of a threshold between humans and other animals in playing on this notion of a "second nature" in contrast with our shared nature with the rest of the animal kingdom. Whatever McDowell (and the rest of the Pittsburg School) hold along these lines, I see no reason to deny that there is some sense, at least analogically speaking, in which certain non-human animals have beliefs and reasons for acting. I do, however, along with the Pittsburg School, want to emphasize that our critically reflective relation to our beliefs and reasons for acting is something unique (as far as we know, and I do take that as an empirical question). See MacIntyre, *Dependent Rational Animals*, 53–61. The place I hold for our animality as a both constitutive and limiting element of our mindedness will become clear as this chapter unfolds.

23. Brandom, *Making It Explicit*, 591.

24. Sellars, "Philosophy and the Scientific Image of Man," 16–17. Sellars' emphasis.

potentially) who are likewise committed to the practice of justifying their sayings and doings. As Brandom puts it:

> The conceptual contents employed in monological reasoning . . . are parasitic on and intelligible only in terms of the sort of content conferred by dialogical reasoning, in which the issue of what follows from what essentially involves assessments from the different social perspectives of scorekeeping interlocutors with different background assumptions.[25]

We occupy the space of reasons only inasmuch as we are able to adopt the perspectives of others, with whom disagreement is a possibility. Normativity carries with it community; reasons-giving is an inherently dialogical practice, because reasons qua reasons must be purportedly binding on other possible reasoners. Do not, however, overplay the role of potential disagreement; the very endeavor to give reasons (as opposed to bald appeals to causality) operates under the assumption that we are engaged in a cooperative endeavor. I can only ask for and offer reasons to the other inasmuch as I presume that she and I occupy a common world.[26]

If Cormac has a thought about Paris, then at least implicitly he has made a judgment about Paris, e.g., "Paris is the capital of the Fifth French Republic," and he is able to give reasons for his so judging that are accessible in principle to his potential interlocutors. By insisting on Cormac's ability "to give reasons," I do not mean to evoke a foundationalism according to which every claim for which someone can take responsibility must be justified ultimately by some final incorrigible court of appeal. Indeed, nothing could be more odious to the Pittsburg School–approach I am out to motivate.[27] Rather, occupying the logical space of reasons is "essentially a matter of being answerable to criticism," "responsiveness to reasons,"[28] or maintaining "a reflective stance at which the question arises whether one ought to find this or that persuasive."[29] That is, making

25. Brandom, *Making It Explicit*, 590–91.

26. For a fascinating scientific discussion of how cooperative intentionality may have undergirded the evolutionary development of distinctively human rationality in a way friendly to the speculations of the Pittsburg School (though not without some disagreements), see Tomasello, *A Natural History of Human Thinking*, 80–123.

27. See Maher, *The Pittsburg School of Philosophy*, 7–20, for a summary of the attack on "The Given" by Sellars and his followers. See also McDowell, *Mind and World*, 3–23.

28. McDowell, *Having the World in View*, 6.

29. McDowell, *Mind and World*, 125.

judgments requires us to be able to take a critical stance toward our judging. Being answerable for his claim that "Paris is the capital of the Fifth French Republic" minimally requires that Cormac can articulate what other claims might commit him to this judgment by implication (What, if anything, are you committed to as a reason for this judgment?), other claims that it further implies (To what other judgements does this judgment commit you?), and other claims with which this position is incompatible (What other judgments does this judgment force you to deny?). Giving reasons for a judgment is placing that judgment in a network of other commitments, both affirmative and negative. Whether or not Cormac derives this judgment directly from some final piece of evidence, as a sapient being he is able to follow the implicatory consequences to which he ought to be committed in virtue of his making this judgment and adjust his commitments (accept new commitments or deny old ones) based on what these implications reveal. Minimally, a denizen of the logical space of reasons is open to revising his or her judgments based on the implications they hold for other judgments. It is difficult to see what else could count as a commitment to a judgment but to accept its implications. For example, by judging "Paris is the capital of the Fifth French Republic," Cormac is likewise committed implicitly to the judgment that "Bonn is not the capital of the Fifth French Republic," and to the degree that he is a participant in *Geist*, he can make this commitment explicit. If Cormac had earlier thought Bonn was the capital of the Fifth Republic, then he would, if he is to occupy the space of reasons, give up that earlier commitment.

Thus, the ability to make any particular move in the logical space of reasons is essentially tied to the ability to make a vast host of other moves, because the conceptual contents of judgments are entangled in overlapping implicative commitments. As Sellars famously puts it, wielding any concept in a judgment presupposes "having a whole battery of concepts" and commitments subject to various other judgments in virtue of that network of conceptual relations.[30] *Geist* is then a "holistic" affair. There is no such thing as having just one concept or being rationally committed to a single judgment. An utterance can only rise to a *bona fide* judgment against the backdrop of a network of judgments and concepts. In order to know how to use the concept of "Paris" in a judgment with any real competence, I will need to know how to work within a complicated network

30. Sellars, "Empiricism and the Philosophy of Mind," §19.

of other concepts, e.g., "capital," "France," "Republic," etc., and following its implications might require me to understand "Bonn," "Germany," "Rhine," etc., since every judgment has both affirmative and negative implications, which we would expect a competent wielder of such concepts to recognize. Minimal facility in judging does not presuppose conceptual omniscience, because knowing one's way around the logical space of reasons comes in degrees. Cormac might be forgiven his ignorance of the implicative relation between "Paris is the capital of the Fifth French of Republic" and "Bonn is not the capital of the Fifth French Republic" due to the poor state of education, without our saying that he simply does not know at all what "Paris" means, e.g., he might be tricked into believing that "Bonn" is another name for Paris. Be that as it may, surely there is some minimum implicative commitment necessary to grasp the concept of Paris. We could not reasonably conclude that Cormac really judges "Paris is the capital of the Fifth French Republic," if he is also willing to affirm that "Lake Michigan is the capital of the Fifth French Republic." In that case, Cormac just does not know what he is talking about, or he is ill-disposed to taking an earnestly critical attitude toward his own judgments (which on this view amounts to the same thing). Someone who cannot distinguish a city from a lake knows what neither a city nor a lake is, and therefore his purported judgments about Paris are lacking sufficient determinacy to be judgments at all. Moreover, someone who is not inclined to avoid such confusions is not really trying to make sense. If you were trying to teach a child to use "Paris" and he kept confusing it with "Lake Michigan," you would conclude either that he misunderstood how to use the word or that he is not trying to play the game in earnest. Notice, then, that to make a judgment about a city, one must, at least implicitly, likewise be able and willing to make some judgments about lakes. Concepts are embedded in worlds of conceptual commitment.

Do not mistake conceptual holism for a coherenentism or idealism spinning freely from any friction with the real, empirical world. Participating in the logical space of reasons is not like moving uninterpreted game pieces around a checkers board. Conceptual relations must be grounded in worldly content, if they are to be cognitively significant. Although they are parts of an inferential nexus, the concepts "lake" and "city" are distinct. That is, one cannot properly use "city" unless she knows that entities falling under that concept do not fall under the concept of "lake." That knowledge, however, is an empirical matter, something we have learned only by the testing of our concepts against the material world. The proposition "x is a city and x is a lake" is not a formal contradiction, even though we competent "concept mongers" (to use one of Brandom's phrases) can see that it is absurd.[31] Thus, that "x is a city" implies "x is not a lake," is a principle of *material* not *formal* logic, as the propositional structure is not what grounds the inference. The work is done by the actual particularities that have played out among lakes and cities, and our language now reflects this fact because of the way the actual world has pushed back against our conceptualizations. But notice that without this material, as opposed to purely formal, connection there is no inferential nexus in which judgments about Paris can be related to judgments about Lake Michigan. Concepts must have material content in order to play a role in anything but a trivial nexus, and hollow stipulation is not thought. As McDowell puts it, significant judgments presuppose "materially sound inferential connections, and command of such connections is inseparable from having substantial knowledge of the world."[32] If Cormac judges that Frank is a dog, he is saddled with the implications that Frank *is not* a fish and that Frank *is* a mammal. But these are material, not formal, relations that only arise through our encounter with the way the world resists and complies with our conceptualizations. Since thinking is judging, and meaningful judgment always involves materially grounded conceptual connections, "thinking *about* something is not a special kind of thinking. It is an aspect of *all* thinking."[33] Thus, the logical space of reasons is held together by two aspects of conceptual content: "the inferential-expressive and the referential-representational."[34] All of this is to say that in taking a critical stance toward our own judgments, we are in touch with more than just our conceptual frameworks. The material world that grounds their materially significant relations gets an equal vote in their semantic determinacy. Or, as it has been said, "Thoughts without content are empty; intuitions without concepts are blind."[35]

31. Brandom, *Making It Explicit*, xi.

32. McDowell, *Having the World in View*, 92.

33. Brandom, *Reason in Philosophy*, 43. Brandom's emphasis.

34. Brandom, *Reason in Philosophy*, 45. See also Brandom, *A Spirit of Trust*, 63–86.

35. Kant, *Critique of Pure Reason*, A51/B76. See also McDowell, "Avoiding the Myth of the Given."

2. Inheritance and Responsibility

Being in the space of reasons requires that one make materially significant inferences, which likewise requires that our concepts and judgments
are subject to revision by "push-back" from the world, so thinking is essentially related to something "beyond our heads." As I have just alluded,
so far Kant agrees. We have, however, also set on the path to more distinctively Hegelian territory.[36] Recall the holistic nature of the conceptual shows that there is no having just one concept. To have a concept is
always to have a nexus of concepts. Thus, no single human individual can
build up the logical space of reasons piecemeal, starting with one concept
and building outward. Initial access to the logical space of reasons, i.e.,
learning a first language, requires someone to be "introduced into something that already embodies putatively rational linkages between concepts constitutive of the layout of the space of reasons, before she comes
on the scene," such that "the language into which a human being is first
initiated stands over against her as a prior embodiment of mindedness,
of the possibility of an orientation to the world."[37]

Wittgenstein somewhat cryptically summarizes this point when he
says: "My judgements themselves characterize the way I judge, characterize the nature of judgment" and "The child learns by believing the adult.
Doubt comes after."[38] In other words, we do not begin reasoning for ourselves. Rather, we learn to reason by working within an already, pre-given
set of accepted judgments we have inherited from our elders. Our first
start is to piggyback on the reasons in our environment, mainly the social
world into which we are being initiated. We do not, for Wittgenstein,
justify our certain judgments by our method of judgment (at least not
at first), but come to understand our method of judgment by holding
ourselves to the paradigmatic judgments we pick up from our mentors.

The human individual can only inherit *Geist* from an already up and
running community of minded human beings. There is an inescapable
social element of mindedness, as I can only enter the space of reasons to

---

36. I am basically gesturing toward the transition from Kant's *Verstand* (understanding) to Hegel's notion of *Vernuft* (reason). See Brandom, *Reason in Philosophy*,
78–108 and *A Spirit of Trust*, 63–86. Kalkavage, *The Logic of Desire*, is also helpful on
this movement.

37. McDowell, *Mind and World*, 125. This is a point that McDowell has certainly
learned as much from Wittgenstein as Hegel; see *Mind and World*, 18–23.

38. Wittgenstein, *On Certainty*, §149 and §160.

the degree that I have taken up a set of practices extant among a group of human beings already involved in the game of giving and taking reasons before I arrived. Our achievement of *Geist* is then to assume a role in a history, as the logical space of reasons is a "repository of tradition, a store of historically accumulated wisdom about what is reason for what," and for a human to be initiated into "that succession, which is the same thing as acquiring a mind, the capacity to think and act intentionally, at all, the first thing that needs to happen is for her to be initiated into a tradition as it stands."[39] A human alone is indeed "a beast or a god," or at the very least she is not fully minded, a participant in *Geist*.

We can now see even more deeply why suggesting that *thinking-about-Paris* is nothing more than *Zeta* is profoundly confused. Thinking can only happen in a historical context, a tradition of making sense of things. There is nothing inherently rational about *Zeta*, or any other physical process, in precision from such a practical history of human beings testing their concepts against the world. No discrete physical event is a thought. Our thoughts are participations in a communal project of making sense that stretches back for centuries. Cormac's judgment about Paris would not have the conceptual content that it does if it were not for the particularities and contingencies of millennia of human history, and his access to that content rides along on the contributions of innumerable other prior participants in that history; we come into the *Lebenswelt* having to off-load much of our cognitive labor onto the senior members of our community. Had fortune broken less fortunately for Charles Martel long ago at Tours, or had the long history of discourse subsequent to those events taken other possible pathways, our concept of Paris would not have the same content as it does today. *Zeta*, without that history, is not a thought of Paris at all, or at least it would not be *our* thought about Paris. "*Geist*, the specifically human mind, brings with it a capacity to create institutions in light of our socially mediated map of how our actions and their explanations fit into the world," such that "the human being transcends its position in any given situation."[40] The human mind transcends any picture-thinking (whether it takes the form of an image of a neurophysiological event on an fMRI or otherwise ghostly imaginings in a disembodied substance), because the historical backdrop against

---

39. McDowell, *Mind and World*, 126.

40. Gabriel, *Neo-Existentialism*, 40.

which meaning can occur cannot be captured in any discrete picture. Our minds are a participation in a history of *being-minded*.

As *Geist* is a historical being, prey to the particularities and contingencies of human affairs and natural happenstance, the tradition of rational reflection into which we are initially introduced must be "subject to reflective modification by each generation that inherits it. Indeed, a standing obligation to engage in critical reflection is itself part of the inheritance," so there is a sense in which *Geist* constantly surpasses the traditions in which it is grounded.[41] Since we know that the tradition of thinking we have inherited did not have to go the way it did, we cannot honestly resist the realization that our way of thinking is not the only possible way of thinking, and therefore our way of thinking may not be the best way of thinking. In other words, being in the logical space of reasons is not only to have a critical stance towards *your* beliefs and judgments (which are always at least potentially *our* beliefs and judgments), but further to extend that scrutiny to the set of historically conditioned norms constitutive of the space of reasons as it has been passed down to you, i.e., the very grounds of your critical stance. *Geist* puts its own history, which is to say *itself*, into question. Though we can only inherit our position in the logical space of reasons, we are obligated to ask whether that conceptual legacy in fact gets things right. For reasons to be *bona fide* reasons, they cannot be just *our* reasons as they happen to have been passed to us. Our reasons purport to be *anyone's* reasons. Thus, *Geist* is perpetually self-scrutinizing. It is the "experience of error" that sets natural consciousness on the long "way of despair" toward true knowledge.[42] The history of *Geist*, i.e., our history of thinking, is a generation-to-generation commitment to be responsible for our judgments, not to our own historically contingent prejudices, but to the world, even on pain of having to revise the very legacy that constitutes our jumping-off point into the life of the mind.[43]

This is not a skepticism that refuses to make a claim on the world for fear of being wrong (no one is more critical of that sort of evasion than Hegel),[44] but a confidence in the ability of humanity to get it right. It is from this standpoint of confirmed optimism that *Geist* can put the central

41. McDowell, *Mind and World*, 126.

42. Hegel, *Phenomenology of Spirit*, §78.

43. I will discuss the connection between tradition, responsibility, and freedom in greater detail in the following chapter.

44. Hegel, *Phenomenology of Spirit*, §80 and §204–6.

concepts of its logical space of reasons into question, but since *Geist* is defined by the space of reasons, mindedness is always self-questioning. To be minded, then, is in part to have a sort of say in what it is to be minded:

> The notion behind the somewhat mysterious term *Geist* can be summarized in roughly the following way: what it is to be a minded (*gestig*) animal is to conceive of oneself in such a variety of ways. Human beings essentially respond to the question of what it means for them to be at the center of their own lives in different ways. What does not vary is the capacity, nay, the necessity, to respond differently to this question. Our response to the question of what it means to be a human minded animal in part shapes what it is to be such an animal. We turn ourselves into the creatures we are in each case by developing a mentalist vocabulary.[45]

Having a mind is to be able to inquire into what it means to have a mind, i.e., to put oneself and one's grounding tradition under critical scrutiny, and to be willing to revise that self-conception based on the results of such inquiry. If one were not willing to so revise her self-understanding, she would be refusing to participate in *Geist*, as it entails a commitment to critical scrutiny and subsequent revision (if need be) of one's concepts and judgments. There is a sense in which we have a vote in who we are, because one can always hide from his own mindedness. It is up to us to commit ourselves to self-criticism and subsequent self-revision, should that be necessary. Nevertheless, our revision of our *Geist* is not an anything-goes-affair. Our conceptual alterations must always, even our revised self-conceptions, be held responsible to the world, if they are to be meaningful. A meaningful logic of our *second nature* is no less a material logic than is a meaningful logic of nature as such. Moreover, the space of reasons, as we have discussed, is always *our* space of reasons, where the "our" extends into history. We are responsible to the world, but also to our contemporary colleagues in sense-making and our shared progenitors from whom we inherit a *lingua franca*. In order for our revisions to be more than arbitrary rantings, there are limits to what we can count as making sense of ourselves.[46] As Wittgenstein puts it, understanding a

45. Gabriel, *I Am Not a Brain*, 3–4. See also the first chapter of Gabriel's *The Meaning of Thought*.

46. The triangulation of semantic responsibility is the central theme of the lessons Brandom extracts from Hegel's *Phenomenology*. The long story is definitely Brandom's *A Spirit of Trust*. He gives more manageable presentations in *Reason in Philosophy*,

concept (using a word correctly) is enabled only "by nature and by a particular training, a particular education,"[47] and our ability to say anything
true at all is always limited by that "form of life," whatever the possibility
of self-scrutiny and revision.[48]

3. Embodiment

Wittgenstein is correct to point out that "nature" is partially constitutive
of the form of life that both enables and limits our giving and taking
reasons and subsequent revisions to our normative commitments. These
capacities "are as much a part of our natural history as walking, eating,
drinking, playing."[49] In other words, *our* theoretically and practically
rational "form of life is possible for beings who are biologically constituted as we are."[50] Of course, "a particular training and education," i.e.,
culture, play an equally important role in our initiation into the logical
space of reasons. We cannot "read off" mind from nature, and we do
not become rational just by showing up as human organisms. Nevertheless, because our form of life is a way of being a certain kind of animal,
the development of our rationality "has its starting point in our initial

---

78–100. See also Brandom's *Heroism and Magnanimity*. The interplay between the
responsibility to and revisability of tradition is a theme that extends beyond recog-
nizably Hegelian circles. For example, it is not hard to read John Henry Newman's
theologically influential *An Essay on the Development of Christian* in this light. See
Alasdair MacIntyre's *Three Rival Versions of Moral Inquiry* for what I take to be an
implicitly Hegelian working out of many of these issues, though in conversation with
very non-Hegelian sources. Throughout these chapters I have taken Brandom's reading of Hegel at face value, but one should note that this interpretation is not without its
significant critics. See in particular Charles Taylor's and Robert Pippin's contributions
to Bouche, *Reading Brandom*.

47. Wittgenstein, *Philosophical Investigations*, 137 (§441).

48. Wittgenstein, *Philosophical Investigations*, §241.

49. Wittgenstein, *Philosophical Investigations*, 16 (§25). See also Wittgenstein, *On
Certainty*, 62 (§475) and (73) §559. Lee Braver's discussion of this aspect of Wittgenstein's thought is superb. See *Groundless Grounds*, 150–62. McDowell is adamant that
this *Bildung* comes at no cost to the philosophical naturalist. See *Mind and World*,
108–26. Gabriel is equally confident in a liberal naturalism that includes *Geist* in its
ontological structure. See his contribution to *Neo-Existentialism*. In later chapters I
will cast some doubt on whether *Geist* comes quite so economically to the philosophical naturalist.

50. MacIntyre, *Dependent Rational Animals*, x.

animal condition."[51] Our form of life is both nature and second nature—a biological and a cultural inheritance, which must be cultivated in us late arrivals on the conceptual scene through an education that is operative within those limitations, which I will refer to broadly as *embodiment*.

Certainly, the pedagogy of *Geist* at some point ends in the explicit grasp of logical cannons for practical and theoretical inquiry; being in the space of reasons means being able to *cite* one's reasons. Nevertheless, for animals like us, initiation into our second nature does not begin with indoctrination into rigorous logical categories, or any other abstract form of learning. The crucial step into the space of reasons is language acquisition, but we do not begin youngsters on that journey by teaching them formal logic. Rather, we mostly learn to speak at our "mother's knee," as it were, through a *caring relationship*. Charles Taylor summarizes the upshot of the psychological findings regarding the relationship between emotional attachment and language acquisition as follows:

> The first and obvious fact is that children can only become speakers by being taught a language. That is, they have to pick up language from a community or family which is taking care of them, its members talking to each other, and talking to them. Without this, the human capacity for language remains without effect. The children can't speak, as we see occasionally with "feral" children, who have been brought up by animals; and moreover they lack all capacities which go along with language.[52]

Peter Hobson, a psychologist studying autism, makes much the same assessment:

> If a child fails to experience interpersonal engagement, the elaborate circuitry of the brain proves to be about as useful as computer hardware working with inadequate software. The computer can still do fancy things of a rather humdrum kind, but it cannot support creative symbolic thinking.[53]

51. MacIntyre, *Dependent Rational Animals*, x.

52. Taylor, *The Language Animal*, 52. Taylor provides an excellent summary of the psychological literature on the close relationship between emotional attachment and language acquisition. I refer to the reader to his notes to follow that literature. For a very helpful presentation of the role of "theory of mind" in language learning (i.e., the presumption of emotional empathy) and the general dependence of rationality on a social, practical, and emotional background, see Von Hipple, *The Social Leap*.

53. Hobson, *The Cradle of Thought*, 48–49. Throughout the following paragraph, I am in debt to Rassano, *Supernatural Selection*, 78–102, where he provides an excellent summary of the literature on attachment and theory of mind as a grounding for

We begin our march toward reasoning by first becoming attached to other people, i.e., "relations of shared emotional bonding" with our caregivers.[54] A confident emotional bond allows "an intense sharing of intentions between the bonded pair," such that the meaning of a word (the content of a concept) can "become an object for us," and only under such conditions does a child realize her linguistic-conceptual capacity.[55] Although "once it is mastered, innovation becomes possible," i.e., we can take responsibility for our normative commitments, it is within a milieu of shared empathy that our natural potency for rationality first comes to actuality, and it is never fully independent of that emotional foundation.[56] As MacIntyre puts it, only through a "responsive sympathy and empathy" with our fellows are we able to "impute to those others the kind of reasons for their actions that, by making their actions intelligible to us, enable us to respond to them in ways that they too can find intelligible," which is the prerequisite of being in the logical space of reasons.[57] In other words, distinctive human mindedness always presupposes a "shared intentionality," constituted by "a uniquely human capacity for sharing emotional, cognitive, and attentional states and coordinating actions relevant to those states."[58] That is, at least in its origins, we cannot neatly separate our uniquely human cognitive capacities from the emotional and biological relationships on which we depend in our early tutelage into *Geist*. It is our innate ability to share ourselves emotionally in the particularities of a communal life that makes possible our shared, materially significant conceptual prowess; which is to say, though potent with possibility for transcendent self-critical reflection, our mindedness is embodied.[59]

---

human cognition. Much of the thinking behind this chapter was greatly enriched by an unpublished lecture Rassano gave at the *Meeting of the American Catholic Philosophical Association* (October 2021), which I had the good fortune to attend.

54. Taylor, *The Language Animal*, 55.

55. Taylor, *The Language Animal*, 56.

56. Taylor, *The Language Animal*, 55.

57. MacIntyre, *Dependent Rational Animals*, 14. In that work MacIntyre makes a sustained and convincing case for the fact that these sorts of emotional connections are necessary not only for our initiation into mindedness, but for our continued sustenance as rational animals. For Wittgenstein on empathy and language acquisition, see *Philosophical Investigations*, 95 (§244ff).

58. Rassano, *Supernatural Selection*, 87. Here Rassano is paraphrasing Tomasello, Carpenter, Call, Behne, and Moll, "Understanding and Sharing Intentions."

59. This is part of what is meant by Hegel's constant demand that *Geist* eventually synthesize the immediate (particular, sensuous, emotional) and the mediate (universal,

Not only attachment, but trust, plays a very large role in the development of distinctively human cognitive capacities. Cognitive scientists and psychologists use the phrase "theory of mind" to refer to the default assumption that other human beings are rational, and this disposition seems to be in the background of our interactions even at very early stages of psychological development. What this amounts to practically is that human beings are actually natural imitators and conformists, not radically individualist rebels. We assume that there is something sensible behind the behaviors of others (especially our elders), and therefore we tend to mimic what they do even when their reasons for doing so are not completely transparent. This tendency to interpret and to imitate the behavior of trusted others charitably is a crucial element in what makes the complicated education necessary for cultural transmission possible. We are such great leaners because we trust teachers and mimic their behavior, even when we do not quite get what they are up to. As psychologist William Von Hippel puts it, theory of mind is an evolutionary boon: "If I understand that another person has knowledge that I don't have, then I also understand that this person might impart knowledge on me. This understanding prompts me to pay close attention to potential teachers and to imitate their actions even if I don't discern their purpose."[60]

Comparative psychologist Michael Tomasello argues that distinctively human linguistic thinking could not have come about without "a number of earlier adaptations for joint intentionality (e.g., joint goals, common conceptual ground, recursive inferences), and that its eventual emergence was part of a larger process in which human activities were conventialized and normativized."[61] In other words, human thinking presupposes an evolutionary background that rewards cooperation and trust; reason-giving is something *we* do. Moreover, this dependence on a background of social cooperation is not only necessary for the species' development of rationality, but likewise for the initiation of each human individual into the space of reasons. Since our thinking requires us to operate within "flexible behavioral organization, cognition, and decision making" which themselves require "time to master a local group's cultural artifacts, symbols, and practices," human rationality requires "an extended ontogeny in which the child and her developing brain are in constant

abstract). For an excellent (even if controversial) discussion of the *Phenomenology* particularly sensitive to this point, see Charles Taylor's *Hegel*, 171–96.

60. Von Hippel, *The Social Leap*, 53.

61. Tomasello, *A Natural History of Human Thinking*, 127.

interaction with the environment, especially the social environment."[62] In other words, due to the particularities of distinctive human (socially oriented) rationality, we are dependent on a protracted childhood, even compared to other sophisticated cognizers among higher apes. *Geist*, whatever its transcendent possibilities, only emerges (either in the species or the individual) in a context of emotional attachment, social trust, and nurturing.

It is far from clear that we are ever free from this grounding in emotional attachment and trust when exercising our cognitive capacities. For example, even after our cognitive powers are up and running, they seem to be sensitive to whether they are embedded in empathetic contexts of joint intentionality:

> A more complex social environment is directly connected to cognitive performance, including working memory. A recent study found that those who had greater levels of social engagement scored higher on measures of cognitive function. Furthermore, ten minutes of social interaction (discussion of controversial issues) was as effective as engaging in nonrelational intellectual activity (reading for comprehension, mental rotation tasks, crossword puzzles) in boosting performance on both speed of processing and working memory tasks.[63]

There is then some evidence that our cognition is always tied to social, empathetic engagement, or at the very least that our cognitive powers are most effectively exercised in that context. It is difficult to envision what would count for shared intentionality without some sort of emotional or empathic grounding. Communication without empathy is not shared cognition of an objective world, but parallel processing of our internal states. That is, our ability to achieve an objective stance is the product of our shared task of checking ourselves in a common practice of reasons-giving that we take up with our fellows, but that presupposes enough mutual regard for us to get along while playing the game of reasons. Thus, human mindedness likely is always dependent on an emotional context to some greater or lesser extent, at least for its optimal function.

Hume was no doubt wrong when he claimed that "reason is and ought to be the slave of the passions," but the ability to assess and control our response to our emotions does not mean that we are capable of

62. Tomasello, *A Natural History of Human Thinking*, 145.

63. Rassano, *Supernatural Selection*, 87.

articulating conceptual content utterly free from an emotional coloring. As we have discussed in the directly foregoing, there is good reason to conclude the proper function of our cognitive powers is likely inextricably bound to emotional ties (or at least empathetic deference to our fellows in the space of reasons). I, however, want to go further to claim that our conceptual contents (not just our cognition of those contents) are likewise entangled with our emotions. I learned how to use the concept of "Paris" by watching war films with my father, attending lectures by teachers whom I admired, hearing anecdotes from cherished and well-traveled friends, reading literature that moved me spiritually, etc. To separate the notion of Paris from that emotional *milieu* is to render the concept meaningless, no less than separating it from the history of the West would empty it of significant content. There are material entailments of the concept of Paris that are partly determined by the emotional significance it has for someone using it to make a judgment. For example, your fond memories of your honeymoon in the City of Lights will rightly guide some of your subsequent judgments about Paris. The emotional bond with other people with whom I share concerns plays an irreplaceable role in initially fixing the content of the concept for me, and it is likely that the concept is forever colored by those attachments. A rat and I might both be in similar neurophysiological states after eating a sugar cookie, and the resulting hormonal release might play similar roles in the reward structures that explain some of our behavioral dispositions, but there is a content to the concept of "cookie" as I use it, and without which I would be unable to use it as I do now, that cannot be separated from emotionally and culturally rich memories of Christmas and the like. These emotional entanglements and how we interpret them are part of what "cookie" means to us, which partly fixes the conceptual content (especially in its material implications).[64] Unless we can take an empathetic stance toward each other, the necessary emotional colorings of our concepts would be lost in our communicative efforts. It is an empathy that binds us to our fellow thinkers in *care* or *concern* for the objects about which we speak and think, and without that emotional embodiment, fully functioning *human* thought cannot gain traction in the world.

64. This is not to say, however, that there is no analogue to such emotional entanglements for the rat (I don't believe that rat thinking is captured on an fMRI any more than ours), but what is distinctive for us is the role our interpretation of these emotional ties plays in fixing material content.

By raising the importance of subjectivity, I am not making an appeal to the infamous *qualia*, or any other supposed atomistic "raw feels," that so notoriously vex physicalists in the philosophy of mind. In fact, I believe hanging our hats on this issue is a source of some confusion regarding the conditions necessary for our mindedness. That is not to say I deny there are *qualia*, nor is it to ignore that *qualia* pose some serious problems for physicalist reductionism.[65] My point is that internally accessible raw feels are not the basic building blocks of human experience, or at least that is not the most important qualitative grounding of our human experience relevant to the space of reasons. In fact, I wonder whether we have all been a bit too quick in assuming we really can introspectively isolate such singular states of *feels-likeness*. Maurice Merleau-Ponty articulates this point well:

> Vision is already inhabited by a sense that gives it a function in the spectacle of the world and in our existence. The pure *quale* would only be given to us if the world were a spectacle and one's body a mechanism with which an impartial mind could become acquainted. Sense, however, invests the quality with a living value, grasps it first in its signification for us, for the weighty mass that is our body, and as a result sense always includes a reference to the body.[66]

Notice here that Merleau-Ponty does not mean by "body" merely the sum-total of someone's physiological parts. Embodiment, for Merleau-Ponty, certainly includes as much, but he has a wider view of the body as our being embedded in a "body schema."[67] On this accounting, the body is "a general system of symbols for the world and through which we can 'frequent' this world, 'understand' it, and find a signification for it."[68] We are embodied not merely by virtue of the fact that our perception presupposes a certain neurophysiology, but more significantly because the supposed simplest or most basic cases of qualitative awareness presuppose a background of emotional, practical, and historical embedding

---

65. For a fairly standard anti-materialist treatment of the *qualia* problems, see Madden, *Mind, Matter, and Nature*, 133–46. See also Scruton, *The Soul of the World*, 40–43, and *Art and Imagination*, 104–6, for a Wittgensteinian approach to *qualia* very much in line with the extended mind position I am motivating in this chapter. See also Rudde, "What It's Like and What's Really Wrong with Physicalism."

66. Merleau-Ponty, *The Phenomenology of Perception*, 52. See also 216–21.

67. See Merleau-Ponty, *The Phenomenology of Perception*, 100–105

68. Merleau-Ponty, *The Phenomenology of Perception*, 245.

to become consciously available to us.[69] When asked, for example, to entertain a case of pure qualitative *redness*, we can only do so by imagining the perennial "red patch," which of course presupposes an overall Gestalt orientation that contrasts the qualitative redness with some border phenomenon. That limit will likewise presuppose all order of orientations, e.g., spatiality, motor function, and prior historical and cultural circumstances. In short, before we can have pure qualitative awareness, we must first be embodied in the sense of being involved in a world of biological, emotional, social, and historical embodiment. *Qualia* are not the experiential rock bottom.

Notice, however, our epistemically significant mental states are no less dependent on prior embodiment than are our supposedly non-intentional *qualia*. In fact, this line of thought should go a long way toward dissolving the hard line between the merely subjective and the semantically significant, which is often taken as a given among mainstream analytic philosophers of mind. None of our thinking is absolutely innocent of an emotional framing; human thinking and emotion are intertwined. Colin McGinn makes this "janus faced" nature of human intentionality clear:

> But these two faces do not wear different expressions: for what the experience is like is a function of what it is of, and what it is of is a function of what it is like. Told that an experience is of a scarlet sphere you know what it is like to have it; and if you know what it is like to have it, then you know how it represents things. The two faces are, as it were, locked together. The subjective and the semantic are chained to each other.[70]

Following Merleau-Ponty, I extend McGinn's coupling of the semantic and the subjective with the enrichment of the latter to include biological, emotional, social, and historical framings, i.e., embodiment. For me, an explicit judgment regarding a scarlet object cannot be completely separated from its invocation of *The Scarlet Letter* and all the experiences tied to my reading of that novel as a high school student. In other words, qualitative experience, cultural involvement, personal attachment, and the intentionality of thought cannot be untangled, nor should we finally

69. For a detailed phenomenological account of the role of emotion in the framing of consciousness at even the most rudimentary biological levels, see Jonas, *The Phenomenon of Life*, 99–107.

70. McGinn, *The Problem of Consciousness*, 29–30. Shaun Gallagher and Dan Zahavi provide an excellent presentation of the link between phenomenality and intentionality in *The Phenomenological Mind*, 93–118.

attempt to do so. All three of these aspects of human thought come online together. To think is to think about something, but thinking about
something is always embedded in a world of meaning, attachment, and
commitment. This claim is not an appeal to qualitative, experiential
atoms as enclosed in the internal, irreducible consciousness of *a* mind.
Whatever we may have to say about all of that, our thinking always has
a deep emotional framing, i.e., the divide between the emotional and
the rational is not as neat as we often tend to expect. Our mindedness
is always embedded in a non-cognitive context from which it draws its
lifeblood. As Evan Thompson puts it, "the subject has to be seen as having a 'life' in all the rich senses of this word—as formed by its individual
history, as a living bodily subject of experience, and as belonging to an
intersubjective 'life-world.'"[71]

Participation in mind then comes at an expense. Of course, it enables us to disclose a world of shared cognitive off-loading, and all the
practical benefits therein. At the same time, however, life in the space of
reasons requires that we maintain an openness to the revision of even our
most cherished conceptual commitments, which themselves, as I have
just suggested, may carry deep emotional and cultural ties for us. The
threat of such revision can only come at the expense of some anxiety, so
there must be something about which we care deeply that moves us to
accept the responsibility and consequent angst of *Geist*, rather than the
calm oblivion of merely natural creatures. A concern for truthfulness,
integrity, dignity, fidelity, or even simply our mortal interests in saving
our own skin binds us to the space of reasons. In any event, there is something in our world for which we care or to which we are attached that
commits us to the burden of rational responsibility.[72]

71. Thompson, *Mind in Life*, 30.

72. If the reader has noticed a transition from distinctively Hegelian to existentialist themes (mainly Heidegger and Merleau-Ponty) in the forgoing remarks, she should
trust this is no accident. These phenomenological themes will become more explicitly
central to our discussion when we consider why the care-structure of human mindedness tells against the notion of machine intelligence in chapter 4. The immediately following section of this chapter likewise will take us into territory originally mapped by
Heidegger and Merleau-Ponty. For a discussion of Heidegger covering a similar scope
of the issues we have addressed in this chapter, see Holland, *Heidegger and the Problem
of Consciousness*. For an excellent introduction to Merleau-Ponty on embodiment, see
John Sallis, *The Logos of the Sensible World*. In those lectures, Sallis also introduces
the problems of transcendence that Merleau-Ponty raises for himself and addresses
(however incompletely) in his later work. These worries will be crucial for us in the
following chapter. See also Sallis's *Phenomenology and the Return to Beginnings* for an
excellent treatment of these issues.

4. The Practical Space of Skills

It is not only our emotional attachments and existential concerns that serve as the implicit non-conceptual undergirding of our explicit logical cannons. Our movements in the space of reasons are also parasitic on our prior ability to move in a *space of skills*. Hubert Dreyfus and Charles Taylor applaud the Kantian-Hegelian holism that inspires the Pittsburg School to insist that our beliefs must be "inhabitants of the space of reasons," but they further claim that McDowell and Co. "have (in our view) failed to take on board the Heidegger or Merleau-Ponty point about the embedding of our explicit beliefs in our background grasp of things."[73] Meaningful concepts must ground *material* inferences, and therefore they originate in and are subject to continual certification by the *material* world stretching beyond our conceptualizations. Putting our concepts up against (or deriving them from) the world always presupposes a background of practical ability for dealing with an already existing world of things (an *equipmental environment*).[74] This notion of a practical

73. Dreyfus and Taylor, *Retrieving Realism*, 57. The tone of this quotation betrays the vigorous debate between phenomenological holists (Taylor, Dreyfus, and Haugeland) and "idealist" or "rationalist" holists (Sellars, McDowell, and Brandom). The primary issue is the priority and autonomy of the space of reasons viz. the "background of things," or what I call the *space of skills*. This debate is, in my view, internecine, and much of what transpires in the following chapters is an attempt at an *Aufheben* of the opposition, though with an additional player in the dialectic (Aristotelianism). Certainly, our ability to operate in a transcendent space of reasons originates and must, in some sense, be referred back to the space of skills and embodiment. That, however, does not undermine the spontaneity of the space of reasons root and branch. See Schear, *Mind, Reason, and Being-In-the-World* for a synoptic picture of the controversy. Lee Braver's contribution to Schear's volume, "Never Mind: Thinking of Subjectivity in the Dreyfus-McDowell Debate" (143–62), comes close to my own view. For another synthetic treatment of the Hegelian and Heideggarian strands of this controversy, see Matthew Crawford's magnificent *The World Beyond Your Head*, 60–68. For a sympathetic, though still critical, treatment of McDowell's position from the phenomenological perspective, see Gallagher and Zahavi, *The Phenomenological Mind*, 133–37. For an excellent presentation of the role of skillful, bodily comportment as a necessary background for human cognition using the resources of Hans Jonas's and Merleau-Ponty's phenomenologies, see Thompson, *Mind in Life*. Merleau-Ponty himself, in my view, did much to anticipate and diffuse this controversy. See in particular *The Phenomenology of Perception*, 126–27, 131–37, and 413–15.

74. I am alluding here to Heidegger, *Being and Time*, 95/67–123/89. Dreyfus's commentary on this part of *Being and Time* in *Being-In-the-World* is highly recommended. For an alternative and likely useful correction of some of the excessive pragmatism in Dreyfus's interpretation, see Harman, *Tool Being*.

background of coping skills necessary for narrowly cognitive acts is what Merleau-Ponty has in mind when he claims that "consciousness is not originarily an 'I think,' but rather an 'I can.'"[75] In other words, our *knowing-that* always presupposes some *knowing-how* with respect to the pre-cognitive world of significance we occupy in virtue of our embodiment. It is this embedding in a set of nitty-gritty skills for getting things done in a world of practical involvement that gives the logical space of reasons *bona fide* material content. Our skillfulness puts us in contact with the world beyond our heads. As Merleau-Ponty puts it, if embodiment is to provide us with a framing for materially significant perception and ultimately thought, then "my body is polarized by its tasks, insofar as it exists towards them, insofar as it coils up upon itself in order to reach its goal, and the 'body schema' is, in the end, a manner of expressing that my body is in and towards the world."[76] In others words, our perceptions and thoughts have semantic content (intentionality) because we are attached to the world by the goals we hope to achieve therein and our successful maintenance of skills for achieving them. Embodiment supports semantically significant acts because it entails our mastery of practically significant acts.

Dreyfus and Taylor motivate this point with the example of asking a youngster, say Cormac, to determine whether the picture in the next room is hung properly. Notice that we would only ask Cormac to take up this task on the assumption that he has a great many "epistemic skills." He needs to know how to gain proper perspective on the picture (standing neither too close, nor too far); he must be able to judge the orientation of the edges of the picture against the lines of the ceiling and walls; he needs to know how to find the room; he might need to know how to use devices, such as door knobs, locks, a level, etc.; and he needs to know better than to barge in, if there is an important closed-door meeting going on when he arrives, etc., etc., etc. That is, "if you should want to challenge him" on his conclusion about the orientation of the picture, i.e., if you were to treat him as a denizen of the logical space of reasons, you are in part asking him to draw on this rich (both social and technical) *know-how* that normally lies in our unnoticed background. Our request for Cormac to produce the semantically significant judgment about the painting presupposes:

75. Merleau-Ponty, *The Phenomenology of Perception*, 139.
76. Merleau-Ponty, *The Phenomenology of Perception*, 103.

his knowing how to do this, his being able to deal with objects in this way, which is, of course, inseparable from the other ways he is able to use them, manipulate them, get around among them, etc. When he goes and checks he uses this multiple ability to cope; his sense of his ability to cope gives him confidence in his judgment as he opens it to us—and rightly so, if he is competent.[77]

In other words, each act of *knowing-that* presupposes a myriad of exercises in *knowing-how*, because concepts only gain material content in transactions with a world that reveals itself to us through skillful, practical maneuvering. The most theoretically spectacular scientific claims presuppose the hands-on practicality of experimental design and execution, if they are to have material significance. Even abstract acts of mathematics and pure logic fall back onto tangible skills of writing and speaking, when one is asked to make his reasons explicit: "*Show* your *work* Cormac, or you won't get full credit for the problem set!"[78]

Moreover, it is not just our formalized procedures for verification that presuppose background practical coping with the world, but even basic perceptions. Dreyfus makes this point drawing on Merleau-Ponty, the Gestalt psychologists, and Piaget: "Before we acquire the appropriate skill, we experience only confused sensations. It is easiest to become aware of the body's role in taste, and touch, but seeing, too, is a skill that has to be learned. Focusing, getting the right perspective, picking out certain details, all involve coordinated actions and anticipations."[79] In other words, the things we see are really there, but we have to learn how to see them. This know-how is an acquired bodily skill that we can only obtain through a training among our senior peers in our form of life. Evan Thompson makes much the same point based not only on the phenomenological data but also the fruits of the dynamic sensorimotor approach to perception adopted by many contemporary neuroscientists and psychologists: "perceptual experience is not an inner event or state of the brain but a skillful activity constituted in part by the perceiver's implicit, practical

---

77. Dreyfus and Taylor, *Retrieving Realism*, 63.

78. This notion of a practical engagement that lies prior to even the most abstract scientific reasoning can be traced back to Husserl's employment of the notion of the *Lebenswelt* in his later phenomenology. See Edmund Husserl, *The Crisis of European Sciences and Transcendental Phenomenology*.

79. Dreyfus, *What Computers Still Can't Do*, 249. See also Merleau-Ponty, *The Phenomenology of Perception*, 52–67.

knowledge of the way sensory stimulation varies with movement" and "what it is to experience the world perceptually is to exercise one's bodily mastery or know-how of certain patterns of sensorimotor dependence between one's sensing and moving body and the environment."[80] Our very ability to perceive the world presupposes that we are already in that world, but *being-in* in this sense is a skillful relationship that necessarily involves bodily engagement. In order to perceive the world, we must be able to work with it such that it can show itself to us. None of this is to say the content of our concepts cannot outstrip their practical undergirding. We can talk about more than we can do, but our talk is always grounded in our transactions with the world, if our judgments are not to be blind. *Geist* is *sui generous*, but it does not operate utterly untethered from its pre-conceptual undergirding: "My first understanding of reality is not a picture I am forming of it, but a sense given to a continuing transaction with it" and its "inseparable presence is undeniable."[81] The logic of the human space of reasons is a *material logic,* and therefore our contents are fixed by our bodily, practical engagement with our world. In other words, our *knowing-that* goes far beyond our *knowing-how* to deal with the material world, but the latter is never completely free of the former. As Merleau-Ponty puts it: "There is . . . a privileged place for Reason. But precisely in order to understand it, we must begin by placing thought back among the phenomena of expression."[82]

Once again, and this has been the point of the argument we have followed for these first two chapters, the notion that having a thought, or even a simple perception, is no more than a particular neurophysiological state, in precision from a broader context, is a non-starter.[83] Just as *Zeta* is a thought about Paris only in the context of a living organism involved in a conceptual, material, and emotional network or milieu, we should add now that *Zeta* only rises to thought when it is likewise embedded in context of epistemic skill in dealing with the world. In fact, *Zeta* is only forged through the coincidence of all of these *worldly* processes. Ricoeur pulls all these vast strands together when he says:

80. Thompson, *Mind in Life,* 254 and 257.

81. Dreyfus and Taylor, *Retrieving Realism,* 70.

82. Merleau-Ponty, *The Phenomenology of Perception,* 196.

83. For neurophysiological evidence in support of what I have argued phenomenologically, i.e., human intelligence is not localizable in any single disposition or structure, but should instead be taken as synchrony among many different components, see Ferguson, Anderson, and Spreng, "Fluid and Flexible Minds."

> Consciousness is not a box in which there are objects. The notion
> of the mental has been construed in relation to the experience
> of being led toward the world and therefore of being outside
> oneself in intentionality. I stand in a very particular relation to
> the world, that of being born into this world, of being in it. The
> great advance of phenomenology was to reject the containing/
> contained relationship that make the psyche a place. Thus, I do
> not at all accept the conception of the "mind"—I deliberately
> put the word between quotation marks—as a container having
> contents.[84]

The problem with both materialism and dualism is they share the presupposition that the mind (*psyche* as Ricoeur puts it) is a sort of *place* within
the thinking individual, wherein thinking occurs. In the foregoing, I
have attempted to expose that error, by motivating the idea that thinking
does not occur in any one *place*, or maybe it occurs in *every place* (in a
richer sense of "place"). Having a mind is not to possess a container for
thoughts, but rather to have a relationship to a *world*, i.e., to be in a *Lebenswelt*. Putnam spoke well when he said that our thoughts (meanings)
"ain't in the head,"[85] but we do better to go further with John McDowell
and conclude that "the mind is not in the head."[86] John Haugland makes
much the same point: "intelligence itself abides 'out' in the world, not just
'inside.'"[87] We inherit, are "born into," a universe of conceptual, material,
emotional, and practical involvements, which always predate our arrival
and which we always share with others.

That shared world is the "place" where thought occurs. It is not
so much that *thoughts occupy* our mental space (brains or individuated
minds) but that *we occupy* a world rife with thought: "The meaningful is
not in our mind or our brain, but instead something worldly" and "we
do not store the meaningful inside ourselves, but rather live in it and are
at home in it . . . the meaningful is the *world itself*."[88] Haugland is not
endorsing a sort of idealism, according to which the world is a mental
projection by a prior existing mind. Indeed, that is exactly what is being recommended against: mind is a participation in a world, where a
world is not merely a collection of material things, but also a network of

84. Ricoeur, *What Makes Us Think*, 119.
85. Putnam, "The Meaning of Meaning," 131–93.
86. McDowell, "Putnam on Meaning."
87. Haugeland, *Having Thought* 232.
88. Haugeland, *Having Thought*, 231.

meaningful relations mediated to us through our shared skills, emotional concerns, and conceptual schemes that are constantly beholden to those concrete martial objects. Think of "world" here not merely as the sum total of entities individuated in time and/or space as in "The *world* came into being with the Big Bang," but as the totality of things that make sense together, as in "Meeting Jennifer in 1998 changed my *world* forever." It is by our participation in such a meaningful world (*Welt*) that we receive thought and become practitioners of mind.

Our worldliness, as participants in *Geist*, holds dire consequences for any reductive or totalizing attempt to explain what it is to be a rational animal. *Being-in-a-world* is not anything that can be fully accounted for by a single science or discipline, even broadly construed. To account for Cormac's thought about Paris would require us to appeal to the findings of neuroscience, history, linguistics, logic, anthropology, psychology (in several of its branches), literature, the fine arts, etc., and a myriad of non-generalizable details in his personal history and the humane relationships that have prepared his place in the space of reasons. In short, there is no science of *Geist*, and nor can there be one.[89] Our shared way of spiritually being in the world is multifaceted (infinitely-faceted?) and wrought with contingency, such that we should hold at arms-distance any claim to have fitted *Geist* into some sort of scientific-disciplinary box. Whatever completes the phrase "The mind *just is* . . ." will always fall short of the mark. There is no singularly unified story to be told about what it is to be one of us. Moreover, we *Gestig* beings are not entirely passive receptors of thought, i.e., we are not hapless vassals of the traditions and vital processes through which *Geist* is given to us. We begin with a world we are *thrown* into, but we then likewise take responsibility for it. Thus, we are always, as responsible inheritors of *Geist*, wary of the possibility that any story we tell about ourselves is quite possibly not the final story, and we are therefore always open to self-revisions as reality pushes back against our thinking. As Merleau-Ponty puts it well: "We must say . . . that our ideas, however limited they may be at a given moment—since they always express contact with being and culture—are capable of being true provided we keep them open to the field of nature and culture which they must express."[90] That openness to the field of nature and culture

89. Here, of course, is where I have said something that departs from G. W. F. Hegel himself, though not for many of the inheritors of the tradition of German philosophizing he partially initiated.

90. Merleau-Ponty, *The Primacy of Perception*, 21.

necessary for truth also opens the door to the possibility of error. Thus, the worldly philosophy of mind makes us

> aware of contingency. It is the continued confirmation of an astonishing junction between fact and meaning, between my body and my self, my thought and my speech, violence and truth. It is the methodological refusal of explanations, because they destroy the mixture we are made of and make us incomprehensible to ourselves.[91]

Thinking is an ever-open field that both grounds us and leaves us on the hook to account for the contingencies of that grounding. To say that we have a final story about *Geist* entails that we have reached the culminating end of history. The latter claim is something that, at this late date, we can no longer seriously entertain outside of the perspective of supernatural revelation, however things might have seemed to forward-thinking Prussian academics in 1807 or neo-conservatives working for the RAND Corporation in 1989.[92] Thus, at least for the foreseeable future, we can only see ourselves as something of a moving target.

Intellectual, social, and ethical maturation is taking up our role in this shared responsibility for the good order of our *Spirit*, our common way of *being-in-the-world*. What distinguishes us from our animal brethren is not the presence of a special part or organ (material or immaterial), but our ability to take this sort of responsibility for our shared commitments (whatever the organic or inorganic preconditions for such a power might be). In the remainder of our discussion, we will follow the consequences for our actions, destiny, and dignity once we stop thinking of ourselves in terms of easy pictures of atomistic repositories for thoughts, and instead see ourselves as participants in a common Spirit.

91. Merleau-Ponty, "Man and Adversity," 205.

92. For a sophisticated disagreement on these points, see Fukayama, *The End of History and the Last Man* and *Identity*. Both texts, even if controversial, provide good entry points into the social and political aspects of Hegel's thought, as mediated through the lens of the influential, even if underappreciated, philosopher Alexandre Kojeve. See also Kojeve's widely influential *Introduction to the Reading of Hegel*.

3

Freedom, Tragedy, and Retrospection

Now as we keep our watch and wait for the final day, count no man happy till
he dies, free of pain at last.

—SOPHOCLES, *OEDIPUS THE KING*[1]

"Everybody is farthest away—from himself;" all who try the reins know this
to their chagrin, and the maxim "know thyself!" addressed to human beings
by a god, is almost malicious.

—NIETZSCHE, *THE GAY SCIENCE*[2]

THE FORGOING TWO CHAPTERS are my attempt to make a cumulative
case that mind, what I prefer to call *Geist*, is necessarily a participation
in a "logical space of reasons," a natural history, a culture, significant
emotional attachments, and practical coping skills that constitute a world
of meaning in which we find ourselves. We also saw that *Geist* requires of us
a sort of responsibility for our status as *gestig* beings. That is, participating
in mind is not exhausted by our passive acceptance of a world, but further
demands that we take-up that world *for ourselves*. To have a mind is to
shoulder commitments to judgments and their antecedent and consequent

1. Sophocles, *Oedipus the King*, 251.
2. Nietzsche, *The Gay Science*, 263 (§335).

implications. These commitments likewise require an openness to revise our judgments, possibly in radical ways, when the world "pushes back" contrary to our expectations. There is then a sort of unavoidable tension at the center of our mindedness. On the one hand, we can only begin with what we are given (a world into which we have been *thrown*); while on the other hand, we must put that world and the judgments to which it commits us under a sort of critical scrutiny and, quite possibly, subsequent revision. This tension is why I have argued that *Geist* is always a moving target, as we can never rule out some future revision of our commitments by an unforeseen resistance from reality. In this chapter, I turn this approach to mindedness toward the notion of freedom. What does the tension between our being thrown into a world of pre-given meanings and biological limitations and our duty for self-scrutiny as denizens of the logical space of reasons disclose about our status as free beings capable of ethically significant actions? I will argue that the answer to that question will do much to disabuse us of many of the dead-ends and confusions abroad in modern thought about freedom of the will.

1. The "Free Will" Debate

I take it that we are not entirely interested in the notion of freedom of the will for its own sake, but mostly because of its implications for our understanding of ourselves as responsible for our actions, and therefore as subject to ethical evaluation. We see ourselves as capable of *ethically significant actions*, i.e., those doings for which we might laud or shame people, and in this way we honor or scorn our and other people's actions in a way we do not appraise the doings of non-human animals or occurrences among inanimate beings. That is not to deny that we evaluate such doings or occurrences at all; one might rightly conclude that a bit of hunting by his pet chameleon was particularly magnificent, or that the destructive movements of a certain tornado were extraordinarily terrible. The difference between our attitudes towards the ethically significant actions of human beings and the non-ethical doings and occurrences of chameleons and tornados is that we do not (in reflective moments or when not waxing poetic) hold chameleons and tornados *responsible* for their doings and occurrences in the same way that we hold ourselves accountable for our actions. Whatever might have happened in the curious case of Job, we are not perfectly serious in calling the whirlwind to account for its destructiveness, and I am not quite doing the same thing when I congratulate my son Cormac on some feat as when I do so for our pet chameleon. Humans, at least those among us who have achieved a certain level of maturity, are responsible for their doings in a way that renders those actions subject to a special kind of normative evaluation.

In the standard debate about freedom of the will currently abroad, it is assumed that this distinctively human responsibility must be explained in terms of a more basic activity, an act of *the will*. That is, ethically significant action supposedly must, in one way or another, be caused by the will of an agent who performs such actions. For example, if Cormac is to be praised for his having acted in such-and-such a way, then Cormac must have willed to have acted in that manner. Likewise, if Cormac is to be shamed for having acted in such-in-such way, then Cormac must have willed to have acted in that manner. It seems rather odd to us either to praise or to blame Cormac for having done something he had no willful intention of doing so. That is the very difference between an *action* and an *accident*. Chameleons, of course, do not accidentally hunt, and there is a sense in which the destructiveness of tornados is not merely accidental, inasmuch as we can see it as subject to certain law-governed explanations. Nevertheless, there is a kind of control we have over our actions that non-human animals and inanimate movers lack. In some sense, what Cormac does is up to him (it is a result of his willing), in a way that the doings and occurrences of chameleons and tornados are not up to them. Indeed, it would be quite odd to say that "The tornado was particularly destructive by accident," because there is no opposing sense in which a tornado could have been destructive *on purpose*. There is a kind of purpose to a chameleon's doings, but there is a sense in which they do not do things "on purpose" in the same way as human beings (or maybe even other higher animals). The difference between the chameleon's purposive doings and those of human beings, according to the standard approach, is accounted for by a special sort of psychological or mental act, an act of the will, that occurs "inside" the agent. In this context, the will is taken as a conscious, deliberative power to weigh or evaluate distinct courses of action, which an ethical agent wields as the final determining factor in a decision. At least, however, that is how a very basic version (maybe even a caricature) of the standard story goes.

Notice that this conscious intention is supposed to play the final determining role in bringing about an ethically significant action. In short, "the will" in the freedom of the will debate is typically thought of as a particular kind of *cause*. At least part of why Cormac has done something ethically significant is that he has willed to perform some action in particular (among the available options). It is then integral to this approach to ethical action that the act of the will occurs antecedently to (or at least simultaneously with) the action. An exercise of the will is a conscious mental event that occurs prior to (simultaneous with) the action it supposedly explains. That would seem to be the case necessarily, as the common assumption in play is that ethically significant action is *caused* by the will in much the same sense that the collision of the cue ball with the eight ball is the cause of the eight ball's subsequent residence in the corner pocket. The exercise of the will is supposed to be that which brings about an ethically significant action; or what makes it such that the action occurs in the sense of a *moving cause* or an *efficient cause* of the subsequent chain of events that constitute a certain ethically significant action. Since the agent's exercise of the will is a cause, in that sense, of ethically significant actions, the exercise of the will certainly must be antecedent to the unfolding, or at least completion, of the action. As the cause of the eight ball's residence in the corner pocket, the cue ball's striking of the eight ball must occur first or simultaneously in the order of time. P. M. S. Hacker makes much the same point when he characterizes the "received empiricist view" as the claim that "some mental occurrence constitutes willing . . . and that willing causes the bodily movement," and thus an ethically significant action should be considered "to be a movement caused by willing, and acting was causing the movement by willing."[3]

This is what I take people standardly to have in mind with talk of the will as it relates to ethically significant actions, but we have not said anything about how all of this relates to *freedom* of the will. Many philosophers are apt to think that being an act of will, even an act of will that is the antecedent cause of an action, is not alone enough to constitute ethically significant action. What is needed is not just an exercise of the will, but a *free* exercise of the will. All along we have said it must have been *up to* Cormac to perform an action, if we are either to praise or to blame him for doing so. Per the going account of its "being up to," whether Cormac performs a certain action is a question of the action's being caused by Cormac's willing that he do as much. But, if the exercise of the will is not itself something Cormac does on purpose, then it is hard to see how we can say that his resulting action is not something he does accidentally. Thus, it would seem Cormac's exercise of his will must be

3. Hacker, *Human Nature*, 147.

free, if it is going to ground ethically significant actions, i.e., it must be up to him as to how he would exercise his will in the sense that nothing else is "making" him do this. The debate over freedom of the will, at least in the mainstream of Western philosophy for the last few centuries, is then over *the cause* of *this cause*. The question is whether the exercise of the will is itself caused by something outside of the agent or whether the agent causes this act of the will independently of all external causes. The standard positions in the free will debate (whether libertarian, compatibilist, agent causal, hard determinist, etc.) are all different accountings of the sense in which the will is (or is not) the efficient cause of our ethically significant actions, independently of factors external to the agent.

I am not interested in getting into which of the standard positions regarding freedom of the will is correct, because I believe they are all built on a flawed assumption about our ethically significant actions, which is itself a failure to understand our status as *geistig* beings. Moreover, I believe these assumptions have caused the resulting understanding of ethical agency to pick an unnecessary fight with the results of neuroscience. *My claim is not that there is no such thing as an act of the will in the sense I have, admittedly, caricatured it above, but more modestly that the standard line of philosophical thinking has placed the emphasis in the wrong place.* This misplaced emphasis on what counts for ethical agency lends itself to undue skepticism about our status as free beings, and subsequent misunderstandings regarding what is most important in our lives.

2. The Neuroskeptical Case against Free Will

By "neuroskeptic," I mean someone who denies that we have freedom of the will based on supposed implications of neuroscientific findings. In recent years there have been no small number of neuroskeptics, both addressing academic and popular audiences.[4] One common source for neuroskepticism is the increasing body of neuroscientific results showing clear neurophysiological substrates for our experience of ourselves as free agents. For example, one recent neuroscientific study indicates that some aspects of the experience of free will are either lost or significantly distorted by lesions in localizable networks in the brain.[5] It thereby seems

4. For a case of the later, see Harris, *Free Will.* I will address much of the academic case for neuroskepticism in what follows.

5. Darby et al., "Lesion Network Localization of Free Will."

that our experience of free will is, in some way or other, dependent on those neurophysiological substrates. One might worry then whether it has been shown that the experience of free will, our intuitive sense of ourselves as ethical agents, is somehow illusory, i.e., freedom of the will just is an occurrence in the brain and nothing more.

That, however, is more than a little hasty. For reasons we discussed in the previous chapters, the fact that there are networks of neurophysiological activity serving as necessary conditions for our sense of free will is not itself evidence that we do not in fact have free will, nor does this show that our sense of free will "just is" the activity of those neurophysiological processes. Wittgenstein is correct when he argues that we cannot "read off" our thinking from our neurophysiology, however closely these phenomena are correlated, and I see no reason why this should be different for our acts of will. The fact that my thinking is correlated with and even clearly dependent on occurrences in my nervous system does not decisively support the conclusion that there is no such thing as my thought or that my thought is no more than the neurophysiological process, and likewise for acts of the will, even free acts of the will.

Moreover, the mapping of the neurophysiological conditions for free will perception might even make a limited contribution to a positive case for the reality of free will. As Massimo Pigliucci puts it, neurophysiological mapping of free will perception shows us how a sense of freedom "can be part of the human experience, because human beings are biological organisms that require a physical substrate to have any experience."[6] In other words, the fact that our sense of free will is something we can see as conditioned by normally functioning, neurophysiological architecture shows us that the notion of freedom is itself not something we must understand in a magical way. Rather, given this progress in neurophysiological mapping, we can see that providing for an experience of free will is part of what the brain is "set up" to do. Of course, there might be perfectly good reasons for the brain to be set up to deliver systematic illusions, but the fact that supporting structures for free will perception have a regular place in our neurophysiological geography is part of what a realist about freedom of the will would expect to be the case. There are versions of free will skepticism that can make sense of such structures too, but at least the free will realist can plausibly claim these actual scientific results do not falsify her position. The nervous system in some respects seems to

6. Pigliucci, *Answers for Aristotle*, 141.

be operating such as we would expect it to, if we supposed there really is such a thing as freedom of the will.[7] Finding neurophysiological structures requisite for free will helps us see how this otherwise difficult and mysterious notion might fit into a scientifically informed stance toward nature. One explanation as to why the brain evolved to accommodate free-will experience is that there really is such a thing to be aware of, just as the brain evolved to track moving objects because there are indeed moving things to be avoided and pursued.

Other neuroscientific findings gathered over the last few decades, however, do seemingly provide much stronger support for neuroskepticism. These findings do not merely point to what for many of us are the expected neurophysiological underpinnings of our free-will perceptions but seem to give us good reason to conclude that these experiences have nothing to do with the causation of our activities, or at least that is how these findings have been frequently interpreted. That is, we have scientific reasons to doubt whether conscious deliberation is in fact a causal *antecedent* of our actions. In 1964, two German scientists, Hans Helmut Kornhuber and Lüder Deecke, set out to investigate the degree to which the brain is actively involved in decision-making processes.[8] To that end, they conducted an experiment in which human subjects were asked to tap with one finger at whatever interval they chose, while any changes in the level of brain activity were recorded. Deecke and Kornhuber found that there was indeed a spike in brain activity leading up to the subjects' finger tapping. They called this increased activity in the subjects' brains the *Bereitschaftspotential* or "readiness potential," as they interpreted it

---

7. It is not insignificant that the neuroscientific study I cite in note 3 employs the notion of a "pathology" of free-will perception, i.e., the normal function of the brain includes support for free-will perception, and its failure to do is pathological. Once again, the fact that free will perception seems to be part of the normal functioning of the brain does not prove anything, but it is good news for the free-will realist to see that the brain's normal function includes structures her position would lead us to expect. I am not, however, attempting to claim the authors of that paper are out to defend anything akin to what I am developing here.

8. For an English translation of Kornhuber and Deecke's original paper, see, Kornhuber and Deecke, "Brain Potential Changes in Voluntary and Passive Movements in Humans: Readiness Potential and Reafferent Potentials." For a very lucid presentation of the scientific issues relating to both Deecke and Kornhuber's and Libet's papers (which we will discuss directly below), see Gholipour, "Does Free Will Exist? Science Can't Disprove It Yet. . . ." As should become clear, I agree with Gholipour that these neuroscientific results do not pose much of a threat to our understanding of ourselves as ethical agents, though for very different reasons.

as the nervous system's preparation to bring about an action. The discovery of the readiness potential was certainly a big deal scientifically, as it showed that the brain really does have a direct role in bringing about an action, and Kornhuber and Deecke's experiments hinted at some interesting philosophical questions. Nevertheless, their discovery of the readiness potential was not initially proposed as a reason to call the notion of freedom of the will into doubt, as their results were perfectly consistent with the proposal that an antecedent act of will is the cause of the readiness potential.

Later experiments conducted by Benjamin Libet, however, do seemingly raise troubling questions about our standing as free beings.[9] Libet was intrigued by the fact that there is a lag between the gathering of the readiness potential and the actual downstream movement. It is not a big gap (a micro-fraction of a second), but in neurological terms, where things happen at the speed of electricity, that is a significant interval. Why is there a substantial gap in time between the decision to act and the subsequent activity? Libet looked into this by varying Kornhuber and Deecke's experimental set-up a bit. He had the human subjects use a sort of clock to record when they consciously decided to move their finger, while their brains were simultaneously being monitored for the onset of the readiness potential. The incredible result Libet found was that the subjects' conscious sense of their decision occurred (though only by a tiny fraction of a second) *after* the build-up of the readiness potential. In other words, it seems that Libet found the brain has already "decided" to perform the action before that subject's conscious sense of having made such a decision. The conscious part of the decision seems to be *after the fact*, so it is difficult to see how it can play any determining role in what will eventually happen. The experience of free will, as it were, is just as much an effect of the realization of the readiness potential as the subsequent physical movements.

Remember the shared assumption of the contemporary free will debate: ethically significant action must be caused by an agent's exercise of the will, where an exercise of the will is an antecedently occurring, resolution to deliberation among the available options. Libertarians, hard

9. See Libet, "Unconscious Cerebral Initiative." Note that Libet himself does not propose that his findings undermine the notion of free agency entirely, as he allows that there could be a sense in which a conscious will exercises a sort of "free won't" as a veto control over what is determined by the readiness potential. For Libet's own accounting of his work and its implications, see his *Mind and Time*.

determinists, and compatibilists, whatever their other disagreements, all agree that antecedent (or simultaneous), conscious deliberation is a necessary condition for ethically significant actions, because such doings must, in one sense or another, be free; and free actions must be caused by the conscious will. Libet's experiment, however, seems to show the conscious act of willing is not antecedent to the readiness potential, and it is therefore not the cause of the action. The threat to freedom and moral agency does not come from the plausibility of determinism or the implausibility of compatibilism or libertarianism. Rather, the problem is the will does not seem to do any significant work in causing our activities. All the real work seems to be done by neurological activity, which is itself temporally antecedent to our supposed acts of will.

Though Libet's work is likely the most influential, a number of other researches have arrived at similar results. For example, C. S. Soon and collaborators were able to predict subjects' decisions before they themselves were consciously aware of their own intentions with a 60 percent reliability using functional magnetic resonance imaging.[10] Daniel Wegner, a social psychologist, appeals to an array of experiments wherein subjects were tricked into thinking they have or have not consciously chosen to do something, which would again seem to show it is not the conscious will that is really running things.[11] There is no small amount of properly scientific, along with philosophical, controversy about these experiments and their interpretation. Serious questions have been raised regarding whether they really do support the philosophical conclusions neuroskeptics infer from them on scientific grounds. I will not wade into those scientific weeds, but not because I doubt there is anything to worry about in that vicinity.[12] I am, nevertheless, happy to concede that Libet-style scientists and neuroskeptical philosophers interpreting their results have in fact shown that their subjects were not acting freely, or in any other ethically significant way. I do not find this terribly troubling because, as I shall argue below, ethical agency worth having has very little to do with the doings that Libet (and other experimenters I have mentioned above) observed on the part of his subjects. In fact, I believe Libet-style experiments do the proponent of a *bona fide* capacity for ethically significant

10. Soon, Brass, Heinze, and. Haynes, "Unconscious Determinants of Free Decisions in the Human Brain."

11. Wegner, *The Illusion of Free Will.*

12. For a critical philosophical discussion of these issues from a defender of free will, see Swinburne, *Mind, Brain, and Free Will,* 105–12.

actions on the part of human beings a service by disabusing us finally of a wrong-headed way of framing our understanding of such a capacity.

3. What Are Ethically Significant Actions?

There are three very important facts about the neuroskeptical case that we need to focus on in order to understand the philosophical implications of the scientific evidence they appeal to. The actions, and I am reluctant to call them actions, the subjects perform in the Libet-style experiments are *arbitrary, insignificant,* and *episodic.*[13]

By *arbitrary,* I mean the performances in the Libet-style experiments are not what recent philosophers call *reasons sensitive,* i.e., they are not doings that can be rationally justified.[14] When asked to tap your finger at an interval of your choosing, without being given any further end this interval-tapping might serve, your decision for one interval over another is not something for which you can give a reason. Supposing Cormac were a subject in a Libet-style experiment. When asked why he tapped his finger at any given moment, as opposed to any other moment in the infinity of perfectly good moments at which he might have tapped, there is no reason he could give. He could only cite a brute fact: "That's just what I chose to do." Maybe Cormac could give "I want to be a good experimental participant," or some such to explain why he is doing any finger tapping at all. Nevertheless, notice that the Libet experiment is not aimed at rooting out the antecedent causes of Cormac's finger tapping in general, but his finger tapping at one interval instead of all the other possibilities. For that explanation, it would seem Cormac could only say "Well, that's just what I happened to decide." Notice, however, that "I chose it" might be a *cause of acting,* but it is not a *reason for acting.* If I were to ask Cormac, "Why did you leave for swim practice early today?" and he replied, "Because I chose to leave early," I would point out to him that he really has not answered my question. Of course, *he* chose to do so; that is why I am asking *him* why he left early. If *he* had not decided the matter, I would not be asking *him* for an explanation. I wanted to know

13. This sort of concern is not novel on my part. For example, though I am not arguing along the exact same lines, see Roskies, "How Does Neuroscience Affect Our Conception of Volition." See also Roger Scruton's discussion of Libet in *The Face of God,* 41–49; and Goff, *Galileo's Error,* 195–205.

14. For a highly influential account of a reasons sensitivity theory of willing among recent philosophers, see Fischer and Ravizza, *Responsibility and Control.*

why he did it, not the causal process that led up to or finalized the decision. Typically, a reason for acting is an end that the agent aims to achieve by such an action. If Cormac were to answer my question with "So that I could get some extra laps for my breaststroke" or "So I could goof around in the pool with the other guys," whatever I might think of the relative worth of these different justifications for his action, either of these replies provides an intelligible reason for acting. That is, they tell us what end he thought he was moving toward when he left for practice early. Notice that tapping your finger at some random interval is not reasons-sensitive in this way, i.e., the performance is arbitrary in that it serves no end, and an agent "acting" in such a way can offer no meaningful justification.

Notice that a reason for acting is typically an end that would plausibly justify such an action; which is to say that reasons for acting are typically taken as *goods* the agent expects (or hopes) will be brought about by such acting. This emphasis on the notion of reasons as goods highlights the *insignificance* of the performances of the subjects in the Libet-style experiments. Only ends that can be seen as being significant to us are intelligible explanations of actions. To say that I acted to achieve some end, implies that such an end is *good to me*. As Aristotle opens what is likely the most historically influential discussion of ethically significant action in the Western tradition: "every action and deliberative choice seek some good."[15] Certainly, a condition of something being a good to me is that it is something I *care* about or it contributes to something *I care* about. In other words, when I ask Cormac "Why did you do that?" I am looking for his reasons (not merely the causes) for his actions, and only ends of acting that have significance to him would serve as a plausible answer to that question. "So that I could get some extra laps for my breaststroke" or "So I could goof around in the pool with the other guys" serve as reasons for Cormac's early departure because we can understand these states of affairs as goods or contributing to goods he is likely to care about (becoming a better swimmer or fun with his buddies).

If Cormac replied to my query about his early departure by saying, "Well, I just wanted the minute hand on the clock to point to the '6' instead of the '9' as I walked through the door," I would need some broader explanation as to why the position of the minute hand could possibly matter to him enough as to justify some particular course of action, before I could see that as part of the actual explanation of his early

---

15. Aristotle, *Nicomachean Ethics*, 2 (1094a1–2).

departure. A correct follow-up to such a reply would be the further question: "How can you possibly *care* about *that?*" In short, reasons-sensitive doings matter or have significance to the agents who perform them in virtue of the goods they serve. An end the agent simply does not care about is not really why that agent performs such an action, or at least it leaves the real justification of such an action unknown. Notice that in the Libet-style experiments, the finger tapping performances of the subjects are quite insignificant to them. It is hard to believe that any subject *cared* about which moment she tapped her finger as opposed to any other of the infinity of possible moments she might have tapped. If similar exercises of finger tapping were involved in an Olympic event in digit dexterity, there would be a ready-to-hand reasons explanation. Nevertheless, under the experimental conditions, nothing is at stake in which arbitrarily chosen moment you tap your finger, and as such no significant reasons explanation can to be given of those movements. Reason-giving is a normative affair, and norms presuppose a level of concern about what they govern.

Finally, the performances in the Libet-style experiments are *episodic*, in the sense that the decision leading up to them takes place at a discrete, *clockable* moment. That is, we are dealing with events that can be shown to have occurred at a specific time, or at least during a definite, hard-edged time interval. The subjects in the Libet-style experiment were clocked at the exact time at which they thought they consciously made the decision to tap their finger (or nearly so). Likewise, the readiness potential was detected at a definite time. Both the conscious perception of the decision and the neurophysiological activity were timed down to the fraction of a second. It is only because the decision to act in these cases can be precisely characterized as a discrete episode that we are concerned with which event (the conscious episode or the neurophysiological episode) comes first. Since the decision to tap your finger arbitrarily and insignificantly is a discrete episode, it makes sense to look for its cause among other antecedent (or simultaneous) discrete episodes. A necessary condition of one discrete episode explaining another is that the one doing the causing comes first in time (or simultaneously). For this reason, the Libet-style experiment takes the conscious episode and the neurophysiological episode in a zero-sum competition for who "goes first," wherein the winner is the "real" decision responsible for the subsequent finger-tapping.

Now, I am not concerned whether Libet-style experiments show that conscious volitions are in fact epiphenomenal in cases of arbitrary, insignificant, and episodic decisions to act. In fact, I would expect that organisms, even rational and reflective organisms like us, would have a mechanism wherein they could determine actions in an arbitrary way on a split second's notice. There is not a lot of time for subtle reasons sensitivity when the saber-toothed tiger shows up on the prehistoric planes. It is better to do something rather than nothing in such a situation; even running in an arbitrarily chosen direction ups your chances of not getting eaten better than remaining stationary while wrought with indecision, or at least you might distract the predator from cherished kin who were lucky enough to pick a safer direction of retreat. In more recent times, we have learned to hedge against the often ill-consequences of making arbitrary snap decisions in the face of an immediate crisis by off-loading information into our environment, e.g., emergency exit signs and the like, but we should expect that we do have a "Just do SOMETHING, ANYTHING!" mechanism in our cognitive toolbox. It is quite plausible that the Libet-style experiments have uncovered the neurophysiological underpinnings of just such a cognitive structure.

True that may be, but how relevant is this type of "decision-making" to ethically significant action? Take, for example, my decision to marry my wife. Was that decision arbitrary? Hardly. I could cite many reasons rendering that course of action perfectly rational, even impeccably justified. A decision to marry a particular person is certainly something we would expect to be reasons-sensitive in this way. This decision had the highest significance to me because it was a consequence of and partly constitutive of my commitment to a form of life. We see this kind of decision as important or grave because it plays such a life-defining role. A decision gains ethical significance in part due to its expression of a commitment to a particular vision of what counts as a good life. Ethically significant actions aim at goods that matter to us because of their role in what we take the very point of our lives to be. Such actions either define our notions of the good life ("Because I have married you, I am thereby committed to a host of other activities so broad as to define the kind of life I will hereafter live") or they are important consequences of our prior existential commitments ("Because I have broad commitments to a certain form of life, I am now committing to marrying you"), and in most cases I expect our ethically significant actions are done out of a mix of these two directions of commitment. The existential gravity of these decisions is why they stand out to us as having ethical significance. Notice that all of this is to say, not surprisingly given our discussions in the prior chapter, that the ability to perform ethically significant actions presupposes that the agent occupies a certain logical space of reasons. That is, ethically significant actions are those doings for which we can give reasons, which must have a significance to us, and the giving and taking of meaningfully significant reasons is to participate in a broad set of emotional, historical, and communal relations along with possessing a great array of epistemic and practical skills. The kinds of doings asked of the subjects of Libet-style experiments are not movements in the logical, historical, emotional, and skillful world of *Geist*, so they shed no light, for good or ill, on the ethically significant decisions of participants in *Geist*. In other words, these experimental results are irrelevant to our status as beings capable of ethically significant decision-making.

Further notice that the decision to marry was not episodic. There is no one *clockable* moment at which I can say I made this decision through a conscious act of will, or at least I am not aware of when such a moment occurred, nor was I when it supposedly did occur. In such decisions there is rarely, if ever, that "Eureka!" moment when one decides all at once to go forward with some course of action. It is often much more like *finding oneself* in a state of having resolved to take such a course. Many of our biggest commitments feel as though they happen to us. There was no specific day and time in the winter of 2000 at which I decided to marry, though I know sometime in that vicinity I crossed the threshold. No doubt there were many millions of discrete mental and physical events whirling around my vicinity during those months. Nevertheless, just as the addition of no one drop of rainfall marks the end of a drought, no one of those episodes amounted to making the decision. There is a fact of the matter, all things being equal, as to whether there was a drought last summer in western Kansas, but it is inherently vague, when specified down to the drop, what quantity of water would have remedied that situation. It is odd to think that a single milliliter of water marks the difference, but that has no bearing on whether there really is or is not a drought.[16] Likewise, it might be inherently vague as to when I make a certain decision, but that does not call into doubt that I made the decision. Indeed, if you reflect on most of the really important decisions you have made in your life, the ones with the greatest ethical significance, the resolutions that have done the most to define or confirm who you are, you will mostly find that there was no discrete "moment of decision," but a sort of *finding-oneself-in* a

16. See van Ingwagen, *The Problem of Evil*, 106–7.

commitment after an indeterminate process of deliberation. In my experience, one usually admits to himself what he has already seemingly resolved to do. Maybe there are such ethically significant decisions occurring at discrete moments, and I am not quite sure how we could decide that question, but my point is only that prior temporal discreteness is not a necessary condition for ethically significant action.

The temporal ambiguity of ethically significant decision-making (or at least some of it) brings us to the final salient feature of morally significant actions. Ethically significant actions, by definition, are reasons-sensitive, but notice they are often, maybe most often, only sensitive to reasons *retrospectively*. As Alasdair MacIntyre puts it: "That it is only in the course of the movement that the goals of the movement are articulated is the reason why we can understand human affairs only after the event."[17] In other words, often the reasons for taking some of the most important actions in my life, those that most define my commitment to a conception of the good life, are not entirely transparent to me while I am making those decisions or performing those actions. The full reasons for an action, the significant goods that fully justify it, might only be available to us consciously after the fact, i.e., after we have performed the action that our reasons can now be seen as justifying. Take the relatively mundane example of performing explicit speech acts (literally speaking sentences beginning like, "I promise I will . . ."). I need not explicitly take up decisions about all the words I utter in such sentences in order for them to gain significance, even though I am committed to their implications. After the fact I can tell you why I have said what I have said, but my commitment to a certain speech act does not require that I have reflected on it root and branch ahead of time, especially down to its component parts. As Hacker puts it:

> We are not aware of performing an act of will (let alone an effort of will or an inner act of trying) or the occurrence of a volition (a mental image or a representation of a kinaesthetic sensation) antecedently to everything we do voluntarily. When one utters a sentence, every word is spoken voluntarily, but it would be ridiculous to claim that one consciously performs successive acts of will, one for each word (or phoneme?).[18]

17. MacIntyre, "Hegel on Faces and Skulls," 234.
18. Hacker, *Human Nature*, 148.

Thus, we can be responsible for something, maybe even something of the highest ethical significance, but our reasons committing us to this responsibility might only be *explicit* to us retrospectively. Indeed, it seems perfectly coherent for us to take our reasons from others, say, wise counsel from a trusted friend, even when what makes those considerations good reasons is not entirely transparent to us. Sometimes, maybe we can give reasons for a selection of mentors, but mostly our counselors are people with whom we have been thrown together by the circumstances of our common world. In such cases, it is reasonable to accept full responsibility for the actions that are justified by these currently opaque reasons. Aristotle points out that even the wisest among us "call upon partners in deliberation on important matters, when we mistrust ourselves as not being adequate to determine the answer."[19] That, however, means the reasons justifying my actions, doings for which I am fully responsible, may be beyond my grasp *as reasons* when I actually perform those actions. My reasons are *mine* because they are features of the world I occupy in virtue of my participation in *Geist*, not because they are always internally explicit to me.

Once again, my decision to marry is just such a decision. Though that decision is perfectly justified by the available reasons, and I can now understand those reasons as justifying that decision, these very same reasons were not entirely transparent to me in the winter of 2000 when I found myself resolved to marry. In fact, though they were maybe quite opaque to me then, two decades later they are far clearer. Indeed, I suspect, God-willing, those reasons will be even clearer to me in two more decades. Like any other movement in the world of *Geist*, the reasons for my decision to marry were not strictly internal to me but had much to do with my occupying a certain place in a human history, i.e., a natural history, an institutional history, and the course of the particularities of my life and the lives of others with whom I share attachments. Making those reasons explicit has been a twenty-year long project of living a certain form of life, which is still open-ended. At this late date, I can make many of the reasons for my marital commitment explicit, even though I doubt I was consciously aware of them twenty years ago, but that is not to say that those reasons were not there in the world I was *thrown into* and *took responsibility for* by making that decision two decades ago. In fact, that I can cite such reasons retrospectively is some reason to conclude

19. Aristotle, *Nicomachean Ethics*, 41 (1112b10–11).

that they were indeed operative even back then: "It is because any exercise of the power to reflect on our reasons for action presupposes that we already have such reasons about which we can reflect, prior to our reflection."[20] Bob the Chameleon's reasons for the particularities of this morning's hunt were "there" operating for him, even though he was not reflecting on them (nor will he ever do so). Thus, I do not need to reflect on something for it to be the reason for my acting; like Bob, the reasons for many of my doings (even some of my most important doings) are off-loaded onto the world in which I participate. Both the mind and the will are extended into our environment.

The point in all of this is that many of our most significant decisions, the sorts of decisions we are raising our children to be able to make, are justified by reasons that may not explicitly be available to us until well after the fact. In short, reasons-sensitivity, in the reflectively significant sense, is often retrospective. As a rational animal, I should be on the hunt to make my reasons explicit, but that is mostly done looking back on what I have already done, when I now know better what I was really up to. My reasons for marrying were partly carried for me by my participation in a certain family, education, church, etc., but those were my reasons, because those institutions were constitutive of the form of life that I live, though at the time very little of all of that explicitly crossed my mind. The Owl of Minerva does indeed make its most important flights late in the day.[21]

We may then conclude that ethically significant actions are non-arbitrary, meaningfully significant, non-episodic, and retrospectively justified. Notice that the sorts of doings considered by the Libet-style experiments are precisely the contrary of such actions: they are arbitrary, insignificant, episodic, and wanting for antecedent justification. The doings of these experimental subjects just are not the type of doings at all relevant to our status as moral agents. This boils down to a classic "apples vs. oranges" confusion. Certainly, Libet and those who follow in his train may well show that in cases of randomly chosen finger-tappings (or trivial situations in which we can be tricked into thinking we decided something we didn't) we are not acting as *bona fide* ethical agents, but nobody should have thought we would be so acting in those cases in the

20. MacIntyre, *Dependent Rational Animals*, 56.

21. Robert Brandom emphasizes the role of retrospective reconstruction throughout his various treatments of Hegel. For his most accessible presentation, see *Heroism and Magnanimity*.

first place. Libet's experiments did not put any significant good in the breach regarding the subjects' decisions, which means that whatever he shows, it has nothing to do with ethically significant actions, nor does it pose any threat to a worthy notion of freedom.

4. Freedom as Threefold Responsibility

Thus far I have attempted to motivate a certain view of the grounds for ethically significant action. Integral to this view is the claim that what makes an action ethically significant is not whether it has been *efficiently* caused by some sort of psychological mechanism internal to the agent independently of outside influences. I am not denying that freedom in that sense is possible or that it isn't a necessary condition for ethical action in some way or another. Rather, I simply see those worries as beside the point of what is most important for securing our self-understanding as beings capable of ethical agency. My concern is the emphasis on that kind of condition for ethically significant action (whatever we think about the plausibility of its satisfaction) disposes us to miss what is cardinally important in this vicinity. Whether or not our wills operate as independent efficient causes makes little difference for how we raise our children, train our future colleagues, or plan our lives in deliberation with our neighbors. Rather, an ethically significant action is a performance that has a special relationship to a form of life. Specifically, an ethically significant action is justified by a commitment to a set of goods that together constitute the good life, or it is something the doing of which commits one (on pain of inconsistency) to such a view of the good. Ethically significant actions are those doings for which one can give reasons, wherein "reasons" are justifications in terms of goods of ultimate concern—acting in accord with a vision of what matters most in life. The perceptive reader will have already noted that I am suggesting we worry less about whether something pushes us from behind as an *efficient cause*, and instead wonder about what exactly pulls us toward it as a *final cause* in a classically Aristotelian manner. What we want for our children, spouses, colleagues, friends, and ourselves is that we be motivated by certain goods that constitute our shared form of life.

I also tried to show you how our relationship to these reasons for our ethically significant actions is often, maybe in many of the really important cases, only *retrospectively* accessible; we frequently piggyback for our reasons on the reasons extant in our world. That is, when I am doing the things that most express or constitute the sort of life to which I am committed, the connection between those actions and their ultimate reasons is quite often not entirely transparent to me. Indeed, even the very goods that compose the form of life we are thrown into are often not entirely within our ken when we need most to decide in favor of them. Until we achieve a certain station in life when retrospective reflection is possible, our reasons for acting are mostly carried by our participation in histories (both cultural and biological) and institutions we have inherited. Because I am an organic product of a natural history, a member of a family, an inheritor of a language and culture, etc., certain reasons are my reasons for acting, even though I might as yet have failed to make those reasons explicit to myself or anyone else, and maybe I will never be able to do so entirely. Throughout much of our lives, we depend on others (both particular others with whom we share bonds of friendship, and institutional others providing contexts within which those bonds of friendship may be established) who have gone before us or along with us to provide the reasons for some of our most ethically significant actions. I take it that this is part of what Aristotle has in mind when he famously claims that a truly self-sufficient person "is either a wild beast or a god."[22]

We humans, however, are not mere automata or unreflective beasts. We can make our reasons explicit. We can, upon reflection, decide that our reasons for acting were not particularly good reasons for acting and the actions that followed on them were subsequently not the right things to have done. We can amend our long-term dispositions for action based on these reflections, though only with a great deal of effort. We can further subject our inherited form of life to critical reflection, and even conclude that it is flawed and possibly requiring substantial revision or even wholesale rejection. Rational conversion is a real possibility. We humans are unique in that we are capable of reflective self-criticism of both our particular actions and the ways of life we suppose to justify them. The process of becoming capable of this sort of self-criticism is ethical education in the most important sense, and it culminates (even if never fully complete) in practical wisdom. Our achievement of wisdom will for the most part come late in life; a skill mostly exercised retrospectively, while looking back upon our own ethically significant decisions and providing reasons on behalf of our juniors who are now set to walk similar paths.

22. Aristotle, *Politics*, 1986 (1252a29).

Once again, I take it that this "Monday morning quarterbacking" phenomenon in our exercise of practical wisdom is part of what Aristotle had in mind when he claimed that happiness (our satisfaction at having lived our form of life well) only comes from the perspective of one's death bed.[23] Certainly, we have to see how things wrap-up ultimately for our projects before we can deem ourselves happy, but we also do not really know how to evaluate those very projects until we have been made wise by carrying them out. Notice that the wise person is someone able to take responsibility for both her actions justified by her form of life and that form of life itself. Since we are capable of reflective self-criticism, we have a sort of ownership of our actions. The wise person sits on her deathbed and looks back over her life and can say "I understand why that has all been done, and, for good or ill, I accept responsibility for it."

All of this is to say we are free beings. I see freedom in this sense as a three-fold responsibility: (a) we are able explicitly to *connect* our actions and the goods that constitute our form of life that would (hopefully) justify them; (b) those *goods really do constitute* a worthy form of life; and (c) those *goods really are our reasons* for acting. In other words, a free person is someone who has entered the logical space of reasons, i.e., a person who can give *legitimate* and *authentic* justifications for her sayings and doings. Someone who satisfies these conditions has moved from being a default participant in the biological and cultural activities constitutive of a certain form of life, to someone who can give explicit justifications for those activities in terms of real goods enshrined as most mattering to those who live in that way. That is, freedom is to be an independent participant in *Geist*. The important contrast to highlight here is between *activity* and *passivity*. The fully initiated denizen of the logical space of reasons does not piggyback on the reasons of others, but comes to take active responsibility for her actions by offering sincere justifications. The free person has reached a point of maturity by moving beyond a passive role of accepting the implicit justifications on offer from her form of life, to an active role of reflectively and critically making those reasons explicit. Part and parcel of this movement from passivity to activity is a willingness to revise one's activities where justifications are found wanting. Surely, any *bona fide* denizen of the logical space of reasons takes reasons to be normative in the sense that the presence or absence of justifications has consequences for practical commitments.

23. Aristotle, *Nicomachean Ethics*, 10 (1098a18).

Aristotle initially defines human happiness in similar terms as I am framing the notion of freedom:

> the function of the human being is activity of the soul in accord with reason or not without reason, and the function of a sort of thing, we say, is the same in kind as the function of an excellent thing of that sort . . . and a human being's function is supposed to be a sort of living, and this living is supposed to be activity of the soul and actions that involve reason, and it is characteristic of an excellent man to do these well and nobly.[24]

That is, the best sort of life (the life that we hope our children will live) is one that is not lived *by accident*. Come what may, a life lived for which one can gives reasons, and not just any reasons but *good* reasons, is the best way of life. For Aristotle, all things being equal, it is better to be good than lucky.[25] We begin by piggy-backing on the reasons in our form of life, and hopefully we will be lucky in the reception of good reasons from this *Lebenswelt*, but the ideal is to be able to take up those reasons explicitly. Whether one thinks that operation in the space of reasons is sufficient for happiness (and Aristotle himself believes it will likely be supplemented by external goods),[26] certainly one can see that living a life that can be justified is integral to the human ideal. Notice, then, that freedom, as I have construed it as a sort of responsibility for one's reasons, is likewise central to any plausible accounting of human flourishing.

The first condition for freedom is a responsibility internal to one's form of life. For Cormac to give explicit justifications of this sort, the goods he cites must actually be the goods of his form of life and they must be actually connected to his actions in the appropriate justificatory manner. In short, part of what freedom requires of Cormac is that he be *responsible to the form of life* he has been thrown into. For example, if Cormac were to justify (and not piggyback on the justifications of others) his decision to marry in terms of, say, his Roman Catholicism, he would need to grasp the goods Catholicism takes as inherent to marriage, his marrying this particular woman would have to be appropriately connected to those goods so as to plausibly bring them about, and he would need to be acquainted with this connection.[27] Using the term loosely, we might

24. Aristotle, *Nicomachean Ethics*, 10 (1098a5–13).

25. Aristotle, *Nicomachean Ethics*, 14–15 (1100a10–1101a20).

26. Aristotle, *Nicomachean Ethics*, 13–13 (1099a31–b5).

27. Of course, all these are merely necessary conditions, as we would also hope that Cormac would actually love the woman he is considering marrying.

think of this condition for freedom as a sort of *syntactical* responsibility, as it requires the explicit grasp of formal and material logical relations between the actions available and justifying goods as specified by the agent's grounding tradition. The free person makes valid moves in the logical space of her form of life.

We might then think of the second condition as a sort of *semantic* responsibility.[28] Here Cormac is not just *responsible to his way of life*, but he is also *responsible for it*. That is, if a proposed set of goods is to justify Cormac's decision to marry, then those goods must not be merely *proposed as* good but must *really be* goods. The logical space of reasons is not solely constituted by trivial, formal logical relations, but more importantly by empirically conditioned relations of material logic, which are themselves sensitive to push-back from reality beyond our direct control. A justification for acting in terms of a merely apparent good (as opposed to a real good) is not a justification for acting, but self-harm. Long-term, maybe irreversible, delusions about what actually constitutes our good is how Aristotle defines the very notion of vice, and he sees it as tantamount to self-destruction in its extreme forms, a permanent state of cognitive drunkenness.[29] Thus, we are not only *responsible to* our form of life, but *responsible for* it. A free being checks her inherited understanding of the good against reality. A cult is not a form of life, and therefore a free person cannot shirk ultimate semantic responsibility.

If we think of the first two conditions for freedom as demands for responsibility to others (the free person is responsible to the others from whom she has inherited her way of life and with whom she shares the consequences of delusion), we should take the third as a demand for responsibility to oneself, a kind of *authenticity*. Nietzsche puts his finger on this condition for *bona fide* freedom:

> Your judgment "this is right" has a pre-history in your instincts, likes, dislikes, experiences, and lack of experiences. "*How* did it originate there?" you must ask, and also: "What is it that impels me to listen to it?" . . . But that you take this or that judgment as the voice of conscience—in other words, that you feel something to be right—may be due to the fact that you have never thought much about yourself and simply have accepted blindly that what you have been *told* ever since childhood was right;

28. The notions of syntactic and semantic responsibility no doubt owes a great deal to Brandom, especially more recent work.

29. Aristotle, *Nicomachean Ethics*, 37 (1111a24–29).

or it may be due to the fact that what you call your duty has up to this point brought you sustenance and honors—and you consider it "right" because it appears to you as your own "condition of existence" (and that you have a right to existence seems irrefutable to you).[30]

Nietzsche's questions are troubling, but they must be addressed, if we are going to take responsibility for ourselves. Even if our form of life can stand scrutiny, that does not necessarily mean that our motivations for adhering to it are pristine, and we must ask ourselves what is really going on "behind the scenes." Maybe Cormac's particular decision to marry instantiates the appropriate connection to the goods prescribed by his Roman Catholic way of life, and that way of life may constitute an actual way of human flourishing. Nevertheless, that could all be coincidental with what Cormac is honestly up to, because those goods are not what really motivate him. Though Cormac's decision to marry *could* be justified by *bona fide* goods of human unity, family, and salvation, he might deep down, as it were, really be motivated by lust, status, money, or what have you. In the latter case Cormac would be *responsible to* and *for* his way of life only accidentally, which is to say he is not acting responsibly at all. If Cormac's actions in such a case were *justifiable* in terms of this form of life, he would merely be lucky, and the movement from being lucky to being ethically responsible is the very mark of freedom.

Once again, if we are sympathetic to Aristotle on this point, it is not just Cormac's freedom but also his happiness that is at stake. We do not raise our children so that they might be accidentally good, but to be good on purpose. Maybe we begin the process of educating someone into a way of life by motivating them with external goods just to get things off the ground. For example, one might need to entice a child toward responsibility with rewards and punishments in the way one might bribe her to learn chess with candy, but mature practical mastery requires that one, to some high degree at least, be motivated by the goods internal to that way of living.[31] Thus, whereas the first two conditions require that the free person can explicitly make the connection between her actions and the goods constitutive of her form of life and (hopefully) the veridical connection between the latter and the world, the third condition requires

30. Nietzsche, *The Gay Science*, 263–64 (§335). Nietzsche's emphasis.

31. Alasdair MacIntyre makes famous use of this example in his discussion of internal vs. external goods as motivating practices or ways of life in *After Virtue*, 181–203.

that she can bring her own true motives to unambiguous transparency, i.e., her satisfaction of the first two conditions is not merely an act of bad faith. An agent operating on bad faith is only lucky, if she achieves the good life, as she is subject to the foibles of her mutable and unanalyzed subterranean motivations. Thus, the happiness constituted by a *complete life* in Aristotle's sense requires that one have self-conscious transparency with respect to her relationship to the goods proposed by her inherited form of life.

In this light, we can see the three-fold responsibility conditions for freedom entail a corresponding three-fold set of knowledge conditions. That is, freedom requires (a) knowledge of one's way of life, i.e., one must know what one is committed to in her way of life and how those commitments are related to particular courses of action on offer; (b) one must have knowledge of how things actually stand, i.e., one must know whether the goods enshrined by her form of life are in fact actual goods; and (c) one must have knowledge of oneself, i.e., one must know whether it really is a commitment to a *bona fide* vision of the good life that motivates his or her acting rather than some other, possibly insidious, motive. Thus, freedom follows on responsibility, but responsibility follows only on knowledge. Or, as I put it earlier, we achieve our freedom inasmuch as we have realized a threefold wisdom: knowing our way of life, knowing how things stand, and knowing ourselves.

5. The Tragic Threat to Human Freedom

We can also see that the great threat to our freedom is not the impingement of efficient causes (whether that threat is provided by a deterministic universal mechanism, or merely the fact that our neurophysiology may do the work we mistakenly credit to our conscious will), but *ignorance*. Indeed, Aristotle puts ignorance among the most insidious threats to voluntary action, on par with the force of external causes.[32] If freedom is wisdom, then bondage is ignorance. Our freedom is undermined when we do not know what we are doing, we do not know whether what we are doing is actually a good idea, or we do not really know why we are doing what we are doing. Whatever might obscure our vision in these matters subverts our freedom. In other words, given the three wisdom conditions for freedom, we can see that we are threatened by a threefold ignorance:

32. Aristotle, *Nicomachean Ethics*, 35–37 (1110b15–1111a29).

We could fail to grasp the goods proposed to us by our grounding traditions and histories (both cultural and natural), which is a failure of education; we can have the misfortune of being thrown into a tradition (along with its biological grounding) with a flawed epistemic relationship to the world; and we could fail to be transparent to ourselves, i.e., we can fail to put our own motives under rational scrutiny. This triple threat of obliviousness is what should worry us about freedom, not the efficient casual underpinnings of volition.

Consider how the tragic drama we find in the Greeks reveals the threat an opaque understanding of the possible distortions inherent in our form of life and our own individual motivations pose to our ultimate well-being. The most obvious example is Sophocles's *Oedipus Rex*. Consider the case of poor old Oedipus, the once great king of Thebes who fell prey to the supposedly blind vicissitudes of Fate. Oedipus saved Thebes from the oppression of the Sphinx with his cleverness and then took on the mantel of monarch, including a marriage to the recently widowed queen. All of that happened not so long after he killed a middle-aged man in a Bronze Age road-rage incident with a magnificent act of marshal skill. Oedipus is the very archetype of the Greek aristocratic warrior in his mix of *thymos*, guile, and physical prowess. In terms of the first responsibility condition for freedom, Oedipus acts magnificently in terms of the form of life he inherited as an ancient Greek. Slaying an arrogant brigand on the road, taking a beautiful, widowed queen as your wife, and saving a city from a plague by an act of wit are paradigmatic instances of being responsible to that way of life, and we have no reason to doubt Oedipus could make many of those goods explicit. Things, however, are not really as they seem with Oedipus. While he sits on the throne, another plague oppresses Thebes, and this time an oracle indicates that the source is not an outside force, but an internal corruption—there is an incestuous patricidal murderer dwelling in the city. Oedipus, of course, vows to excise this malignancy, but, as the story unfolds, we find out that it is actually Oedipus himself who brought on this pestilence. It was his father, then the king of Thebes, whom Oedipus slew on the roadway, and it is his mother with whom he has conceived his children. We readers of Sophocles' play are not surprised by this outcome, because we know the backstory: it was long ago foretold that Oedipus would slay his father and lay with his mother, and we know the true account of his meteoric rise. It appears Oedipus, despite his personal magnificence and efforts to circumvent the prophecy of his grim destiny, was the victim of a rigged game. He was fated to these crimes since before he was born, just as his own children (all of whom fall on very rough times in Sophocles' other episodes in the trilogy) are destined for tragedy.

Oedipus comes to ruin through a systematic distortion of his understanding of who he is and what ultimately accounts for his motives. Oedipus's agency may have been thwarted by a kind of ignorance, but it is hard to excuse him entirely from responsibility for what he should have known. He knew the prophecy of his patricide and incest, and it is hard to take seriously that Oedipus never noticed a striking resemblance between himself and his wife, nor the odd coincidence that he just so happened to kill a man about the age of his father, etc. Maybe appearances were deceiving for Oedipus, but he should have known better than to take everything at face value. Sophocles gives Oedipus only the thinnest veneer of innocence, and that is no accident. Oedipus's sin is ultimately willful self-ignorance. He was not willing to look at the hard, "subterranean" facts of what was really going on with respect to his own thinking and acting. Thus, we should not take tragic fate as an external agency that forces our hand, but something we participate in by our unwillingness to look at unsavory facts about our nature and personal motivations. It seems, then, Oedipus had, prior to the revelations in the drama, completely failed to put himself under significant rational scrutiny, or maybe he willfully ignored the revelations wrought by that scrutiny. In any event, it was that, possibly willful, self-ignorance that accounts for Oedipus's terrible fate.

Tragedy is then not merely the operation of fate in our lives that might bring us to an ill-end even though we have made the best possible efforts to the contrary. Rather, tragedy is a result of a failure to take responsibility for one's form of life and oneself, i.e., an abdication of our freedom by refusing to take seriously our responsibility for our form of life and our responsibility to ourselves. By not examining yourself, i.e., your reasons and motives, you leave your life to the play of fate. If things come out well for you, that will be merely accidental, as you have never taken possession of yourself. Even if Oedipus really did kill a brigand, save the city, and marry the beautiful queen (all great deeds), he is only lucky that he is not a party to incest and patricide. For all he knew, though he easily could have known better, he was really a complete lout. Why didn't Oedipus ever put two and two together regarding the curious series of events that formed the most pivotal events of his life, the curiousness of which is so blatantly obvious to the reader (an impartial external observer of that life)? One can only conclude that ultimately Oedipus did not want to face hard questions about himself, and therefore his ultimate motives are dubious indeed. It is no accident that Sophocles has the tidings of Oedipus's horrifying wrongdoings originate from the Oracle at Delphi, where the motto "Know thyself" was inscribed and Socrates later claims to have learned that "The unexamined life is not worth living." Sophocles, on my reading, goads us to ask of Oedipus, "Really, what have you actually been up to?" and to see that failure to ask such a question of ourselves will lead to similar ruin.[33] Tragic fate is therefore not an entirely external imposition. Rather, cases like Oedipus show that "we conspire in our fate" through our willful self-ignorance or lazy indifference to unflattering truths about ourselves and our form of life, and therefore, "fate requires our freedom in order to bring our destiny down upon us."[34] We are partly responsible for our tragic falls because of our inauthenticity.

Our freedom and happiness are then threatened by our ignorance, and in particular ignorance of ourselves and the way our own delusions may distort unwelcome truths about our form of life and our deepest motives. Alasdair MacIntyre highlights that in the Aristotelian-Thomistic tradition, the alleviation of such cognitive blind spots should be among our utmost ethical concerns:

> Education in the virtues consists in key part in making those so educated aware in detail of the possibilities of error and of the errors which each of them will be particularly inclined, because of temperament or social role, or whatever. Here the traditional insights of Aristotelian Thomism need to be enriched by more recent findings.[35]

For MacIntyre, today the Oracle of Delphi calls us to a "sociological self-knowledge" that amounts to "a grasp of the nature of roles and

---

33. I do not put these remarks forward as anything even approaching a responsible piece of interpretive criticism of Sophocles' drama. The reader should take these thoughts as merely my impressions upon reflecting with the text. This reading of *Oedipus* in particular, however, is supported by Simon Critchley's in *Tragedy, The Greeks, and Us*, 12–15, 272–73. Though I have not read Sophocles exactly as he does, and I have made a different use of the notion of tragedy, Brandom's considerations on Sophocles and its role in Hegel's approach to freedom and responsibility are certainly in the background. See Brandom, *Heroism and Magnanimity*, 20–36; and *A Spirit of Trust*, 636–758. For a philosophically informed approach to tragedy (Antigone in particular), see Benardete, *Sacred Transgressions*.

34. Critchley, *Tragedy, the Greeks, and Us*, 15.

35. MacIntyre, *Ethics in the Conflicts of Modernity*, 191.

relationships in which one is involved, of the shared assumptions of those with whom one interacts, of what in those roles, relationships, and assumptions obstructs the exercise of rational agency, and of what the possibilities are of acting so as to transform them."[36] That is, to achieve freedom we must be willing to put our self-conceptions to the test, to be sure that we truly are responsible to reality and to our truest motives when giving reasons, which will include a possibly painful and anxiety-ridden process of achieving self-transparency.[37] This is the cost of the dignity of *Geist*, and we must be willing to consider the results of the social sciences in particular, as they are our best resources for gaining a glimpse of an unvarnished picture of ourselves.

If I am subject to self-delusion, then how am I ever to trust *myself* in overcoming my self-delusions? Couldn't whatever revision of my understanding of my own motives that I opt for be itself just one more convenient bias, an evasion of the ugly realities of my true desires? Well, sadly, yes, but this is where friendship comes into play. Again, MacIntyre:

> But our self-knowledge too depends in key part upon what we learn about ourselves from others. . . . And it is insofar as I am overprotective of myself in resisting disclosure to just such others that I am liable to become a victim of my phantasies.[38]

In other words, I need critique by others in order to achieve self-knowledge—to liberate myself form my self-aggrandizing fantasies. I am unlikely to achieve an objectivity about my actions and motives simply by an act of introspection. We are subject, like Oedipus, to our own, possibly incorrigible, self-imposed ignorance of ourselves. Other people, however, are not distorted by our own personal shortcomings (though they have their own blind spots too), so they must be our source for self-criticism. Notice that MacIntyre emphasizes the fact that our resistance to disclosure is one of the primary obstacles to overcoming our self-imposed delusions. That is, I cannot consider the other's critique of my doings and motives until I have honestly disclosed myself to her. Honest disclosure, however, only occurs in contexts of trust and mutual good will, which is to say, it is our friends on whom we depend to provide us with *sympathetic subversions* of our own convenient biases. No one is in a better position than my wife to tell me, "We both know you have

36. MacIntyre, *Ethics in the Conflicts of Modernity*, 213.

37. I see MacIntyre's exhortations as much akin to Harry Frankfurt's in *On Bullshit*.

38. MacIntyre, *Dependent Rational Animals*, 94–95.

long envied Smitty's success, and that is why you are considering voting against his promotion, not your supposed commitments to professional excellence." Subversion of our possibly flawed self-understanding is a necessary, though dangerous, drug that carries many terrible side-effects unless administered properly. The proper application of this powerful therapy is a context of love and trust, where we know that the point of the critique is not the subversion of our personality as we know it, but to help us avoid tragic self-destruction. As MacIntyre puts it, the best protections against our most grievous errors are "friendship and collegiality"[39] and "the judgment of preceptive and ruthlessly critical friends."[40] I must be able to trust you to tell me the truth that I most need to hear (however painful that subsequent self-realization may be) and I need to trust you to do me no harm in your pronouncements on my character.[41]

There is a ring of paradox in the view of freedom I am sketching for you, at least to our modern ears (though I doubt that Aristotle, St. Thomas, Hegel, Heidegger, or Wittgenstein would hear the slightest irony). We associate the notion of freedom with independence, and I have highlighted this in the emphasis I have put on freedom as a kind of responsibility. The free person is someone who can take responsibility for her sayings and doings (responsibility *to her form of life, for her form of life*, and *to herself*) by offering sincere justifications, and certainly responsibility is a kind of independence. If I am to become responsible for my sayings and doings, then I am able to exercise practical rationality in offering the relevant justifications independently. The free person no longer piggybacks on other people's reasons for her ethically significant actions. We begin dependent on others to carry our reasons, but our freedom is the achievement of independent ownership of those reasons. Notice, however, that responsibility to myself (purging myself of delusions about my true motives) requires that I admit a special kind of dependence I have on others. I must submit myself to others and trust that they are both wise and good-willed. My freedom can only be achieved inasmuch as I can depend on trusted friends. And the idea that I can one day free myself entirely from the creeping temptation of self-delusion is a dangerous fantasy. I am forever beholden to my friends, to some degree or other, to spot my lies to myself. Freedom is then a kind of independence

39. MacIntyre, *Dependent Rational Animals*, 96.

40. MacIntyre, *Ethics in the Conflicts of Modernity*, 113.

41. See too Brandom on trust and forgiveness in this regard, in particular *Heroism and Magnanimity*, 49–78.

that is always parasitic on a kind of dependence, and our path toward wisdom is always one we will walk shoulder-to-shoulder with our friends in a shared "fear and trembling." There is no final guarantee that we have achieved the proper relationship to the world and ourselves, so anxiety is inevitable. *Geist* abides within these tensions.

6. Self-Consciousness and Evolutionary Psychology

Thus far, I have treated the responsibility conditions for freedom mainly at the levels of the human individual and specific cultural traditions by focusing on whether our form of life or our personal motivations might be subject to systematic distortions. Now, however, I will emphasize these sorts of questions as aimed at our common biological and evolutionarily conditioned heritage. I will attempt to show that rather than posing a threat to our understanding of ourselves as free and responsible agents, the deliverances of evolutionary biology and psychology, even when they are incongruous with our preferred self-images, are necessary conditions for the kind of self-knowledge integral to ethically significant agency. Freedom is to know oneself, and that includes even the most unvarnished facts of our animal existence and natural history.[42]

Allow me to recycle the example I introduced in the last chapter to mark the distinction between reasons and causes. Suppose I claim that "Smitty believes in the multiverse *because* of the evidence in the astrophysics literature." In this case, I am giving an account of Smitty's belief that takes him as an agent in what is often called the "space of reasons." The space of reasons is the realm of logical norms linking beliefs in justificatory or entailment relations. By accepting a certain belief in the space of reasons someone likewise accepts other beliefs appropriately linked by entailments and/or justifications. Smitty's understanding of and ascent to the evidence in the astrophysics literature commits him to the belief that there is a multiverse. Notice, however, that the connection between nodes in the space of reasons is *normative* not *predictive*. That is, someone might be acquainted with the same literature as Smitty and yet fail to draw the inference to the multiverse. To say that understanding of and ascent to the evidence in the astrophysics literature justifies a belief in the multiverse is not to make a prediction of what someone *will* believe,

---

42. Throughout this section I am greatly in debt to Robert Brandom's unpublished paper "Reason, Genealogy, and the Hermeneutics of Magnanimity."

but only to indicate what they *ought* to believe based on the *norms* of the space of reasons. One might say, "Given what Smitty read, he ought to believe in the multiverse," but that does not entail that Smitty actually so believes. This sense of "because" presumes some act on the part of Smitty. Where normativity goes agency follows. Norms are satisfied, not because they cannot fail to be satisfied, but because someone is committed to their satisfaction. That is, the logical-justificatory relation between the evidence in the astrophysics literature and the belief in the multiverse is insufficient to assure that Smitty will believe the latter based on the former. Rather, Smitty must be committed to and competent in the application of these norms; the norms of the space of reasons are available as explanations of Smitty's belief, only if he is actively involved in the application of those norms (though often only explicitly in retrospect). Thus, if we are going to subject our beliefs (both theoretical and practical) to explanation in the space of reasons, which I believe is an ineliminable perspective for us and a condition of our full-fledged ethical agency, we must at least be able to *see ourselves* as agents. Mature residence in the space of reasons entails a certain *self-conscious awareness of the reasons for our beliefs and our relationship to them.*

Suppose now I say "Smitty believes in the multiverse *because* he has been drinking cough syrup all morning." In this case, I am not placing Smitty's belief in the space of reasons, but in what has been called the "space of causes." As above, I am giving an explanation as to why Smitty holds the belief, but not in normative terms. The fact that Smitty has been drinking a great deal of cough syrup does not in and of itself speak to the truth or falsity of the resulting belief. Smitty might get lucky, and it turns out that there really is a multiverse, but that is merely coincidental to his drinking the cough syrup. The drinking of the cough syrup in no way certifies or recommends Smitty's belief. Furthermore, Smitty's belief in this case is not his doing, but something that happens to him. To put Smitty in the space of causes seems to take him as a passive party with respect to his beliefs. If it is the cough syrup (along with other external factors) doing all the work, then there is no normative commitment behind Smitty's belief in the multiverse. Given the prior conditions (Smitty's recreational use of over-the-counter cold remedies, maybe coupled with his recent reading of science-fiction novels, etc.) such an outcome was inevitable. The important point to notice here is that once we move from the space of reasons to the space of causes, Smitty as an agent has dropped out of the picture. When we are looking at things from the space of causes, there is no need for a self-conscious linkage between the belief and its causal grounds.

What is the relation between the space of reasons and the space of causes? Let us begin with what I call an *exclusionary* account. Immanuel Kant famously claims that "Thinking for oneself means seeking the supreme touchstone of truth in oneself (i.e., in one's own reason); and the maxim of always thinking for oneself is *enlightenment*."[43] Behind this call to Enlightenment is the assumption that human cognitive powers can operate independently of all non-rational influence, and we have the volitional power to renounce the easy temptation to offload our rational spontaneity onto the ready authorities in our immediate surroundings (whether these be institutional or biological). The only limitations on human reason, according to Kant, are the intrinsic limitations of reason itself. Reason is self-limiting in terms of its absolute scope of possible applications, i.e., nothing external to reason determines what reason can or cannot cognize and the actual applications it makes. In other words, nothing external to the rational individual ultimately determines what she does indeed think or will. As Kant puts it:

> Man now finds in himself a faculty by means of which he differ-
> entiates himself from all other things, indeed from himself in so
> far as he is affected by objects, and that faculty is reason. This, as
> pure self-activity, is elevated even above the understanding . . .
> with respect to ideas, reason shows itself to be such a pure spon-
> taneity that it far transcends anything sensibility can provide.[44]

All of this is to say that Kant takes it that the space of reasons and the space of causes are mutually exclusive territories. There is no overlap between them. In fact, for Kant any underlying causal etiology for a belief undermines its normative-agentive status, since for him freedom is the "achievement of autonomy, reason's complete self-legislation, or its declaration of radical independence and self-sufficiency."[45] Kant accepts an entirely deterministic, Newtonian view of nature. Since, however, he agrees that the space of reasons is an ineliminable element in our self-conception, he concludes that the world as described by the natural sciences must be *phenomenal*, while the transcendental seat of rational agency must occupy a noumenal realm of absolute reality. In short, for

43. Kant, "What Does It Mean to Orient Oneself in Thinking," 14. Kant's emphasis.

44. Kant, *Groundwork for the Metaphysics of Morals*, 80.

45. Pippin, *Modernity as a Philosophical Problem*, 55.

Kant, there is a zero-sum game afoot between the space of reasons and the space of causes, and the space of causes will need to yield ultimately to the space of reasons.

Exclusionary stories, however, can go the other way. One might grant the zero-sum struggle between the space of reasons and the space of causes while forfeiting the former for sake of the latter. Several decades after Kant's answer to the question of enlightenment, Friedrich Nietzsche opens his *Genealogy of Morality* not with an optimistic exhortation to the exercise of our dignifying rational powers, but with something of a caution to anyone presuming such an outlook:

> We are unknown to ourselves, we knowers: and for good rea-
> son. . . . We remain of necessity strangers to ourselves, we do
> not understand ourselves, we must mistake ourselves, for us the
> maxim reads to all eternity: "each is furthest from himself,"—
> with respect to ourselves we are not "knowers?"[46]

Certainly, one of Nietzsche's targets is Socrates who claimed to speak on behalf of the Oracle's injunction to "Know thy self," but there is also an important contrast here with Kant (who, for Nietzsche, is not accidentally associated with Socrates). Nietzsche broods over the standing of the *knower*, the supposed rational self, and he denies the transparency that Kant presumed that transcendental self has to itself—*knowers* are *unknown* to *themselves*. That is, Nietzsche questions the supposedly unmediated relationship the knower bears to the reasons for her cognitions. For Kant, human rationality is thinking for oneself, which requires a certain transparency of oneself to oneself and freedom from the space of causes, but here Nietzsche denies this transparency and therewith Kant's optimistic assessment of our standing as autonomous agents. Nietzsche suggests that there is always an underlying and archaic causal etiology constituting the real reason for our beliefs and actions. The space of reasons is a useful fiction, a mere convenient phenomenon, masking the hidden reality of the space of causes.

Nietzsche, like Kant, is convinced that the space of reasons and the space of causes are mutually exclusive, and he eclipses the former with the latter. For our purposes, it is noteworthy that Nietzsche claims in part to have arrived at this position for broadly Darwinian reasons. Nietzsche is certainly critical of the specific mechanisms of evolution by natural selection (he does not believe that survival is the end selected for, but

46. Nietzsche, *On the Genealogy of Morality*, 1.

the diffusion of indifferent power),[47] but the idea that even the cognitive structures of organisms, including human beings, have evolutionary etiology is something Nietzsche accepts wholesale. Indeed, the *Genealogy of Morality* is an extended evolutionary explanation of the space of moral reasons in terms of the space of causes, and that book is really a sequel to the more general evolutionary explanations he gave for theoretical reason in the "Truth and Lie in a Nonmoral Sense" and the *Gay Science*. We should see Nietzsche as an evolutionary psychologist, whatever we think of his actual competence in the field. He is offering causal explanations of human agentive and epistemic capabilities based on an evolutionary process beginning in ultimately non-agentive and non-epistemic capabilities in earlier animal species. For Nietzsche, and for many contemporary evolutionary psychologists, this connects our rational, moral, and religious beliefs with rather less than flattering origins. At least for Nietzsche, and maybe some contemporaries, that is part of the debunking power evolutionary psychology has for what we would like to think of as our dignified place in the space of reasons.[48]

Be that as it may, the important point is the shared exclusionary premise between the Kantian and Nietzschean positions. Both thinkers presume that the space of reasons and the space of causes cannot overlap for a rational agent. Thus, where there is a causal etiology of belief available, both Kant and Nietzsche banish such a belief from the space of reasons. Kant believes that self-consciousness is necessary for rational agency, i.e., the reasons for my thinkings and doings must be *my reasons*, so a self-conscious agent is therefore a transcendental subject existing and operating outside of the space of causes. Nietzsche agrees that reasons must be *my reasons*, but he believes an honest assessment of our biological and psychological conditioning precludes such pristine transcendental self-consciousness, since our thinking and willing are ultimately explained by non-rational and amoral causal etiologies. For Nietzsche, the very notion of a space of reasons is a mere phenomenon fobbed on us by our evolutionary past and therefore does not provide a significant explanation of our beliefs and actions.

Nietzsche and Kant's shared exclusivism seems to leave us with no good option. On the one hand, Nietzsche's version of exclusionism is

47. See Nietzsche, *The Genealogy of Morality*, 8–11.

48. For accounts questioning whether evolutionary explanation really does debunk our practical and theoretical rationality, see O'Hear, *Beyond Evolution* and Rassano, *Supernatural Selection*.

wrought with self-referential problems (though I am not sure this really troubles him): Is he giving reasons for us to conclude that that space of reasons is illusory? I don't think it's quite as easy as all that to get rid of Nietzsche, but at the end of the day his story cannot be made to make sense.[49] At least in its extreme Nietzschean manifestation, the conjunction of the supposed exclusivity of the spaces of reasons and causes and an evolutionary reduction of our cognitive faculties to non-cognitive underpinnings, seems to undermine its own rational credentials. That is, there could be no place in the space of reasons for us to *conclude* that we do not in fact operate within the space of reasons. On the other hand, Nietzsche's critique of Kant's transcendental defense of the space of reasons as a last-ditch, rearguard effort to save the Platonic project at the very expense of cognitive contact with the real world is likewise hard to resist. Kant's transcendental exclusivism may preserve our place in the space of reasons, but it seems he leaves us only able to reason about ourselves—the productions of self-limiting, self-conscious reason only contact a phenomenal world of its own construction. All we can know of nature is really our own image staring back at us. Exclusivism forces the unhappy dilemma between self-referential incoherence and transcendental narcissism.

Kant's and Nietzsche's exclusivisms are totalizing positions, i.e., they both claim that all of what is most fundamental must be collapsed into either the space of causes and or the space of reasons. They see the world in terms of all-or-nothing monism. Maybe, however, that *either-or* could be a *both-and* consistent with the exclusionary premise. One could argue that the world is for the most part under the exclusive jurisdiction of the space of causes, save for a small preserve, say human rationality, that is cordoned off as the space of reasons. The space of reasons and the space of causes would then be separate accountings of two *bona fide* and yet distinct regions of being. I don't think there are grounds to rule this dualist exclusivism out of hand, but like all forms of dualism it carries with it the complicating issue of how to account for the relation between the space of reasons and the space of causes, and "a distinction becomes a dualism when it is drawn in terms that make relations between the distinguished items unintelligible."[50] We shouldn't expect a salvific story to be very close at hand, given the perennial problems of dualism in all its manifestations.

49. We will take up in detail this self-reference problem for Nietzsche's debunking of normativity in chapter 5.

50. Brandom, *Spirit of Trust*, 660.

Failure to give such an account would seem to leave the space of reasons spinning off in empty reflection of itself. Furthermore, the dualist solution is not entirely immune from the Nietzschean invective unmasking it as rearguard Platonism: as our evolutionary explanatory field expands into the psychological realm, the dualist's insistence on an autonomous space of reasons increasingly appears to be *ad hoc* and desperate. That isn't necessarily a dealbreaker for the dualist, but we do have good reason to look for a way of making sense of the claims of evolutionary psychology in non-exclusionist grounds.

What have we learned from the mutual collapse of the Kantian-Nietzsche positions? On the one hand, any attempt to reduce the space of reasons entirely to the space of causes is self-referentially incoherent. On the other hand, the claim that the space of reasons is utterly autonomous from the space of causes renders the former empty and platitudinal (an imposition of our autobiography on nature).[51] If we affirm only the space of causes, then our supposed reasons are not really the reasons for our beliefs. If we utterly liberate the space of reasons from the space of causes, then our reasons reflect a transcendental fantasy lacking any external grounding. What would it be to avoid both these errors?

A possible answer to this question would be to say that the space of causes is the *content* of the space of reasons. That is, *the space of reasons is the space of reasoning about the space of causes.* To put it in the terms of the debate I am tracking here: the self-consciousness necessary for standing in the space of reasons implicitly entails an awareness of the underlying causal etiologies of my beliefs. This is essentially Hegel's reply to Kant and the proto-Nietzschean position he anticipates in the *Phenomenology of Spirit*.[52] The idea is that for the space of reasons to have a grounding in more than its own transcendental fantasies, I must be aware of the possible causal etiologies that may be operating behind the scenes. The fact that our cognitions are grounded in non-cognitive underpinnings is partly what assures that our thinking has a grip on something outside of us. If I am not open to possible distortions from within, then I am indulging a sort of cognitive narcissism, i.e., my concepts lack the material

---

51. Of course, this is a very quick caricature of the Kant's and Nietzsche's actual positions.

52. Brandom's "Reason, Genealogy, and the Hermeneutics of Magnanimity" and *A Spirit of Trust* (547–82) are particularly insightful treatments of Hegel's prescient reply to genealogical/evolutionary subversions of rationality, even though I am not proceeding in the very same way in this chapter.

content needed for cognitive significance. If these causes are possibly distorting, then self-conscious exercise of rational agency requires acquaintance with these possibly distorting influences. The willingness to explore this possibility of causal debunking is part of what assures the denizen of the space of reasons that she is not merely staring at her own conveniently attractive reflection. The world, including what the world says about the nature of our cognitive equipment, gets a vote in the standing of our reasons for our beliefs and actions. Reason is not merely an expression of our autonomy, and we must admit that things might be going wrong via. causes beyond our rational control. That admission is part of what grounds the space of reasons in a world outside itself, i.e., by conceding that there could be something very wrong with us, we put thinking up against reality. In short, part of the self-consciousness necessary for the space of reasons is an awareness of how our sense of reason might be systematically distorted. Self-consciousness worth having is, in part, awareness of where we are liable to go wrong simply because of our given nature. This liability is once again part of the cost of embodying world-bound *Geist.*

This does not imply a sort of Cartesian methodological doubt forcing us to rule out the possibility of error before accepting a belief. I am not suggesting that one must rule out all *possible* grounds for doubting oneself before accepting a belief. Rather, the point is that the *willingness* to investigate the possibility that one's cognitive equipment may be off when there is some suggestion of as much is part of what ties the space of reasons to substantive content. I admit that I could be wrong, but I need not actually look for systematic distortions behind all of my beliefs unless there is a suggestion of such problems in my vicinity. If I have indeed been drinking cough syrup all morning, then I should put my "reasons" for certain conclusions about astrophysics to scrutiny to determine whether there is a less than flattering explanation for why I have accepted these beliefs. When there are hints that there may be a problem, rational self-consciousness requires that we investigate things and become aware of any distorting influences. Rational self-consciousness should be grateful for the suggestion that it may be under the influence of distorting causal etiologies, as this possibility is what protects it from the genealogist's charge of transcendental narcissism.

Notice, however, that none of this is to deny the spontaneity of the space of reasons. In fact, the suggestion that rational self-consciousness is responsive to its possible subversion by causal etiologies implies that it is always somehow transcendent to those potentially undermining factors. The suggestion presupposes that rational self-consciousness can step back and take a higher order perspective on what it believes and why it believes it. As I have argued above, this notion of rational transcendence is ineliminable, so long as we are claiming to have good reasons for our claims. Thus, although the space of causes gets a vote in what we are and what we believe, as rational self-consciousness we likewise get a say in the matter. It is up to us regarding what is to be done with the revelations by our investigations into what is going on behind the scenes of our beliefs and actions. Being in the space of reasons is the synthesis of content and conceptuality, causality and freedom, givenness and spontaneity. The Oracle counseled well when it bade us to "Know thy self." Sleepwalking is not rational self-consciousness, and our wakefulness can understand and respond to its underlying liabilities.

Might evolutionary psychology reveal unflattering truths about the etiology of our most cherished beliefs? For example, that morality and religion have their origins in organization for warfare or the maintenance of oppressive social control or that our desire for community comes from a primal tribalism. From the philosopher's armchair I can see no reasons to deny these possibilities. Is it likewise possible that these origins still cast shadows over our minds, leaving us with racist, sexist, xenophobic and otherwise unsavory and violent dispositions? This too is not something we can easily dismiss, and there is every suggestion exactly that is true. In light of the above discussion, we should be grateful for these revelations. For it is only by accepting the responsibility of rational self-consciousness to subject itself to possible debunking by genealogical subversion that we can hedge against falling into our own transcendental narcissism. It is evolutionary psychology, even if it has an unflattering story to tell about the origins of our thinking, that today may be the best means to save us from the tragic fate of Oedipus. Without these insights, we will at best be lucky, but the examined life, the kind of life that is worth living, is lived by reason and not by chance.

4

The Anxiety of Not Being a Machine

In the sweat of your face you shall eat bread till you return to the ground,
for out of it you were taken; you are dust, and to dust you shall return.
— *THE BOOK OF GENESIS*[1]

The trouble with artificial intelligence is that computers don't give a damn.
— JOHN HAUGELAND, *HAVING THOUGHT*[2]

W E ARE AWASH WITH reports of the latest smart gadgets enabled with
"AI" capabilities poised to emancipate us from our long bondage
to such labors as reading maps, driving an automobile on the morning
commute, employing an indexed reference book to find information,
winnowing the myriad options for music playlists, finding sexually
compatible partners, writing academic essays, and even the crushing
burden of ordering our groceries online. Moreover, we now employ AI-
driven machinery to identify criminal suspects or likely terrorists, select
political rhetoric and reach voters in ways that sway our most cardinally
important elections, and to enhance our ability to apply lethal force on
the battlefield. As we off-load our cognitive and manual labors onto our

1. Genesis 3:19.
2. Haugeland, *Having Thought*, 48.

digital technologies, our collective awe at this late deliverance from the curse of Adam is not without its ambiguities. Could the AI capabilities of all these machines eventually surpass our abilities to outsmart them? Some people claim that our machines will soon or already have achieved self-conscious sentience. Have we set the grounds for an apocalyptic future, in which we undo ourselves by creating a "race" of killer robots beyond our control? Is it ethically acceptable even to take such risks? A bit less grandiose, though still serious, concern is raised by considering more subtle consequences of our being relieved of our ordinary burdens by smart devices. One might wonder whether it is good for us to have our decisions made, even in mundane matters, by machines acting on our behalf. What will come of our sense of agency or pride in just organizing ourselves practically, as we increasingly delegate those responsibilities to our mechanical servants? Will we develop the epistemic skills necessary to ground our space of reasons in a real world? Are democratic institutions sustainable now that we have means to manipulate the voting population via. algorithmic formulae that reach beyond the possibilities of unaided human calculation? What comes of our sense of the gravity of warfare when we have smart machines that buffer us entirely from the grim work of killing other human beings? At the same time, our development of "smart" devices is only an extension of the distribution of our cognitive labors into our structured environment, which, as we have discussed earlier, is part and parcel of much of the human species' distinctive genius. To suggest that we put the brakes on these technological developments is not only practically infeasible (the proverbial genie is out of the bottle), but it would likewise run contrary to the distinctively human power to extend our cognitions into an environment we have designed for the task, which is integral to how our mind works. In any event, we cannot fall into the spell of thinking that the human dependence on technology is something new under the sun. This has been true of us at least as long as we could be actually defined as the "speaking animal."

These questions, however worthy, are not what concerns me at this point in our discussion, though they will arise again in the following chapter. Whether jigging our environment with putatively intelligent devices is a net loss or gain for human flourishing, our gravest danger or our greatest opportunity, is not my immediate concern. The possibility of developing machines that materialize the utopian and dystopian fantasies of science fiction is a moot question: we clearly will soon do so, or maybe we have already done so. The only question now is how to interpret that situation: Is this our ultimate demise or our final fulfill-ment? Is our distinctively modern technological way of being a dream or nightmare? Those are questions that I will forestall for the moment. For now, the question is whether *in principle* there could be a machine that is in fact intelligent, at least intelligent in the same sense as we hu-man beings are intelligent. Can a machine *really be* intelligent? Not just operating *as though* it were intelligent or doing the work normally done by intelligence, but actually *being intelligent.*

Many things, however, can be meant by "intelligence," and I believe there are senses in which it is obvious that there are already intelligent machines, e.g., machines that can solve formalized problems, manipu-late tokens in games, learn and process new information, and even teach themselves in some limited cases. I suspect that when most advocates of artificial intelligence claim there are now *bona fide* smart machines (or at least there could be), what they mean is that such machines are intelligent in that conventional sense. Moreover, this is the sense of "intelligence" that most psychologists and cognitive scientists have in mind too. Thus, when the question of whether artificial intelligence is a possibility (or even a current actuality), what is being queried is whether machines could match higher animals, and humans in particular, in such functions as abstract problem solving, computations, information gathering and retention, learning, etc. That is all well and good, and as you shall see, I am fairly optimistic about an affirmative answer to those sorts of ques-tions about AI. Intelligence as conventionally construed, however, is not what concerns me. Whatever we might say about machine *intelligence*, I wonder whether they can have *minds*. Or better, can machines reside in the space of reasons along with us? Is it possible for a machine to par-ticipate in *Geist* in the way that human beings do? Thus, the question concerning artificial intelligence really comes to the question of whether machines can be *rational* in the same sense in which human beings are rational. I am happy to concede that machines may already be intelligent in a non-trivial sense, but I maintain the question of *artificial-mindedness* is still far from closed. The worry then is whether there is or could be machine mindedness. Is artificial *Geist* a possibility?[3]

---

3. Putting the question in this way is odious, as it presumes that "artificial" is a hard-edged category contrasting with the equally hard-edged category "natural." That framing is itself an expression of a central assumption of modernity, which is shared with its critical parasites (postmodernism and reactionary premodernism). All of that is a long story to tell and ancillary to our immediate concerns, so I will leave it aside

In what follows, I will argue that an affirmative answer to this question is quite implausible. I will make that case not by defending the typical objections to machine intelligence offered by AI skeptics. Indeed, I will side with the replies to some of those objections. Instead, I will appeal to the notion of distinctive human rationality and freedom that I developed in the previous chapters. In those discussions, I suggested a picture of human freedom understood as a three-fold responsibility (to one's form of life, to the truth, and to oneself), and that this notion of freedom is inseparable from the account of mindedness that I developed in the first two chapters, i.e., participating in mind is to be a responsible denizen of the logical space of reasons. Once we came to understand that notion of mindedness, we were able to see that the supposed neuroscientific and evolutionary cases against distinctive human freedom are non-starters; not because there is some flaw in the sciences, but rather due to a truncated understanding of what counts as significant freedom and rationality abroad in these debates. In this chapter, I will follow a similar strategy: the relevant scientific fields have gone a long way toward showing that machines are "intelligent," but that has precious little to do with what marks distinctively human *mindedness*. More specifically, I will argue in what follows that the suggestion that a machine might be embedded *in* and responsible *to* and *for* a world in the way that we participants in *Geist* are, even if not demonstrably impossible, strains credulity. This distinctive, non-mechanical status, as I will argue, comes at an expense, for it calls on us to accept the possibility of tragedy and the requisite anxiety that follows on this realization, but it is our anxious responsibility that marks our greatest dignity. That dignity, however, is not at all undermined by the occurrence of smart devices, however "intelligent" they may be.

_____

for now. Suffice it to say, however, the supposed technological vs. pure nature dualism is among the many expressions of the dualist sorting that forms the picture that holds us captive, and we do well to jettison this dualism along with its brethren. For an insightful and influential discussion of this point, see Latour, *We Have Never Been Modern*, 109–16. Moreover, as we discussed earlier, it is difficult to take the extended-mind thesis seriously without ambiguating the relationship between technology and our natural environment, i.e., the latter has been partly the effect of the former, and vice versa, as long as humans have walked the earth.

1. Why Would Anyone Think Machines Can Think?

Damespiel

Players   **Pieces**
A and B A^1—A^{12}
              B^1—B^{12}

Set Up
$A^1 = 1$, $A^2 = 3$, $A^3 = 5$, $A^4 = 7 \ldots A^{12} = 23$
$B^1 = 64$, $B^2 = 62$, $B^3 = 60$, $B^4 = 58 \ldots B^{12} = 42$

A-Moves
Player A moves initially and thereafter follows a completed move by Player B.
"x" is a start, "y" is a finish.
"$(A^1 = x^1)$" means "A^1 starts in x^1."
"$(A^1 = y^1)$" means "A^1 ends in y^1."
$(A^1 = x^1)$, only if $A^1 > 0$.
For any two pieces, A^1 and A^2, $(A^1 = y^1) \neq A^2$, unless $A^2 = 0$.
A-Move Positive: $(A^1 = x^1) + 9 = (A^1 = y^1)$
A-Move Negative: $(A^1 = x^1) + 7 = (A^1 = y^1)$

B-Moves
Player B follows a completed move by Player A.
"w" is a start, "z" is a finish.
"$(B^1 = w^1)$" means "B^1 starts in w^1."
"$(B^1 = z^1)$" means "B^1 ends in z^1."
$(B^1 = w^1)$ only if $B^1 > 0$.
For any two pieces, B^1 and B^2, $(B^1 = z^1) \neq B^2$, unless $B^2 = 0$.
B-Move Positive: $(B^1 = w^1) - 9 = (B^1 = z^1)$
B-Move Negative: $(B^1 = w^1) - 7 = (B^1 = z^1)$

Limits
For any series of y, y^a-y^b, if $y^b = (8, 16, 24, 32, \ldots 64)$, $(1, 9, 17, 25, \ldots 57)$, $(1, 2, 3, 4 \ldots 8)$, or
   $(57, 58, 59, 60, \ldots 64)$, then the move ends.
For any series of z, z^a-z^b, if $z^b = (8, 16, 24, 32, \ldots 64)$, $(1, 9, 17, 25, \ldots 57)$, $(1, 2, 3, 4 \ldots 8)$, or
   $(57, 58, 59, 60, \ldots 64)$, then the move ends.

Vaulting
For any pieces, [if $(A^1 = x^1) = (B^1 - 7)$ and $((B^1 + 7) = (A^1 = y^1)$, then $(B^1 = 0))$] and [if $(A^1 = x^1)$
   $= (B^1 - 9)$
   and $((A^1 = x^1) = (B^1 - 7)$, then $(B^1 = 0))$]
For any pieces, [if $(B^1 = w^1) = (A^1 + 7)$ and $((A^1 - 7) = (B^1 = z^1)$, then $(A^1 = 0))$] and [if $(B^1 = w^1)$
   $= (A^1 + 9)$
   and $((B^1 = z^1) = (A^1 - 7)$, then $(A^1 = 0))$].

Promotion
If any $(A^1 = y^1) = (57, 59, 61, 63)$, then A^1 may make B-Moves and is designated as A^{1*}.
If any $(B^1 = z^1) = (2, 4, 6, 8)$, then B^1 may make A-Moves and is designated as B^{1*}.

Winning
If A cannot move, then B wins.
If B cannot move, then A wins.

So why would anybody think that artificial intelligence is a real possibility, let alone an actuality, in the first place?[4] To get a grip on that ques-

---

4. I am going to build the case for AI in a conceptual or intuitive manner. For an excellent historical account of why AI became a priority in the philosophy of mind following on the origins of modern philosophy (along with the subsequent development

tion, consider the rules for a simple game. *Damespiel* is a number game I invented. It is set for two players, A and B. Each player has twelve "pieces" initially defined by predetermined numeric values, which can be tracked through various arithmetic operations. For Player A, the initial values are odd numbers from one to twenty-three, and for Player B, the initial values are even numbers from forty-two to sixty-four. Stipulations are made for turn-taking. Basic moves are made by either adding or subtracting from the starting values. It is only metaphorical to talk about "moves" here, as *Damespiel* is not played-out spatially, but arithmetically. Player A moves by adding either seven or nine to the staring value of one of her pieces. Player B moves by subtracting either seven or nine from her pieces. A turn is a succession of such moves for a single piece until the player elects to move no further, a limit is reached (as defined by certain stipulated ending values), a promotion occurs (as defined by reaching a certain range of limits and resulting in permission for that piece to make the same type of moves as the opposing player's pieces), or no further legal move can be made. An additional type of move, vaulting, can be made as specified by certain relations (being either greater than or less than by either seven or nine) between the value of one of a player's pieces starting value and the value of one of her opponent's pieces. The result of a vault gives the player's piece either the greater or lesser value by either seven or nine, and the opponent's piece a value of zero, which permanently renders that piece ineligible to make moves. A player wins by rendering her opponent unable to make any legal moves. Upon introduction, *Damespiel* appears pretty complicated, but with a bit of scratch paper we could get the hang of it and play with some competitive vigor.

You may have noticed something interesting about *Damespiel*. Its moniker is actually the German word for checkers; literally, "lady game," as in Germany a crowned piece is called a "queen." That is no accident on my part, because every element of checkers has a corresponding element in *Damespiel*. Positive and negative moves for A and B are equivalent to left and right diagonal moves for red and black pieces in checkers. Vaulting corresponds to jumping in checkers, promotion to crowing, numeric values to positions on a checked grid of black and red squares, limits to the edge squares on the grid, a value of zero to being captured, etc. If we played a game of checkers while making corresponding moves in

of mathematics and computer science), see John Haugeland, *Artificial Intelligence*, 1–124. Much of what I do in this chapter, as will become clear, is done under Haugeland's good influence.

Damespiel, the games would come to the exact same results in terms of winning and losing. Of course, checkers is built on spatial relations between the pieces as situated on a grid, and *Damespiel* is built on arithmetic, but there is a perfectly good sense in which they are the same game. We could call all the elements of *Damespiel* by the names of their checkers equivalents. We could even play a game of *Damespiel* symbolically on a checkerboard with checkers pieces, all the while making our decisions according to the reckoning appropriate to *Damespiel* behind the scenes. Likewise, we could do the same going in the other direction. Suppose you were playing someone in what you thought was a game of checkers, but behind the scenes he was reasoning by *Damespiel* arithmetic and not spatial relations on a grid *a la* checkers. Would you say that no game of checkers had occurred? Would you say that he was not playing by the proper rules? Hardly. I think you are more likely to say that *Damespiel just is* checkers, albeit described or defined in different, though formally equivalent, terms from how we typically specify the procedures for playing checkers.

All that is necessary for two games to be effectively the same is that their rules are *functionally equivalent*, or at least that is the standard story.[5] Two systems of rules are functionally equivalent, just in case every move in one of the "games" has an equivalent move in the other, and vice versa. Any playing of one of the games can then be mapped onto a playing of the other in a one-to-one correspondence. Of course, there might be different processes of reckoning going on behind the curtain of each game, but that doesn't seem to matter. As long as the moves come out in the right correspondence, then the games, in an important sense, are the same. Operating by spatial patterns of checkers or the arithmetic relations of *Damespiel* are both equally good for playing the game. There are in fact indefinitely many, maybe infinitely many, ways we could specify rules to play games functionally equivalent to checkers, and they would all be equally good candidates for how one plays. In fact, we could specify a set of rules in which the pieces are pixelated images on a monitor and moves for these pieces are determined by positions of electronic switches. Not only could we do so, but these endeavors have been quite

5. The notion of functional equivalence and the account of the mind built around it, functionalism, are immensely important to contemporary philosophy of mind and cognitive science, along with the AI debate. For an introduction to these issues (including references to key sources), see Madden, *Mind, Matter, and Nature*, 122–31, 147–61.

commonplace for decades. Such a set of rules is more or less the sort of thing that operates behind the scenes of the games application that comes standardly on personal computers. (I realize I am getting dangerously beyond my meager technical pay grade here!) Certainly, those programs are spelled out in different symbols than either checkers or *Damespiel* (and with far greater rigor and sophistication than my primitive version) but it is functionally equivalent to both. If you turn the application on and play a game, you will be operating by the checkers principles while the computer will be running the program, but you will be playing the game. One might ask, however, whether you are *both* playing the game: is the computer playing the game of checkers with you, or are you just playing solitaire checkers?

What has all this to do with the question of artificial *Geist*? Really, the question about whether you play checkers *with* your computer is the same query. Those who claim that artificial intelligence is a real possibility argue that *functional equivalence is sufficient for cognitive equivalence*, such that you and your computer are playing together. How would you determine whether someone knows how to play checkers? You would not ask her to give you a formal statement of the rules of checkers, specifying legal moves and the like. Indeed, you probably would not care at all about what sort of reckoning may be going on between her ears. You could not even evaluate such a statement of rules until you saw how they played out. Rather than asking for a statement of the rules by which she is playing, you would sit her down and try to play the game. In fact, someone might be utterly unable to state the rules of checkers with any specificity at all, and yet be able to play. If she can make moves that are sufficiently intelligible as moves in checkers, you would deem her as knowing how to play the game. Functional equivalence would be enough. Likewise, how would you know whether someone can do long division? You would give her problem sets and see whether she produces the right answers. You would not query the internal process, but just check whether she could pull-off the operation. There are indefinitely many processes of reckoning that one could use to get those results, and which one is going on in the student's head is irrelevant to whether she can do long division. Of course, you might require your pupil to "show her work" according to the standard notation for long division, but that just pushes the question back to a higher order: there are indefinitely many sets of rules any single system of notation could be used to express, all of which come to the same answers to any finite set of problems. That is, even if the student wrote out the long division problem in the proper notation, that doesn't entail that she interprets the notation in the same way you do. We only know that we are doing the same thing with that notation because we already share an implicit, background agreement as to what we are up to.[6] Thus, it looks like all we need to recognize competence in long division is functional equivalence.[7]

Notice that you can play checkers (or *Damespiel!*) with your computer, just as well as you might play checkers with your human friend. Indeed, when it comes to chess, there are computers that likely can play chess better than any human friend you might have (even if your companion is a grandmaster). Thus, artificial systems are functionally equivalent to human beings when it comes to games like checkers and chess. Moreover, I am sure the calculator application on the laptop on which I am writing this chapter can far surpass my meager abilities for long division. Have a look at more applications on your "smart" device of choice. The machine behind that annoying lady's voice on my mapping application is pretty good at finding its way to the airport in Boston. If I'm at the wheel, we better let "her" handle the navigation. By the same criteria I would use to determine whether you can play checkers or find your way to Logan International, I would likewise have to judge that your smart phone or laptop is equally competent. Your smart device is functionally equivalent to you in these ways, and as such we should conclude that inasmuch as these are intelligent activities on your part, they are likewise intelligent activities on the part of the machines.[8]

6. I am helping myself to Wittgenstein's arguments regarding rule-following, though he is not attempting to defend functional equivalence as sufficient for psychological equivalence. Rather, his point is to show that we make psychological attributions, such as ". . . understands long division" based on external, performative criteria, not an appeal to inner mental states. See Wittgenstein, *Philosophical Investigations*, 80 (§185ff.).

7. As an aside, note that the externalist position I have developed in the foregoing likely implies that what goes on "behind the scenes" for your opponent has less to do with whether she is playing checkers than what you two are doing together "out" in the world. Thus, it seems that my line of argument does much to motivate the proposal of artificial *Geist*. There is something to this point, and we will see a bit below that an externalist position does not sit well with standard objections to strong AI. Nevertheless, we will ultimately see that it is difficult to take seriously the idea that a machine is *being-in-the-world* in that phenomenological sense that undergirds the idea of *Geist* as I am framing it. Thus, do not conclude that the position I am developing is friendly to the possibility of artificial *Geist*.

8. For a very clear introduction to the basic case in favor of the possibility of *bona*

2. What about Meaning? Syntax vs. Semantics

That's all a bit too fast. Notice that in the case of games like checkers, there need be no sense in which the tokens (the pieces) *mean* anything. The red as opposed to the black discs do not refer to anything outside of the game, or even anything within the game. They are not *signs* of anything; they are literally in-*sign*-ificant. Checkers pieces are just items that can be moved in terms of a set of rules. Moreover, the rules by which we move these insignificant tokens are themselves insignificant. That is, the rules of checkers are arbitrary stipulations that signify no real relationship among the intrinsic natures of the pieces. Nothing that happens in checkers is either true or false because checkers has no bearing on anything that happens in the world external to checkers, and the rules of checkers themselves are merely arbitrary stipulations. Checkers operates by a rigorous, even if it is pretty simple, set of rules—what we technically call a *syntax*—but it has no *semantic* value; it does not *say* anything that is either true or false. Checkers is not a logical space of reasons because its rules are not a material logic, i.e., checkers is not sensitive to empirical "push-back" from the world. The same could be said about long division: a student could learn how to manipulate certain symbols, say Arabic numerals, according to the rules of long division all the while being indifferent to what any of it means, without ever caring whether he or she actually made a true utterance in this notation. Your mapping application is subject to the same concern. We could teach a young child to become perfectly competent to find locations on a fictionalized map according to an entirely arbitrary set of directions and coordinate system. Such a child would be operating by a formal syntax without really *saying* anything, but that certainly would not be the same thing you would be doing when you read a map in order to navigate through a new city. Your reading of the map would turn out to be either true or false, or at least it would *matter* to you whether it took such semantic values. In short, it is entirely possible for something to operate by a rigorous formal syntax (rules) while lacking semantic value (signifying nothing). We defined *Geist* partially in terms of semantic responsibility (to have a mind is to make claims about beings and to care whether those claims are true or false), and *prima facie* machines are not semantically enriched enough to take such responsibility.

---

fide AI that covers the ground I have introduced here along with other considerations, see Dennett, "Consciousness in Human and Robot Minds," 13–30.

Thus, functional-syntactical equivalence might be sufficient for games like checkers, but only because such games are meaningless. Any ability that entails semantic value (such as reading a map or actually understanding and applying long division) will require more than just functional-syntactical equivalence in order to be equivalent to what *we* do when *we* think, even when operating by the same syntax. Furthermore, it is not just that a system must be such that it *could* take semantic value, but it must *actually* take such value. What a child does when reading a map as part of an arbitrary game *could* be true or accurate, but when you read that map on your way to a foreign city for the first time, your reading was *actually* true (or false). In the former case, the semantic question just doesn't arise, i.e., the child at play doesn't really *care* whether the map gets things right. *Geist*, i.e., residing in the space of reasons, entails *semantic commitment*. Minded beings purport, at least implicitly, to make true claims, which is more than just operating by rules that can be formalized to run on various types of hardware. Thus, whatever else one might say about *intelligence*, mere functional equivalence does not speak to *Geist* or *mindedness*, as I have developed the notion in the previous chapters.

The mention of semantics, as opposed to syntax, or we might as well have said "meaning" as opposed to "grammar," raises the real issue in question. Humans do more than play empty syntactical games devoid of meaning. We talk, write, and otherwise depict the world. Our medium for doing this, or at least our most obviously means of expressing it, is language. The primary way we cultivate rationality in our children is first and foremost by inducting them into linguistic practices. The way we primarily detect rationality in others is by looking for signs of linguistic competence. Certainly, we might decide someone (a human or even a non-human animal) is rational based on an observation of his or her non-linguistic behavior, but in such circumstances, we are likely still framing our interpretation in linguistic terms. For example, I might think of my pet chameleon as acting rationally by climbing down from his tree, because doing so is appropriate for a hunter of insects who *believes* that "There are crickets at the bottom of the cage." In that case, which is fairly typical, I am supposing a justification for the chameleon's actions, i.e., a plausible answer to a linguistically structured demand to make sense of what he has done. Apparently rational, non-linguistic behavior is always something for which we expect an agent could give a reason, so we ascribe "beliefs" as justifications for such actions (even if in doing so we are overestimating or significantly mischaracterizing the cognitive powers of chameleons), and the ability to give reasons for acting is a linguistic power. Rational agents are linguistic agents, inasmuch as being rational places the agent in the logical space of reasons, i.e., the agent is able to answer questions as to why she acted (including her speech acts) as she did. At least, I take it as fairly obvious that residence in the logical space of reasons is a necessary condition for being rational in the sense that humans may be distinctively rational, as we have discussed at length earlier in this book. Notice that linguistic competence that places someone in the logical space of reasons requires semantic commitment. Certainly, when challenged to give reasons for why I have said something is true, a perfectly good reply is because other things that I have said (or might have said) are *true* and appropriately related to my later utterance. Thus, human rationality is intrinsically related to linguistic competence, which includes both syntactical rules and meaningful semantics.[9]

Is this conclusion good news or bad news for the proponent of an affirmative answer to the question of artificial *Geist*? Well, it certainly does complicate the story a bit. It looks like machine competence in meaningless games like checkers, number crunching, or even highway navigation do not do much to move the needle in favor of mechanical *Geist*. It is not enough to show that computers can operate by syntax. To answer the artificial *Geist* question affirmatively, we would need some reason to believe that computers could be programed to display fully human linguistic competence, which requires both syntax and semantics. The question is not whether computers can operate according to rules, however complicated, but whether computers can *mean* something by doing so. How would we know whether a computer *means something* by its conformity to a rule? The fact that we mean something by the rules we program into the machine would not do the trick, because that would just show that the computer's operations *mean something to us users of the machine*. The question is whether *the computer can mean something on its own*. How, one might ask, do we determine that anyone else means something?

Mundane situations such as asking an instructor "What did you mean by that term you introduced?" are not what we have in mind here.

9. That is not to say, however, that linguistic competence and residence in the space of reasons are all-or-nothing affairs. One can be more-or-less in the space of reasons. Moreover, I am not denying that there are "pre-linguistic" or ever-implicit reasons. Rather, the point is only that full-fledged rationality, for us, involves linguistic competence.

Presumably, one goes to the class with the expectation that the instructor is semantically committed, but we are wondering about what marks someone or something as holding semantic commitments in the first place. Consider a situation in which an anthropologist has encountered a population of previously unknown hominids. Their utterances seem to have nothing in common with any language known to her previously, both in terms of syntax and semantics. After some months of immersion, she manages to discern fairly stable practices, linking typical utterances into predictable patterns. There is a grammar or syntax in play here. Maybe these beings, like us, mean something. Meaning requires semantic value, so now the anthropologist needs to look for some way they might be trying to say something about the world. She notices that every time a rabbit runs across the forest floor the members of the tribe shriek "Gavagai!" Suppose further that this fits the apparent grammatical ordering and structuring of utterances our researcher has discerned earlier. We now have a case in which the rules of the foreign tongue seemingly allow an utterance of true statements. Of course, the anthropologist does not know for sure that the tribe means "rabbit" by "Gavagai," but she has a good bet as to when they might be making a true statement under their rules (or at least they are trying to do so). As she makes more discoveries of seemingly semantic patterns, it will be clear that this population occupies a logical space of reasons in some ways similar to her own. That is, they, like us, are rational animals.[10] The idea here is what John Haugeland calls the "Formalist's Motto: If you take care of the syntax, the semantics will take care of itself."[11] That is, if a system (organism or machine) operates in a syntactically rigorous manner that we can interpret in a way that makes semantic sense, we need nothing more to conclude (at least as a working hypothesis) that such a system is in the space of reasons.

This point is the basic idea behind what has become known as the Turing test, named for Alan Turing, one of the great founding figures in computer science.[12] Suppose you are having a conversation with someone

10. I am playing here with a famous example from Quine (*Word and Object*, 23–72), though I am not claiming to make the exact same use of it as Quine himself. The point here, which is something to which Quine would have sympathies, is that we can get a good, verifiable hypothesis of meaning up and running by seeing how a certain syntax plays in semantic contexts. Please also note that I am not claiming that this is how actual field linguists or anthropologists do business, nor that they should do so.

11. Haugeland, *Artificial Intelligence*, 106.

12. For Turing's statement of his influential views on this issue, which I am about to caricature, see his "Computer Machinery and Intelligence," in *Mind Design II*, 29–56.

about Russian literature via a keyboard and a monitor. Your interlocutor speaks with what you interpret as some insight about works by Dostoevsky and Chekhov. You have a pleasant conversation and sign off. Afterwards, a computer scientist informs you there was no human being originating the responses to your questions about *Crime and Punishment*, but only a machine running a very sophisticated program, but you could not tell the difference. The computer program was functionally equivalent to a human being discoursing about Russian literature, and in doing so, the machine made utterances that turn out to be true, or at least plausibly so from your limited expertise. On Turing's view, we would then have the same basis for saying the computer was rational as we would for a litera-ture professor. The point is that if a computer program for some subject matter could be run such that a neutral observer could not discern its responses from those given by a human being, then we should conclude that the system is intelligent in the same sense as a human being (even a human expert on the subject matter) in this respect. The Turing test is just to put computer programs under such scrutiny. As Haugeland sum-marizes this criterion: "whether a system has a mind, or how intelligent it is, is determined by what it can do . . ." and surely "a system is intelligent, if it can carry on an ordinary conversation like an ordinary person," leav-ing aside normalcy biases we might have for the mode of presentation, e.g., tone of voice.[13] No doubt there are different processes going on in-side the computer "expert" on Russian literature and a human expert on the same subject matter, but if we gave a computer the same benefit of the doubt that our anthropologist gave the newly found hominids, might we not find that we have the same grounds for concluding that the computer is rational? Wouldn't it be little more than bio-bias or stubbornness to deny the computer's rationality in speaking English, while granting it to the speakers of a radically different language?

There are now machines that we should likely say have passed lim-ited Turing tests. Certainly, there are no programs yet that can match us in discussing Russian literature and other such areas of interest. Nev-ertheless, shouldn't we say that a machine passing a limited Turing test is "minded-ish," and this should shift the burden of proof against the person who is inclined to deny machine mindedness? Robert Brandom is not utterly optimistic about the prospects of *bona fide* AI, but he does seem inclined to answer this question affirmatively:

13. Haugeland, "What Is Mind Design?" 3. Note that this is not an endorsement of the view as such by Haugeland, but his summary of Turing's position.

> There just is no point in insisting that something that is genu-
> inely indistinguishable (including, crucially, dispositionally
> counterfactually) from other discursive practitioners in conver-
> sation—no matter how extended and wide-ranging in topic—
> should nonetheless not be counted as really talking, and so
> thinking (out loud), and deploying a meaningful vocabulary.[14]

It is always hard to adjudicate philosophical issues that come down to
worries over the burden of proof, but, in this case, I do believe the burden
falls on the artificial *Geist* skeptic. Maybe we are just "wet computers," or
at least what we thought was distinctive about us is at bottom no different
from what machines can do and maybe already are doing. At the very
least, as machines increasingly become functionally indistinguishable
from us in our many cognitively complex tasks, this seems to be a possibility we cannot rule out without some very good reason in principle.[15]

3. The Chinese Room Objection

Among the most interesting objections to the Turing test is the "Man in
the Chinese Room" thought experiment, first proposed by the philosopher John Searle.[16] Suppose Cormac is utterly ignorant of Chinese; he
doesn't speak a word of Chinese, and he does not understand a single
symbol in the Chinese alphabet. Imagine a scenario in which Cormac is
in a room with two windows. In one window people outside the room
(who are native Chinese speakers) insert questions written in Chinese,
with an indexing number attached. Cormac then refers to an exhaustive manual and finds a perforated answer to that question in Chinese
according to the indexing number, which he then tears along the dotted

14. Brandom, *Between Saying and Doing*, 74. Note that Brandom, however, goes
on to claim on the same page that "it is a long way from acknowledging the criterial
character of the Turing test for sapience to endorsing the computational theory of the
mind on which classical symbolic AI is predicated."

15. Once again, one could admit that the burden of proof favors the artificial *Geist*
proponent based on the plausibility of the Turing test, and even grant that the machines have or likely will pass such tests, while at the same time remaining skeptical
about *bona fide* artificial *Geist* overall. For example, Brandom himself worries whether
a pragmatically sensitive system can accommodate non-algorithmic learning. See *Between Saying and Doing*, 82–87.

16. Searle defends this line in a number of places. See his "Minds, Brains, and Programs," 417–24; *Minds, Brains, and Science*, 28–41; *The Rediscovery of Mind*; and *Mind:
A Brief Introduction*, 62–71.

line and slides it out the second window. The manual is exhaustive and reliably accurate. Thus, to people outside the Chinese Room, it seems the system passes a Turing test for Chinese. The native speakers of Chinese posing the questions and evaluating the answers would have every reason (based on the interpretation of the "room's" utterances) to conclude that there is a *bona fide* competent speaker of Chinese in play; the outputs are syntactically rigorous and make good semantic sense.[17]

Its proponents, however, think this thought experiment shows the absurdity of the Turing test as a criterion for ascribing intelligence. Clearly, Cormac does not understand Chinese, nor does any part of the room, i.e., no component of the system understands Chinese. So where, one might ask, is the understanding of Chinese in this system? It seems to Searle that the judgment that someone is actually speaking Chinese is simply wrong based on the data available to the outside observers. His point is that the simple fact that a system can follow the syntax or rules of Chinese, does not entail that any part of the system understands what even a single Chinese symbol means, even if that syntax is interpretable as semantically valuable. Sure, maybe Cormac can follow Chinese syntax, but he has no clue what is being "said," i.e., he has no Chinese semantics. The utterances of the Chinese Room are not meaningful *to Cormac*, but only to the native Chinese speakers outside the room. They can understand the Chinese Room's utterances and interpret them as semantically significant, but the Chinese Room doesn't understand them. We might also highlight that neither Cormac nor any other part of the room is committed to any of these utterances. Since, Searle argues, Cormac operating within the Chinese Room is analogous to a computer subject to a Turing test, we should conclude that, like Cormac, "the programmed computer . . . does not understand Chinese either," and because "the program is purely formal or syntactical and because minds have mental or

17. One might worry, even at this point, whether the native Chinese speakers would conclude that the Chinese Room satisfies the Turing Test. Satisfying the test requires the system to be able to deal with such questions as "What color hat am I currently wearing?" but that is not something that could possibly be accounted for in Cormac's indexed book of replies. For the thought experiment to have traction, the Chinese Room needs to be sensitive to the contingent empirical situation, which is a capacity that many smart devices already have in hand, e.g., mapping applications that are sensitive to changes in the traffic flow and adjust the recommended route accordingly. In short, the original version of the thought experiment underestimates what can be expected from computers. Maybe the thought experiment can be easily adjusted to accommodate this concern.

semantic contents, any attempt to produce mind purely with computer programs leaves out the essential features of the mind."[18] In other words, the thought experiment purports to show that the Formalist's Motto is false: good syntax is not enough to take care of semantics.

Searle's argument is the source of a decades-long controversy, but I will mainly focus the most standard objection: the argument is clearly invalid, in virtue of committing the Fallacy of Composition, i.e., it infers that since no part of a whole has a certain attribute, the whole itself lacks that attribute.[19] For example, the fact that no member of the children's choir sings loudly does not imply that the children's choir does not sing loudly. Thus, the fact that Cormac, part of the Chinese Room system, does not understand Chinese does not alone imply that the Chinese Room (the system as a whole) fails to understand Chinese. I am not saying that the Chinese Room does understand Chinese, but only that Searle's thought experiment does not give us any reason to conclude that it does not. Searle's argument is simply invalid. The only way to infer the absence of an attribute at the level of the whole system from the absence of that attribute among the parts is if some reason can be given why in this case the attribute at the level of the whole depends on that same attribute being present at the level of the parts. Something like this is the case in the relationship between a wall and its composing bricks (the solidity of the wall presupposes the solidity of the bricks), but it is not the case in the relation between a painting and its composing paint "splotches" (the representational and even some of the qualitative properties of the painting could be utterly absent at the level of the paint splotches). Certainly, what is going on inside the Chinese Room is not at all like what goes on inside a human Chinese speaker, but the whole point of the AI advocate's position is that lower-level, material difference can be overcome by higher-level functional equivalence. Thus, just saying that no part of the Chinese Room system is at all like the components of a human's understanding of Chinese simply begs the question. Certainly, no single part of a system running the rules for *Damespiel* knows how to play checkers, but the system does. No individual part of your brain knows how to speak English, but you do. There is something different going on inside the Chinese Room from what goes on in a human speaker of Chinese,

---

18. Searle, *The Rediscovery of Mind*, 45.

19. For a very good summary of the standard objections to Searle's thought experiment and the dialectic that follows in the literature, see Copeland, *Artificial Intelligence*, 121–37.

but there is something different going on materially in machines running checkers on different software. Nevertheless, they both produce something we rightly interpret as checkers.[20]

4. Relevance, Care, and Authenticity

It seems we are running out of reasons to doubt the possibility of *bona fide* artificial *Geist*. Should we just give up and take the consequences of our posthuman future seriously? I, for one, am not quite yet prepared to do so. My reason for this is not because I believe there is a way to undermine the Turing test as a criterion for ascriptions of linguistic competence, nor do I have absolute grounds to believe that the construction of a machine that passes such a test is impossible. I do, however, think that there are good reasons for being doubtful about an affirmative answer to the question of artificial *Geist*. In what follows, my intent is not to prove the impossibility of an artificial mind, but to raise considerations showing that it is at best a remote possibility, if it is a possibility all. In other words, I want to discuss how high the bar really is for a computer to pass a legitimate Turing test for human intelligence, where what we mean by "intelligence" is participation in *Geist* as we have discussed it in the forgoing chapters, i.e., rationality. We will see that constructing a machine that we can interpret as having full human linguistic and practical competence appears to be a very tall order, and in some cases it is difficult to envision what would even count as doing so. We will shift the burden of proof again strongly in favor of the skeptic regarding artificial *Geist*.

20. I am, broadly for the reasons discussed in the foregoing paragraph, less confident in Searle's thought experiment than when I defended it in an earlier writing. See Madden, *Mind, Matter, and Nature*, 150–55. Though Markus Gabriel does conclude that the debate over the Chinese Room ends in a stalemate, he nevertheless believes that broader resources from Searle's philosophy of mind can serve to move the needle in favor of the AI skeptic, i.e., Searle's account of consciousness as a biological phenomenon is sufficient to show that any artificial system lacks *bona fide* intentionality; see Gabriel, *The Meaning of Thought*, 63–65. In principle, I agree with Gabriel here, and I will basically defend much the same position in the next section of this chapter. His reading of Searle, however, seems to be too charitable. That is, Searle's narrow notion of biological life and seeming internalism about the mind (remember his presumption of the plausibility of the brain-in-the vat hypothesis we discussed in chapter 1) are insufficient to reveal the real problems with the very idea of artificial *Geist*, and I hope the following discussion makes as much clear. In any event, I am not claiming that Gabriel's position shares these liabilities. In fact, much of what he argues in *The Meaning of Thought* is complementary to what I am attempting to achieve in this book.

The considerations I raise go under the monikers of *pragmatic relevance, giving-a-damn,* and *authenticity.*

(a) *Pragmatic Relevance*

Consider driving your car down the road. How many objects in your environment are you aware of when doing so? We know that in some sense of "aware" you are conscious of far more than what is occurrent before the "mind's eye," as it were. You are not explicitly conscious of the trees you pass, the leaves blowing in the gutters, the address numbers on all the houses, the children playing on the lawns, etc., etc., but we know that a great deal of that information is taken in by your nervous system. Very few of these data rise to the level of explicit awareness, though they are *ready-to-hand* in the background. As soon as one of those kids steps off the curb, hopefully that awareness will become explicitly present in your consciousness on the quick. The point is that consciousness of your environment is sorted in terms of relevance to the task at hand. We are confronted with a vast myriad of phenomena, and we are able to have an intelligible experience by sorting out what is relevant to what we are trying to do at the moment. As Hubert Dreyfus puts it, "most of what we experience must remain in the background so that something can be perceived in the foreground."[21] Do not let how complicated an ability that is pass by too quickly. How many pieces of currently irrelevant, but potentially relevant, information are being tracked by your nervous system right now? Notice how easily your consciousness can move from one frame of relevance to another, e.g., smoothly transitioning from the lane change you are making to the insipid commercial on the radio. It is easy to miss how complicated this task is, just as it is easy to fail to appreciate the fluidity with which you make these transitions constantly. How many different frames of relevance can you transfer to and from? Dreyfus makes this point in detail:

> It has to do with the way man is at home in his world, has it comfortably wrapped around him, so to speak. Human beings are somehow already situated in such a way that what they need in order to cope with things is distributed around them where they need it. . . . This system of relations which makes it possible to discover objects when they are needed is our home or our

21. Dreyfus, *What Computers Still Can't Do,* 240.

world. The Human world . . . is prestructured in terms of human
purposes and concerns in such a way that what counts as an object or is significant about an object is a function of, or embodies, that concern. This cannot be matched by a computer, which
can deal only with universally defined, i.e., context-free, objects.
In trying to simulate this field of concern, the programmer can
only assign to the already determinate facts further determinate
facts called values, which only complicates the retrieval problem
for the machine.[22]

Dreyfus's point, following Heidegger and Merleau-Ponty, is that human
experience (and subsequent practice) is always pre-sorted, as it were,
by pragmatic concerns ultimately grounded in basic human needs. Our
thinking is presented with indefinitely, even infinitely, many possible semantic engagements with the world, but we winnow those dizzying possibilities down based on pragmatic sorting. Moreover, we move among
these various pragmatic sortings with utter facility in a way it seems
highly unlikely that any algorithm can capture, because they are always
based on our particular bodily and culturally conditioned prior attempts
to deal with the world. Again, as Dreyfus puts it, "our present concerns
and past know-how always already determines what will be ignored, what
will remain on the outer horizon of experience as possibly relevant, and
what will be immediately taken into account as essential."[23] That is, we are
always temporally and contingently situated such that our next move is
partly determined by our personal history and current needs. The principles of relevance that make sense of our sense-making are ever-moving
targets because of the fluidity of our needful, practical situation. It is difficult, though maybe not impossible, to envision how this historicity of
our consciousness could ever be captured in an algorithm.[24]

Notice that this phenomenon is most profoundly reflected in our
linguistic practices. The number of true utterances in any given situation

22. Dreyfus, *What Computers Still Can't Do*, 260–61.

23. Dreyfus, *What Computers Still Can't Do*, 263.

24. Certainly, Heidegger and Merleau-Ponty are due the credit they get for phenomenologically ferreting the temporal/historical aspect of human conscious experience, but many of the rudiments of this account are already present even in some of
Husserl's earlier lectures. See Husserl, *The Phenomenology of Time Consciousness*. See
also Latour, *We Have Never Been Modern*, 67–79, for an analysis of how the dualist
sorting distorts our understanding of temporality in ways leading us to equally misguided understandings of our relation to both nature and artifacts (which, for him, we
should be careful not to distinguish too sharply).

that can be made with even a truncated English vocabulary boggles the mind. Take merely the vocabulary of the average fifth-grader and allow all the humans who ever existed to do nothing but form sentences from those resources for the entirety of human history. Their utterances over all those centuries would not have exhausted what can be said with even that basic vocabulary. In fact, you have probably never said the exact same sentence twice, excepting circumstances of explicit self-quotation or recitation. Thus, almost everything we say is a novel utterance, and yet relevant to the varied and overlapping contexts that constitute our world.[25] Moreover, this infinite plasticity leaves us with vast options for what can be said with semantic value at any given moment. Whenever you enter a room, how many true statements could you make? There are, no doubt, thousands of utterances that would get something right, but among that multitude of true statements regarding your implicit environment, how many are you even tempted to utter? A miniscule fraction. Unless we have some way of narrowing all the possibilities of what could be said, nothing could meaningfully be uttered. Notice, however, that you likewise change relevance frames effortlessly in a single coherent conversation. We can move effortlessly in and out of relevance frames in which "Smitty's shirt is stained," "The interview is in an hour," and "The atomic weight of chlorine is 35.453" all make sense in the flow. We can both stay on topic and change topic with equal facility, which implies the background sorting of likely millions of linguistic possibilities.

Here, then, is the point: What would it take to specify a set of rules that captures the plasticity of relevance sorting implicit in any human conversation? How many such rules would have to be specified? How would appropriate transitions from one frame of relevance to another be specified? Our "situation" (the world in which we meaningfully and pragmatically engage) is "organized from the start in terms of human needs and propensities which give the facts meaning, make the facts what they are, so that there is never a question of storing and sorting through a list of *meaningless, isolated data*" like what we would envision a computer doing.[26] The problem is not just quantitative, though the sheer number of algorithms to be specified is daunting. The problem is also qualitative. All of these frames of relevance seem open-ended, e.g., there really is no hard line between what is relevant to a conversation about chameleons

---

25. Brandom, *Reason in Philosophy*, 74–75.
26. Dreyfus, *What Computers Still Can't Do*, 162. Author's emphasis.

and a conversation about the Battle of Austerlitz. I bet there is a coherent conversational flow leading from the one to the other while making perfectly good sense. How will a syntax for such an open-ended process be specified? The notion that this will be done someday strains credulity. That is not to say it is impossible (and indeed there are very smart people spending their life's work on solving these problems), but the odds seem to favor skepticism at this point.

Our human linguistic competence always operates in a *practical holism*. The truth of an utterance is insufficient for it to make reasonable sense; it is not enough that a statement be true, as it must also be an *appropriate* statement of truth. A mark of rationality is therefore not only truth-telling, but *appropriate* truth-telling. That is, a single utterance is meaningful only in light of what has been said and what could be said next; we always speak in a temporally conditioned situation. The temporality of human speech requires that meaning does not only float up from the individual utterances to the conversation as a whole, but also sinks down from the conversational wholes to the sentential parts. In other words, intelligent utterances are always parts of an overall meaningful frame of reference, and in any given situation there is an indefinite number of "wholes" within which one might operate. That conversational whole is defined (albeit without hard edges) pragmatically: utterances are relevant to what we are doing in our conversation, which is connected to both human needs and our prior, contingent development of skills and know-how. We communicate meaningfully in a conversation only because we are operating under an implicit and yet open-ended agreement about what we are trying to achieve by speaking to each other, and we are skilled "craftsmen" at our linguistic tasks. Capturing that contextual plasticity and contingency of the pragmatics of linguistic competence is a major difficulty for AI. Not a deal breaker, but a big problem. Maybe intelligent machines can be or have been constructed, but they will not be rational in *our* way unless they are able to sort myriad semantic possibilities according to needs and contingency while in the open-ended flow of the *Lebenswelt*.[27]

Moreover, even if the programming difficulty posed by open-ended sortings for pragmatic relevance can be overcome (and maybe it will),

27. There has been much work done on these problems since Dreyfus first raised this objection. For his update on why he believes all the progress in AI engineering in the subsequent decades have not undermined his philosophical point, see Dreyfus, "Why Heideggerian AI Failed."

our ways of sorting are based on biological needs that have been conditioned by our natural history. Is a system, even if it sorts the world in a functionally equivalent way, really doing the same thing as we are, if it does so without a significant connection to our evolutionary past? I doubt that we can separate the semantic content of our thinking from our natural history. Non-living, non-evolved beings are not thinking how we think, and they are not thinking what we think, because our thought is always in the service of a sort of inherited *concern* over our well-being and mortality that we share with all living things.[28] The same issue arises regarding our cultural history: Can we separate the semantic content of our thoughts from the cultural context in which they come to be? I suggested in chapter 2 that these questions should be answered negatively. Thus, even if a machine could be engineered to operate with complete facility and skill through the same range of pragmatic sortings of semantic contexts as we do, it is far from clear that such a machine would be thinking as we do. At the very least, it would not necessarily be in *our* logical space of reasons. *Geist* is worldly, and it is far from clear that machines are embedded in worlds in the way necessary to participate in such mindedness. Our mind is embedded in our history, and machines lack our history (even if they are themselves always a part of it).

(b) *Giving-a-Damn*

John Haugeland famously claims, "The trouble with artificial intelligence is that computers don't give a damn."[29] Here is how he explains this quip:

> A single [speech] act cannot be embarrassing, shameful, irresponsible, or foolish in isolation, but only as an event in the biography of a whole, historical, individual—a person whose personality it reflects and whose self-understanding it threatens. Only a being that cares about who it is, as some sort of enduring whole, can care about guilt or folly, self-respect or achievement, life or death. And only such a being can read. This holism, now not even apparently in the text, but manifestly in the reader, I call . . . *existential holism*. It is essential, I submit, to

28. See Jonas, "Cybernetics and Purpose" and "The Burden and the Blessing of Morality."

29. Haugeland, *Having Thought*, 48.

understanding the meaning of any text that (in a familiar sense) *has* meaning.[30]

Haugeland's point is that pragmatically defined frames of relevance, from which our individual utterances derive meaning from meaningful wholes, is to a very large extent itself determined by what we *care* about.[31] Because I am concerned about my honor, I am undertaking some dangerous feat, which leads me to be concerned about some narrow subset of the entities in my environment. You can make sense of my talk about these entities only to the degree that you likewise share a commitment to this project, or at least you can empathize with it. I make sense to you because you get what I'm up to pragmatically, but that can happen only if you have some grasp on what I *care* about. My fear of death draws my attention to certain dark possibilities for the next decade, which might not otherwise invade my concerns. This fear attunes me to constituents of the world that were previously outside my ken, and yet they are disclosed by my mood as being there all along. My love for my wife diverts my consciousness from occurrences that might have otherwise aroused one's ire and brings to mind other welcome occurrences that escaped the notice of just about anyone else. All these moods narrow the possibilities of experience and thereby bring to the foreground particular entities among the vast plurality that could be the objects of our experience, only because they are ordered to things about which one has deep care or concern. It is our existential concerns that set our practical agendas, which in turn constitute our world.[32] As we have discussed, human mindedness, *Geist*, can only occur in such a meaningful world.

Allow me to play on the superficial linguistic similarity among "sign," "signify," and "significance" to make Haugeland's (really Heidegger's) point: a sign can only sign-*ify* something inasmuch as it is illuminated by a world of sign-*ificance* to us.[33] It is only because I care about myself (the kind of person I wish to be), I care about other people, or I care that certain things occur in the world that I take up a pragmatic stance that allows my speech to make intelligible sense, or at least that is one way we

30. Haugeland, *Having Thought*, 58–59.

31. This is certainly implicit in much we have discussed above with Dreyfus. See *What Computers Still Can't Do*, 272–80. Moreover, both Dreyfus and Haugeland are following Heidegger on this point.

32. See Heidegger, *Being and Time*, 83–84.

33. Heidegger, *Being and Time*, 107–14.

do the sorting, and maybe the one most important for and distinctive to us. Pragmatic stances (or what we will call linguistic practices) are what allow us to determine meaningful utterances non-arbitrarily, and our existential care is what makes our determination of linguistic practice non-arbitrary. It is our concern for who and what we are, our care for other people, and what we value in the world that finally determines the significance of our signs; among all the possibilities, it is the significance of what we *give a damn* about that primarily sorts the relevant from the irrelevant. There may be other ways of sorting the relevant from the ir-relevant, but the *human* way of sorting only follows from the fact that our own being and the being of what we love is an issue to us.

To fail to care about what you are saying, is a failure to *mean* any-thing at all. The logical space of reasons in which we operate is defined by our care for the meaning not just of our utterances but of our lives. In fact, living in the context of what makes our lives meaningful is a neces-sary condition for our making meaningful (non-arbitrary) utterances. This is what Wittgenstein mostly meant when he famously claimed that our words have meaning only in *a stream of life*.[34] Again, as Haugeland puts it: "Apart from a few restricted domains, like playing chess, analyz-ing mass spectra, or making airline reservations, the most ordinary con-versations are fraught with life and all its meanings,"[35] which is to say, "Love is the mark of the human."[36] Maybe the algorithm behind Expedia can out-perform us in winnowing the options for a flight to LAX, but can an algorithm be produced that would sort the world in terms of the ex-istential concerns that motivate the trip? Even if a machine could, would it be doing what *I* am doing? Would it *care*? It is hard to articulate even what an affirmative answer to that question might take without indulging the sort of materialist reductionism I argued against in chapter 1, so once again I am skeptical about *bona fide* artificial mindedness.

(c) *Authenticity*

A kind of structure of meaning has arisen for us as our discussion has unfolded. Individual utterances are meaningful inasmuch as they par-ticipate in pragmatically defined linguistic practices, but these linguistic

34. Wittgenstein, *Zettle*, 32 (§173).
35. Haugeland, *Having Thought*, 59.
36. Haugeland, *Having Thought*, 2.

practices themselves are intelligibly meaningful only inasmuch as they participate in our basic existential concerns, i.e., we care about them. Here is a self-indulgent example. I spend a great deal of my time working within the linguistic practice of *being-a-philosophy-professor*. The practicalities of that way of being sort my utterances non-arbitrarily so that I can exchange meanings with other people involved in those practices, mostly students and other professors of philosophy, or at least that is my hope. The game of *being-a-philosophy-professor* fails to deliver any real meaning unless it is itself non-arbitrarily selected among other linguistic practices. What makes that determination? Why am I making *philosophy-professor-type* utterances rather than talking about chameleons or jiu jitsu, or whatever else might be a worthy topic of conversation? It is my *care for* or *commitment to* something—say, a concern for a certain kind of truth, or a wonder about certain enduring questions. Maybe my admiration for a long-remembered mentor still holds me to it. It is because I share such concerns with those to whom I speak that I can use the linguistic practice of *being-a-philosophy-professor* to say anything at all. That is just my case, but we could say the same things about *being-a-chemist*, *being-a-welder*, *being-a-mother*, *being-a-Catholic*, *being-a-socialist*, etc.: these practices allow us to say something meaningfully intelligible about the world because they are connected to something we care about.

If care is what sets us toward a practice, then we should care about that practice. For example, if your concern for human suffering commits you to the practice of medicine, then the practice of medicine should itself be a concern of yours. You should care about the practice of medicine, because that is what takes care of the humans you care about. Likewise, if my concern for wonder is what grounds me in the practice of *being-a-professor-of-philosophy*, then I should likewise care about the practice of being a professor itself, as that practice is how I care for those wonders.

What does it mean to care about a practice? How does one show concern not just for beings, but for ways of articulating being? It certainly is not the thin, facile care I have for those people I send Christmas cards to every year (even though I have not really known them for two decades) or the *faux* concern I feign for exclusively Facebook "friends." That's not the "Real McCoy," as they say. That is *inauthentic*. What is real, authentic care? Notice a subtlety in the word "care" as it is linked with various prepositions. One *cares about* the Green Bay Packers' score, or cares *about* the price of lumber, but a garden can be something I *care for*, and I can *care for* my children, or *care for* my teammates. Likewise, my pet chameleon is *in my care*, or a therapist's clients are *in her care*. What does it mean to *care for* something, or to have something *be in our care*? It is, as we put it in a quite familiar turn of phrase, *to take care of* something: to cultivate it, nurture it, see to its flourishing, etc. In short, *caring for* something is taking *responsibility* for it. Sending barely initialed Christmas cards to your all-but-forgotten college roommates, liking someone's profile on Facebook, and keeping someone's crushing tragedy in your "thoughts and prayers" are mostly not authentic forms of care. All of that is just going through the motions. It's playacting care, behaving *as-if* care, the simulation of concern without semantic value, mindlessly going through the motions. Rather, raising a child, cultivating a garden, taking your aged parent into your home, becoming a therapist, joining the Marine Corps, are all taking responsibility for something one cherishes, not merely making the outward, but probably empty gesture, of care. Authentic care is taking responsibility for something or someone, or even some *way of being*.[37]

What does it mean to care authentically for a practice? How does a doctor take responsibility for the practice of medicine? First, and most commonly, the doctor cares for medicine by trying as hard as possible to be a good doctor, i.e., she takes responsibility for her adherence to the norms and practices of *being-a-doctor* as they have been handed down to her. If care for human suffering is what sets someone to the practice of medicine, then she should care about being good at the practice of medicine as a means to alleviating human suffering. Likewise, if a reverence for wonder is what sets me to be a professor of philosophy, then it seems I should care enough about the practice of *being-a-professor-of-philosophy* to work at being good at cultivating wonder in myself, my students, and my colleagues. Someone carelessly going through the motions of a linguistic practice, not caring one wit about the practice itself and whether she is in fact doing it right, is not really saying anything. She is just babbling or play-acting, even if her utterances have the outward form of intelligible speech—just like my mass-produced Christmas cards or offers of "thoughts and prayers" on Facebook. If I am going to say anything

37. See Heidegger, *Being and Time*, 78–86, 241. Haugeland's reading of Heidegger in *Dasein Disclosed* has deeply influenced me on this point and much of what I am motivating in this section. I do not claim that his interpretation is getting Heidegger right (it is quite controversial on that score), but only that his reading provides a very effective vocabulary for articulating the issues we are discussing. Once again, Harman's *Tool Being* should be contrasted with the version of Heidegger we get from Haugeland and Dreyfus.

semantically significant through a linguistic practice, I must be taking responsibility for getting it right. Earlier I called this *being responsible to a form of life*, and I argued that it is integral to our very participation in mindedness and freedom, *Geist*. Real freedom and rationality require us to hold ourselves to the standards of our inherited world.

Notice that there is a higher-level sort of responsibility one can take for a practice, a more profound sort of care. Is it possible that the practice of medicine as it has been handed down to our contemporary doctor turns out to be deeply flawed? Could the medical practice she finds herself thrown into actually lead to consequences contrary to her concern for human suffering? Could she be doing more harm than good regarding what she cares about the most? Might she have dedicated her life to cultivating a practice that simply gets the world wrong? Yes, in fact this sort of revelation has come to us before; think of leeching, bleeding, cutting holes in the head to relieve bad vapors, and even some of the famous mistakes of modern medicine (e.g., thalidomide). Should the doctor ask these questions? Well, probably not on her way into the OR to perform an emergency appendectomy. Nevertheless, should she ask these questions at some point? I think she must, if she really does care about medicine, which is to say, if she is to *truthfully be* a doctor. Thus, one must ask stark questions and face possibly dark answers about her form of life, if she really cares about it. This is what it means to refuse to live in a sham world. Earlier, I called this *being responsible for a world*, and it too, so I have argued, is integral to our status as participants in *Geist*. We need to hold our forms of life to a semantic responsibility to the way reality pushes back.

These considerations also raise to prominence the third type of distinctively human responsibility that we discussed earlier, i.e., authenticity. If I really care about a practice because it cultivates something else that concerns me, then I should not tolerate a situation in which that practice really is not worth caring about because it does not actually serve that for which I really care. Otherwise, I'm steeping myself in illusion and going through the motions. Not raising the issue of semantic responsibility is to leave open the question of what really motivates you to engage in a certain linguistic practice. If I do not really worry about whether the methods and claims of my practice are true or ultimately useful, then it seems *my real motives* for engaging in this way of being are, at best, opaque. Studied indifference to the possibility of the failure of our definitive practices is not to care about them at all. This self-imposed ignorance is likely only to bring ruin onto what we claim to love, much as Oedipus's lack of authenticity brought a plague to Thebes. Taking responsibility for a practice is not just being good at the practice, but also being concerned with whether the practice is itself really any good, and only in that self-critical light can we reach clarity about our own motivations. If we dodge worry about the semantic value of the judgments defining our practices, then we are not persisting in our form of life because it is ordered to the good, but for some other unstated motive. Does the practice of medicine actually serve what our doctor most cares about? Does it disclose the world in a way that addresses those concerns? Does the practice of *being-a-philosophy-professor* as I have been thrown into it actually cultivate the wonder I cherish? I could be very good at being a professor of philosophy, even if that practice does not indeed do any good for the things I most care about. If I don't ever address that latter possibility, then maybe I am really only doing this because of the long holidays and the security of ten-ure. Failure to ask these questions about the linguistic practices that make our speech rationally intelligible is a way of dodging responsibility for them, and therefore an expression of indifference, not care. When Mick Jagger said, "I know it's only rock-'n-roll, but I like it," I think he probably should've added ". . . and I don't really care about it either." Moreover, if the argument I am pressing is correct, we should also point out to Mick that his rock-'n-roll subsequently fails to say anything intelligible at all, and we mistrust his motives for taking up the practice in the first place. Somehow, I think The Stones probably did care a bit more than these lyrics express. Authentic care is being responsible for our practices to the world we care about, and that possibility is what distinguishes distinc-tively human, semantic values. *Geist* entails responsibility, and respon-sibility entails care. Indifference erodes the fundamental conditions for mindedness.

Whatever we make of the intelligible content of Mick Jagger's lyr-ics, we have arrived at the following important point: the possibility of making sense presupposes our embracing of the possibility that our very means of making sense might ultimately be senseless. To get meaning off the ground (to participate in *Geist*), we must live in a human world, but that world must also be a *real* world. "Being real" about things or "keeping it real" as we say, requires us to accept the possibility that much of what we cherish could run afoul of reality. Humans mean things in the most meaningful way, only because we can put the linguistic prac-tices by which we define ourselves and address our ultimate concerns under critical scrutiny. The willingness to suffer this scrutiny is authentic care, and the possibility of such concern appears to be a condition for distinctively human rationality in its full maturity. We are the beings whose being is always an issue for us.[38] We ask ourselves questions about ourselves, and quite dark questions at that. This does not mean that we must be inherently skeptical. Our physician can resolutely go forward in her responsible practice of medicine, even while being open to the possibility that someday the world may reveal that very practice as bankrupt regarding her deepest concerns. I can continue to practice as a professor of philosophy, without shunning the possibility that the profession has outlived its cultural usefulness. Openness to the possibility of failure is not the same thing as the admission of failure, any more than admitting the immanent possibility of death is giving up on life, though accepting these grim possibilities is necessary for authentic participation in our lives. All that is necessary is a legitimate desire to know whether one's way of life really is a way of being responsible for what is most worthy of our concern. Maybe, in the end, your beloved practices get it right. Who can tell unless we ask? Unless we put ourselves under the scrutiny of such questions, we shun the very possibility of thinking and otherwise just go through the motions as if we were automatons.

Of course, there are dark possibilities that come along with authentic care. Our physician may put the practice of *being-a-doctor* at issue, subsequently to find that it is a failure; it does not get the world right as revealed by her concerns. I may have found that *being-a-philosophy-professor* is no longer a legitimate way of cultivating wonder. In these cases, *being-a-doctor* and *being-a-philosophy-professor* have become absurdities as we find ourselves in them. What is one to do with that state affairs, i.e., when one's way of being seems to have suffered a sort of death?[39] It would seem one would need to revise these practices radically, but that would certainly be easier said than done. Institutional reform is famously difficult. Does one just abandon the practice? Maybe, especially in the case of professions like medicine or academics. Notice, however,

---

38. Of course, here I am paraphrasing Heidegger, *Being and Time*, 32. Equally, it should be obvious that much of this discussion of authenticity finds its origins in that same text.

39. The notion that a way of being (a "Dasein" taken as a social practice) can suffer death and the connection of this possibility to authenticity is an important theme in Haugeland's interpretation of Heidegger. See *Dasein Disclosed*, 179–86. As always, this reading of Heidegger is controversial, though I find it philosophically illuminating.

abandonment does not displace the original deep concerns that bound us to these practices in the first place. I do not think one can just give up on the alleviation of human suffering or the cultivation of wonder the way one changes brands of shoes, nor should one even consider doing so! Certainly, giving up broader cultural or religious practices will be even more difficult to entertain than the loss of one's profession. One could just stick to it, "keep on keeping-on," with the practice of medicine or being a professor of philosophy. That, however, is consciously to accept a state of "play-acting," and it might even be to participate in doing harm to things and persons you care about. In any event, ignoring the revelations of authentic self-criticism is to subject oneself to the whims of fate, as did Oedipus. No, there is no good course of action for someone who has asked the kind of question required for authentic care and come to a grim answer. Thus, authentic care comes only with anxiety, but that is the price one must pay to say anything meaningful at all. Maybe we have arrived at the place for the virtues of hope and faith: persisting in practices as if they were meaningful simply because giving up on what you care about is not an option. Maybe remaining resolute will one day reveal something you have missed.[40] Nevertheless, without putting ourselves at risk out of love for what we care about (and thereby accepting the requisite anxieties), we will go through our lives merely babbling, like robots. The price of love, really caring about something, is quite steep.

Well, I have gone a bit far afield, but not too far as that last passing reference to robots suggests. If indeed a machine is to be produced that has the same rationality as human beings, i.e., participating in a *human* space of reasons, it will have to sort the world in terms of pragmatic relevance, but that likewise requires that such a machine sorts linguistic practices by existential care. Furthermore, existential care entails at least the possibility that such a machine is capable of authentic responsibility for its own being. Can a computer put itself into question? Can it face the grave consequences of seeing its way of life as a failure? Could machines question their own motives for running their programs? What would it be like for a computer to do any of that? I have no proof for the impossibility of a computer having an existential crisis, but I find the very suggestion

---

40. Jonathan Lear provides profound reflections on how authenticity in the face of the collapse of one's form of life can be an occasion for hope in *Radical Hope*, and in doing so he is gathering many of the same Aristotelian and Heideggarian strands I have attempted to pull together in this and the previous chapter. I, no doubt, do not claim to have woven this fabric as well as Lear.

almost laughably implausible. As Haugeland puts it: "cognitive science and artificial intelligence cannot succeed in their own essential aims unless and until they can understand and implement genuine freedom and the capacity to love."[41] Of course, that does not absolutely rule anything out, so I guess we must live with the question as to whether our way of being is significantly distinct for what machines might, however implausibly, be able to achieve. That is a bit uncomfortable; it leaves us humans with our humanity in question. In the end, we might come to *nothing* special in comparison to machines. Is entertaining that possibility so bad? Can we own up to that? Might the fact that the question of artificial *Geist* always lingers show us something about ourselves? How else would you *care for* humanity but to take responsibility for the question of whether humanity is *worth caring for* more than our artifacts? Doesn't the anxiety spurred on by this question lead us a long way toward answering it? Doesn't this perplexity reveal you as *something*? Are these questions a machine can ask itself, or do these concerns only arise for Spirit?

41. Haugeland, *Dasein Disclosed*, 274.

5

Dignity and Meaning in the Face of Techno-Nihilism

It is only this new consciousness at a higher potential, this abstract reflex of everything intuitive in the non-perceptive conception of reason, that endows man with that thoughtfulness which so completely distinguishes his consciousness from that of the animal, and through which his whole behavior on earth turns out so differently from that of his irrational brothers. He far surpasses them in power and suffering.

—ARTHUR SCHOPENHAUER, *THE WORLD AS WILL AND REPRESENTATION*[1]

Human nature is the set of delegates and its representations, its figures and its messengers.

—BRUNO LATOUR, *WE HAVE NEVER BEEN MODERN*[2]

We already have human technologies that are both physical and "psychic" (in the sense of influencing the consciousness of the observer). An example of such a technology is given, very simply, by your television set. It determines

1. Schopenhauer, *The World as Will and Representation*, §8.
2. Latour, *We Have Never Been Modern*, 138.

what toothpaste you use, how you shave, who you go to bed with, and how
you will vote in the next election.

—JACQUES VALLÉE, *MESSENGERS OF DECEPTION:*
UFO CONTACTS AND CULTS[3]

T HERE ARE PLENTY OF worries about the consequences of technology
abroad today. The threat of environmental degradation following
on the emergence of techno-industrial society has been a going concern
for at least a century, and we can find the roots of such concern already
in the Romanticism of the early nineteenth century. The application of
biotechnology to human beings, especially during the embryonic stage
of our lives, has raised the two-edged promise of both the alleviation of
grave suffering and the instrumentalization of human lives at their most
vulnerable point of development, or at least that is a worry for many of
us. Similar technologies raise the prospect of genetically engineering
"designer babies" made to custom specifications, which leaves one to
wonder what comes of parenting when our children are readily treated
as artifacts contrived to fit our specifications. We are all familiar with
the ill-consequences personalized digital technology has had for how
we spend our time and the substance of what fills our thoughts, not to
mention the emerging evidence of the developmental harm done to
children reared mostly in front of screens. What will come of our *Geist*
as we increasingly initiate ourselves without actual human attachment?
What comes of our grounding traditions when we bombard ourselves
with images and "conversations" that are the intellectual and aesthetic
equivalent of what McDonald's is to the pallet (engineered solely for
sensuous effect with disregard to nutrition)? Speaking of which, to this
standard list of technological woes, I also add our current obesity and
opioid epidemics plaguing us in the United States and to a lesser extent
other Western nations. Certainly, the availability of easily produced and
distributed food stuff is one of the great boons of the technological age, but
it has also addicted us to cheap pseudo-foods that are causing havoc on
our bodies and our healthcare systems. The development of pain-relieving
wonder drugs like OxyContin has done much to spare us many horrid
torments suffered by prior generations, while the availability of those same
drugs has also sent untold human lives down a spiral of degradation, often

3. Vallee, *Messengers of Deception*, 67–68.

with mortal consequences. Of course, one should also mention both the promise of nuclear power and how the chaotic geopolitics of the twenty-first century have reminded us of the looming possibility of belligerent Armageddon we too quickly forgot after 1989.

Those are all grave concerns, and they are particularly pressing as the increasing speed of technological advance seems to pile problems up faster than our intellectuals can even enumerate them, much less articulate strategies for resolution. There is, nevertheless, nothing utterly new in these challenges. Going back at least to the tale of the Tower of Babel in *Genesis* and the ancient Greek myth of Icarus's ill-conceived flight to the sun, humanity has long known that technological innovation almost always carries unforeseen consequences and the specter of disastrous hubris. Surely the particular implements we have contrived in recent decades pose new threats (maybe even qualitatively more perilous), along with previously unforeseen promises, but the double-edged sword of technological innovation has troubled philosophers perennially; e.g., remember Socrates's reservation about the written word because of its consequences for memory.[4] The good and bad of technological advancement are the fruits, both nutritious and poisonous, of our perennial standing as cognitive extenders. That is not to underplay the gravity of the material consequences of recent technological advances, but to say that those consequences are nothing new and, as such, they likely do not challenge us with a demand for a novel kind of philosophical reflection on these issues.

In any event, I want to return to the concerns expressed by Wittgenstein's invocation of "the darkness of this time" with which I initiated our conversation, and you will remember that he associated this darkness with technology. We began with the proposal that technology is not only a practical but a *spiritual* problem, and our question is what has technology done to our understanding of ourselves, our self-consciousness. Whatever our devices might be doing to the environment or our circadian rhythms, our concern now is what it leads us to think about ourselves.

4. It would be interesting to reconsider Socrates' misgiving about the written word as a threat to our cognitive powers in light of the extended-mind approach to cognition that I have drawn on throughout this book. In that light, the off-loading of our memory onto written records was no more a cognitive diminishment than the original development of the spoken word, which itself was an off-loading of our cognitive burdens onto a collective or cultural memory. Yet, the following should show that Socrates' worries were not in principle entirely misplaced. These issues are illuminatingly considered in Ferraris, "Total Mobilization."

At least on Wittgenstein's reckoning (among prominent others), our distinctively modern technological way of being has undermined our self-understanding, and thereby left us alienated from our most natural sources of meaning, in part, by foisting upon us a defective understanding of what counts for mindedness. In short, the claim is that our current inklings of nihilism are a result of a self-alienating understanding of mind. In the foregoing chapters, I have tried to bring the broad contours of a non-alienated understanding of mindedness to light, but now I turn to an account of why particularly modern forms of technological organization have served to obfuscate what should be obvious to us—ourselves.

Heidegger, in his most influential treatment of technology as a philosophical problem (among his many confrontations with this problem), frames this issue by leading us toward a "questioning concerning *technology*, and in so doing we should like to prepare a free relationship to it. The relationship will be free if it opens our human existence to the essence of technology."[5] Heidegger is not out to track the consequences of particular devices for human flourishing, at least not in this line of questioning.[6] Instead, he is asking what technology *is*, in its essence, and "Technology is not equivalent to the essence of technology. . . . That which pervades every tree, as tree, is not itself a tree that can be counted among all the other trees."[7] In other words, the inquiry we are embarking on begins with wondering not about this or that device and its effects on our form of life, but a concern for what technology essentially is, and, as Heidegger hints at in the first passage I quoted in this paragraph, what our relationship to the world must be, given our reliance on and obsession with technology. Heidegger does not take technology as something *neutral*, a metaphysically innocent set of devices that we can evaluate by disinterested utilitarian criteria. He does not deny that there are such things, nor does Heidegger doubt the importance of such reflection, but these considerations do not arrive at the essence of technology. In fact, Heidegger eventually comes to see the essence of technology not as a

5. Heidegger, "The Question Concerning Technology," 3. Author's emphasis.

6. He does take up something like those issues in his "Memorial Address," where he notes that even the nascent media technologies of the post-war era tend to make everything seem near, which occludes what is truly near to us. For an excellent discussion of this moment in Heidegger's critique of modern technology that relates it to "The Question Concerning Technology" and contemporary developments in media technology, see Kisiel, "How Heidegger Resolved the Tension between Technological Globalization and Indigenous Localization"

7. Heidegger, "The Question Concerning Technology," 4.

definition of a class of objects, but as an attitude toward Being. Technology, in the sense we are interrogating it, is an attitude or mood, as Heidegger uses that notion in his earlier work, that *reveals* a world: "If we inquire, step by step, into what technology . . . actually is, then we shall arrive at revealing."[8] In other words, technology, for Heidegger, is primarily a form of care or concern that winnows and sorts the world for us, such that certain entities come to the foreground in our intelligible discourse. This is not, so Heidegger hopes, the only possible revealing, but it is the way he believes things are sorted for us modern Westerners. Heidegger is not wondering about the consequences of our modern technological devices, but the stance toward, or take on, Being that leads us to fill our world with such things.

If, indeed, the essence of technology is our stance, i.e., the background that sorts being into a world for us, then the demand for self-scrutiny and authenticity as conditions for distinctively human freedom and rationality would require us to take up the question concerning technology. What does the essence of technology say about what we are, at least implicitly? If the essence of technology is our way of revealing the world, does it actually fit with what we explicitly claim to care about? For Heidegger, there are high stakes riding on how we answer these questions, because technology as a stance has a particularly blinding effect:

> Everywhere we remain unfree and chained to technology, whether we passionately affirm or deny it. But we are delivered over to it as something neutral; for this conception of it, to which we particularly like to do homage, makes us utterly blind to the essence of technology.[9]

There is something about the technological stance that makes it difficult for us to see that we have a technological stance, and we are thereby particularly subject to the tragic inauthenticity I have cautioned against in the last two chapters. Technology as an attitude is, as Heidegger says, *the danger* because it occludes itself as a stance; it leaves us thinking that there is no other possible way to look at the world; a sort of oblivion to the questioning necessary for human-being.[10] It is a stance that undermines the questioning of stances, and thereby robs us of the possibility of authentic responsibility for our place in the logical space of reasons. The

8. Heidegger, "The Question Concerning Technology," 12.
9. Heidegger, "The Question Concerning Technology," 4.
10. Heidegger, "The Question Concerning Technology," 28.

hiddenness of the contingent nature of the technological stance (when we are in its grip) binds us, in an unreflective and subhuman way, to a single unquestioned take on things. For all we know, we are no better off than poor Oedipus, walking through the world in a sort of convenient oblivion. By seeing the truth of our stance, the essence of technology, Heidegger believes we can begin a process of liberation. Freedom and truth stand in "the closest and most intimate kinship."[11] The willingness to face such possibly unflattering truths about ourselves and our self-constituting stances toward the world (which in this case is that technology is a destiny for us moderns) is, as I have argued throughout the foregoing, part of what marks us as participants in *Geist*, as opposed to brutes or machines.

As such, I am going to raise the "question concerning technology" in the spirit in which Heidegger does so, but I will not primarily do so in conversation with Heidegger's text by that name. Certainly, "existentialist critique of modern technology" invokes Heidegger's "Question Concerning Technology," and I am going to proceed differently not due to any dissatisfaction with that seminal work. Indeed, my admiration for and reliance on that text (and other later works by Heidegger treating this issue) will be apparent at critical junctures in what follows.[12] In this chapter, however, I plan to discuss a lesser-known work fitting that description. I do this in part because Heidegger's essay is already the object of a great deal of insightful commentary, and there are also other sources emphasizing other aspects of the problem that we do well to attend to.[13] In particular, I have in mind Keiji Nishitani, who was a leading member of Japan's Kyoto School, where he long held a chair for philosophy and religion.[14] He was both a Zen master and one of the most insightful Japanese interpreters of Western philosophy and theology in the last century. Not surprisingly, given his Zen background, Nishitani was particularly important in the Japanese reception of Christian variations on mysticism

11. Heidegger, "The Question Concerning Technology," 25.

12. The reader new to Heidegger's later thought may find the first two lectures of *What Is Called Thinking?* (3–27) among his most concise and lucid statements of his critique of technology.

13. Richard Rojcewicz's *The Gods and Technology* has done much to teach me about Heidegger's critique of technology in ways that overlap with many of the lines of thought I have pursued in this book. See also Zimmerman, *Heidegger's Confrontation with Modernity*.

14. Nishitani's principal work engaging Western though is *Self-Overcoming Nihilism*.

and existentialism; his writings are full of discussions of both Eckhart and Kierkegaard, along with the usual list of nineteenth- and twentieth-century European philosophical luminaries. There is also a clear affinity between Heidegger's and Nishitani's work, and Nishitani actually studied briefly with Heidegger in the 1930s. Though he is certainly influenced by Heidegger in the broad structure of his existentialist phenomenology, as far as I am able to tell, Nishitani's critique of our technological way of being is largely independent of Heidegger's, and we should take him as an original thinker in his own right on this issue. I am going to frame our discussion in terms of Nishitani's critique of the modern technological attitude, both for its intrinsic merits, and because it dovetails with insights found in the Aristotelian-Thomistic tradition that I plan to bring to bear in our consideration of the essence of technology, which will help us to remember what our technological stance occludes.

1. The Happy Paradox of Technology

In a major essay, "Nihility and Sunyata," Nishitani develops a conception of technology as a mark of human distinction.[15] Indeed, Nishitani makes the case that *mechanical technology* is both the most striking expression of human dignity and the high point in the evolution of the universe itself. Technology is then not the sum total of our contrivances, but an expression of human distinctiveness, and we should see here already resonances with the externalist/extended-mind account I have been developing throughout this book. Nishitani begins by accepting at face value a basic modern understanding of the universe as governed by mathematically expressible physical laws describing patterns of blind efficient causality. That is, the laws of nature, considered in themselves, are purely descriptive principles determining how things at the most fundamental physical level just so happen to operate inexorably in the universe we just so happen to have on hand. Nature, considered in terms of its most basic physical constituents, is non-teleological in its primordial state; it serves no good or purpose as it initially shows up. The laws of nature in themselves "are what they are" so to speak. Considered in this way, the universe runs entirely on indifferent "push from behind," without any "pull" toward a good or ultimate meaning.

15. Nishitani, "Nihility and Sunyata."

We should not, however, be too quick to write the universe off as meaningless on Nishitani's philosophy of nature. Even though the laws governing the physical universe are non-teleological, they are *mathematically specifiable*. Thus, while this basic structure of things as it initially appears on the scene, as it were, is a meaningless *nihility* (to use Nishitani's own phrase), going nowhere ultimately, it is nevertheless *rational* in some broad sense since it can be captured by mathematical reason. That is, the laws of nature are rational inasmuch as they are intelligible in the sense that they can be understood or made explicit. Though in and of itself, the universe is not going anywhere, it is a sensible place because it is subject to scientific explanation, and therefore it has an *implicit* rationality or meaning from its very beginning. In Aristotelian terms, we might say that the physical world on its own is unintelligible, though it has an essential, though originally unrealized, potency for intelligibility.[16] The problem, however, is that at the elemental level, there is nothing to whom the universe can make sense, nobody to make the implicit rationality of the universe explicit in thought. The laws of nature govern the basic physical constituents of the universe without any expression or apprehension of their rational character. That is all well good, but an intrinsically rational universe composed entirely of nonliving things would be truncated and pathetic—an eternally undisplayed masterpiece.

That sorry state of affairs is, happily, not to be found in our universe, as Nishitani points out that in the activities of living things there is "a kind of *appropriation* of the laws of nature. It is a kind of *apprehension* prior to apprehension proper, an apprehension to which the ambiguous term 'instinct' is usually applied."[17] The living organism does not merely follow the laws of nature in the way of an iron ball hurtling inexorably to the center mass of the earth. That is not to say that protozoa exercise some sort of free will or abstract understanding while they gobble micronutrients. The point is that the living thing exploits or uses the laws of nature for its good, and it does so by conforming itself to those laws of nature.[18] Through the evolutionary process organisms appropriate their

16. Of course, this is not to say that Aristotle believes there is an original, uncognized state of nature in which material being was only potentially intelligible.

17. Nishitani, "Nihility and Sunyata," 80.

18. Hans Jonas, however, plausibly argues that even at these very basic levels, we should understand organisms as expressing a "needful freedom," i.e., their metabolic processes liberate them from their particular set of material constituents, while saddling them with the burden of a continuous search for nutritive replacements. See

nature to the laws of nature to serve their good. In a way, then, the laws of nature are reflected in the evolutionarily conditioned natures of living things. Organisms are living conformities to physical laws.

In this light, consider this following highly characteristic passage from Thomas Aquinas:

> *True* expresses the correspondence of being to the knowing power, for all knowing is produced by an assimilation of the knower to the thing known, so that assimilation is said to be the cause of knowledge. Similarly, the sense of sight knows color by being informed with the species of color.
>
> The first reference of being to the intellect, therefore, consists in its agreement with the intellect. This agreement is called "the conformity of thing and intellect." In this conformity is fulfilled the formal constituent of the true, and this is what *the true* adds to being, namely, the conformity or equation of thing and intellect.[19]

On Aquinas's account, "truth," in its paradigmatic meaning, denotes a conformity or assimilation of a thing with an intellect. Literally, for Aquinas, the form or principle of the object of knowledge comes to be, in some sense, in the subject of knowledge (the knower and the known bear a *formal identity*), and the occurrence of this relation is truth.[20] In the case of a finite creature, the cause of this assimilation runs from the object to the subject of knowledge (finite intellects have truths to the degree that their thinking is caused to conform to the things), but in the case of the divine intellect, the causal relation moves in the other direction (things are true to the degree they conform to God's mind).[21] Again, knowledge is then the occurrence of such a conformity relation between things and intellect; it is the coming to be of truth in a mind.[22]

Consider Nishitani's account thus far in light of these insights from Aquinas. In the very being of the protozoa (along with everything else in the biosphere) there is then an *implicit* knowing or apprehension of

Hans Jonas, "To Move and to Feel: On the Animal Soul."

19. Aquinas, *Truth*, Q.1, A.1 (6).

20. An interesting question for another inquiry is to ask whether for Aquinas it makes any sense to say this conformity, which for him is a kind of identity, occurs "inside the head."

21. Aquinas, *Truth*, Q.1, A.2 (9–12)

22. Though, once again, one wonders how we should take the "in" as opposed to "outside" regarding the mind in this account of knowledge.

the basic principles of the universe. Though the non-intellectual animal cannot make this conformity between itself and the rational principles of the universe explicit, the living thing in its very being is a conformity to nature, a quasi-apprehension of nature in its essence. As I said earlier, there are reasons for Bob the chameleon's doings, but they are always merely implicit in his activities. Bob's dispositions for action, however, are a proto-knowledge, or a kind of *sense-making*.[23] Thus, with the emergence of living things, and their practical appropriation of the laws of nature, the intrinsic rational nature of the universe reaches a higher level of expression, i.e., it becomes *implicitly known* and its truth comes closer to being *revealed*. The universe comes closer to making sense, as there is an order of being to which it can make sense, even if only implicitly. As Nishitani puts it:

> these controlling laws become manifest in living organisms as something lived and acted out in a sort of "instinctive appropriation." The laws of nature only appear when these organisms live and act, and thereby embody and appropriate those laws. Instinctive behavior is the law of nature become manifest.[24]

Once again, to invoke scholastic terminology, we might say along with Nishitani that organisms represent an increased perfection of the universe, because, as implicit apprehensions of nature, they have a more perfect (explicit) participation in the rational principles governing the universe than do non-living things. With the beginning of life, the universe starts to *make sense* in a way that it previously did so only potentially.

Notice, however, that the arrival of life brings not only quasi-apprehension, but also *meaning*, because the expression of laws of nature in instinctual behavior:

> displays a purposive or teleological character. The rational order of existence comes to assume a teleological character on the field wherein living organisms come into being and instinct becomes active. Physico-chemical laws are here synthesized in a teleological structure and become, so to speak, its raw material.[25]

---

23. For a discussion of the role both phenomenologists and some contemporary biologists see sense-making as central to all living beings, see Thompson, *Mind and Life*, 128–65. See also Cunningham, *Darwin's Pius Idea*, 131–77.

24. Nishitani, "Nihility and Sunyata," 80.

25. Nishitani, "Nihility and Sunyata," 80–81.

For Nishitani, the miracle of life is constituted not only by the implicit apprehension of the rational principles of the universe, but by the further fact that these rational principles are for the first time put to the service of purposes benefiting living things. Organisms, by their ontological appropriation of the laws of nature, introduce value into the universe. The protozoa conform to the rational principles of the universe to obtain their good and avoid harm; even this simple life-form aims at something. Thus, the universe is not just the blind play of particles beholden to mathematical principles, but a place wherein a drama unfolds—the story of the flourishing or extinction of *proactive* beings based on the degree to which they can express the rational nature of the universe in their behavioral dispositions. Once again, this point is reminiscent of Aquinas as he paraphrases Aristotle: "Good expresses the correspondence of being to the appetitive power, for . . . the good 'is that which all desire.'"[26] With emergence of life, there is a conformity between the organism and the rational structure of the universe itself, for the sake of the benefit of the former. In other words, the organism is the locus of the universe's coming to be implicitly self-apprehensive and meaningful.

Merleau-Ponty also makes much the same point about the introduction of value and meaning that follows on the emergence of life: "Already the mere presence of a living being transforms the physical world, makes 'food' appear over here and a 'hiding place' over there, and gives to 'stimuli' a sense that they did not have."[27] The world has taken a *normative* turn: "Biological autonomy thus necessarily includes the bringing about of norms,"[28] and we might think of those norms as hybrid entities emerging from the interaction between the evolution of living beings and the laws of nature to which they conform. Those norms are not yet explicit, but they are operative in the natures of living creatures. The universe, however, comes to be in a novel way as the object of desire. Here too, Nishitani would agree that this is a higher participation and greater perfection of the universe. We can see that the physical universe itself rises to a higher plane (that of intelligibility, meaning, and normativity) toward which it was previously only implicitly disposed, once the first organisms come to be: "Living is a process of sense-making, of bringing forth of significance and value. In this way, the environment becomes a place

26. Aquinas, *Truth*, Q.1, A.1 (6).
27. Merleau-Ponty, *The Phenomenology of Perception*, 195.
28. Thompson, *Mind and Life*, 158.

of valence, of attraction and repulsion, approach or escape."[29] In other words, organisms bring the previously un-cognized and meaningless universe a step closer to being an explicitly intelligible and normatively rich world.

Human beings are appropriations of the rational principles of the universe in our very being as animals. Moreover, our animality constitutes a locus of meaning, value, and purpose in what would otherwise be a meaningless and blind world (or at least according to Nishitani). Though our metabolism, respiration, reproduction and the like are perfections of material reality, we are not special in this way. As much can be said of everything from the lowliest of single-cellular life forms all the way up to the most sophisticated of primates. True enough, but Nishitani argues that the rational and teleological character of the universe takes an even greater leap with the emergence of humanity, because of our uniquely technological way of being. By producing even the most basic tools and contrivances, human beings consciously appropriate the rational principles of the universe to specific practical ends.[30] We are not merely programmed by our biological history when we produce technological innovations, but apply our explicitly rational apprehension of the laws of nature to novel situations. As Nishitani puts it, "Unlike simple instinct, technology implies an intellectual apprehension of these laws of one sort or another. When pre-civilized man learned to make tools and use them . . . this skill contained in the embryo an understanding of the laws of nature *qua* laws."[31] Thus, with human technology, nature's rational character is not only expressed implicitly but *explicitly*. Human contrivance requires not *proto-apprehension*, but apprehension *simplicter*. Human beings have a power to stand back from their productive activity and ask "How can we do this better?" in a way that makes the underlining principles explicit objects of comprehension. That is, the laws of nature "become manifest as laws through the technology of man . . . unlike the case of instinct, the laws have become manifest in activity by being

29. Thompson, *Mind and Life*, 74.

30. This in not to say that human beings are the only tool-making animals. Rather there is something distinctive about human tool-making, namely the intentional appropriation of physical laws, which probably can be connected to our distinctive working memory. For an excellent introduction to these issues, see Rassano, *Supernatural Selection*.

31. Nishitani, "Nihility and Sunyata," 81.

refracted through knowledge."[32] In short, with human technology, the rational and teleological nature of the universe is no longer an implicit, instinctual appropriation, but a conscious and autonomous manifestation. In scholastic terms, we can say that there is a profound interplay between formal and final causality that comes into play with the advent of human technological innovation. The human being, through its distinctive rational powers, is able to grasp the forms of natural beings (which ground the laws of nature) and exploit this knowledge so as to further his or her own pursuits of the ultimate good for its kind. Technology, because it is an intersection of formal and final causality, is an expression of distinctively human theoretical and practical reason. Technology expresses our distinctive nature as both knowers and doers. Technological beings like us reside in the space of reasons, as they make the normative structure of the world as they understand it explicit in the process of crafting their devices.

Technology, however, is not only an expression of our particular human perfections. Nishitani would say that the universe is itself perfected in human technological activity, because by such activity we "rationalize" the universe; as our technological innovations take hold of ever greater expanses, nature becomes an ever more explicit apprehension of a rational and purposive order. Since it results in relatively stable and self-operative entities, the highest form of this activity is the construction of *machines*. As Nishitani puts it:

> The rational character of existence exhibits a manifold perspective whose *teleological* character becomes increasingly more marked as it ascends the levels of being until it eventually comes to complete actualization in the machine, where the purposive activity of man functions in a purely mechanical manner. Here the rule of the laws of nature may be said to attain its final and deepest point.[33]

In other words, with the machine, the laws of nature become both fully explicit and completely meaningful, but that only happens through human practice presupposing an intellectual apprehension of the rational principles undergirding the universe.

Again, we can see a symmetry with Aquinas's views here. Aquinas thinks that human intellectual apprehension represents a perfection of

32. Nishitani, "Nihility and Sunyata," 81.
33. Nishitani, "Nihility and Sunyata," 82.

the physical universe, not merely because our technological implementa-
tion of that knowledge brings a sort of intentional order (though I doubt
he would deny that), but further due to the fact that things come to a sort
of perfection in our act of cognizing them:

> Nothing becomes conformed with itself, but conformity re-
> quires distinct terms. Consequently, the nature of truth is first
> found in the intellect when the intellect begins to possess some-
> thing proper to itself, not possessed by the thing outside the
> soul, yet corresponding to it, so that between the two—intellect
> and thing—a conformity may be found.[34]

In other words, for the intellect to conform to the thing (and thereby
enact the truth necessary for the knowledge relation), the intellect must
come to be in a way that is both distinct from and yet grounded in the
thing. On the one hand, something must come to be that is not the object
simply as it is without the intellect, otherwise there would be nothing
significant about knowledge. In such a case, knowledge would merely be
one more causal relation, which as we have discussed is insufficient to
ground the logical space of reasons; explanations in the space of reasons
come in terms of *reasons*, not causes. On the other hand, whatever it is
that comes to be in the intellect must somehow incorporate the thing,
otherwise the logical space of reasons will spin *frictionlessly* in triviality,
to borrow an apt phrase from John McDowell.[35] Aquinas splits this difference as follows:

> It is true that our mind receives knowledge from sensible things;
> nevertheless, the soul itself forms in itself a likeness of things,
> inasmuch as through the light of the agent intellect the forms
> abstracted from sensible things are made actually intelligible so
> that they may be received in the possible intellect.[36]

That is, objects in nature are only *potentially* intelligible, i.e., they are
singulars that can be brought under universal concepts, but once they
are apprehended actively by an intellect, they come to be in or for that

34. Aquinas, *Truth*, Q.1, A.3 (13).

35. McDowell has shown some sympathy to Aquinas's epistemology, even if he is
not willing to go all the way with its metaphysical implications. See McDowell, "Sellars's Thomism," 239–59, and *Perception as a Capacity for Knowledge*; O'Callaghan
"The Identity of the Knower and the Known," 1–30; and Kerr, "McDowell and Aquinas: Philosophical Concurrences." The original engagement of the Pittsburgh School
with Thomism is Sellars, "Being and Being Known," 41–59.

36. Aquinas, *Truth*, Q.10, A.6 (28).

intellect as *actually* intelligible, i.e., they are shown in their universality. For Aquinas, this too is a perfection of the physical universe. Through the distinctively human act of knowing (though the Angelic Doctor himself would certainly add the angels to this story) the world comes to be in a higher, more perfected way. In other words, in our knowing, i.e., in our *making explicit*, the rational structure of the universe moves from being merely implicit to being explicit. Our knowledge is an idealization of the world, and this distinctively human cognitive act is the background presupposition of our mechanical technology.

Nishitani sees something of a felicitous paradox in all this: "The higher we proceed up the chain of being, the deeper the reach of the rule of law; but at the same time, the more fully actualized the freedom of things that use those laws."[37] In other words, the greater living things are able to conform their activities to the laws of nature (to act as apprehensions of nature's laws), the greater they are likewise liberated from those very same laws of nature. By learning to understand, anticipate, and exploit the workings of nature and bringing their behaviors in line with these patterns, creatures are then able to live in ways that allow them to flourish far beyond what merely blind adherence to natural law would allow. Moreover, the machine is the high point of this happy irony: "It is only in human work that it is clearly seen that obedience to the laws directly implies freedom from their bondage. Nowhere is this more radically apparent than at the level where technology becomes mechanized."[38] Our technological contrivances are indeed ways of consciously and autonomously obeying the laws of nature (intentional conformity to a norm, not mere determination; a free participation), but it is these very techniques, especially our machines, that subsidize our pursuit of other ends that reach beyond anything anticipated by our participation in the laws of nature.

Aristotle famously observed that leisure (freedom from merely making a living) is a necessary condition for philosophy.[39] It is our machines that have provided us the time and space for lives of relative leisure, at least as compared to the lives of our less mechanical ancestors, and this "extra time" is what allows us to indulge truly humane, contemplative pursuits. Thus, mechanical technology is a conscious, explicitly

37. Nishitani, "Nihility and Sunyata," 82–83.
38. Nishitani, "Nihility and Sunyata," 83.
39. See Aristotle, *Metaphysics*, 3 (981b8–24).

intentional, obedience to nature, that at the same time opens for us a realm of being that transcends nature. Moreover, both our leisurely contemplations and our applied engineering stem from the same ability to grasp the nomological structure of nature. To return to Brandom's way of drawing the distinction, we are not merely *sentient animals* following nature to the satisfaction of our biologically based desires. Rather, we are *sapient animals* who use nature to liberate ourselves from nature by our explicit grasp of its normativity. Thus, the human technological way of being "is a rule over nature more far-reaching than the self-rule of nature itself. Hence, we see here in greatest clarity a relationship according to which subordination to the control of law directly implies liberation from it."[40]

2. The Unhappy Paradox of Technology

Mechanical technology then occasions what is most perfect and most distinctive in human nature: our conscious obedience to the laws of nature liberates us from the demands of mere survival for the sake of higher contemplative goods. Culture is expensive, and it is bought and paid for by the machine. Our technologies are what allow us to off-load our labors onto our environment (including some of our cognitive burdens) so that we can free ourselves for more distinctively humane endeavors. We should also note how mechanical technology expresses the curious "halfling" status of the human person. We are neither beast nor god; angel nor brute. We are natural beings, yet we are not *merely* natural beings because of our free participation in the normativity of nature. The technological and the contemplative are also both expressing of the distinctive, *Geist*-making power to make normativity explicit. I take it that this is why Nishitani finds technology so intriguing: the machine occasions our fullest transcendence through our deepest involvement with the mundane. Whatever its merits may be, there really is no more apt expression of the mysteriously embodied nature of humanity than our technological way of *being-in-the-world*. Remembering the extended-mind thesis, we can see that technology and human nature cannot be disentangled, and our most distinctive cognitive developments are intertwined with our mastery of techniques for enriching our surroundings informationally. The very evolution of the human organism is involved in a feedback loop

40. Nishitani, "Nihility and Sunyata," 84.

with our innovations in technology. Thus, "technology is the fruit of our nature. Every movement of our body and every sound of our voice is technological. Human nature . . . has displayed an originary technicity that we are free to adopt and even called on to develop."[41]

Technology, however, is not only our liberator from nature, but it ultimately threatens our re-enslavement to an even greater degree than that of our pre-mechanical ancestors; it is integral to human nature, while at the same time threatening to undermine it. In other words, there is also an infelicitous paradox of human technological being. With the introduction of machine technology on a grand scale "we must speak of the controller becoming the controlled."[42] As our interpretation of nature becomes ever more abstract and mechanical and our reliance on the resulting machine technology continues to expand to the point of saturating our lives:

> the laws of nature reassume control over man who controls the laws of nature. The situation is usually referred to as the tendency toward the mechanization of man, toward the loss of the human. Needless to say, it points to one of the basic features constituting the contemporary "crisis of culture."[43]

What is this mechanization of humanity of which Nishitani speaks? No doubt, once we have turned the corner toward a machine-based civilization, there is a sense in which our lives are not liberated for the sake of humane pursuits but ensnared by what is supposed to be our very source of autonomy. As much as saving us time, our machines dominate our time. This is certainly a common critique of technological society, and one that no doubt has much traction.[44] (How many times have I delayed the writing of this chapter in the service of software updates for my laptop?)

Fair enough, but Nishitani has something more profound in mind, and remember our concern is not the effects of particular technologies but grasping modern technology as a stance toward being. Consider the following remarks:

41. Esposito, *Persons and Things*, 118.
42. Nishitani, "Nihility and Sunyata," 84.
43. Nishitani, "Nihility and Sunyata," 85.
44. See Carey, *24/7*, for a discussion on how the machine world has dominated our time and distorted our sense of temporality.

there appears a mode of being wherein a man situates himself on the freedom of nihility and behaves as if he were using the laws of nature entirely from without. It is a mode of being of the subject that has adapted itself to a life of raw and impetuous desire, of naked vitality . . . the growing affirmation of a prereflective human mode of being that is totally non-rational and non-spiritual, the stance of the subject that locates itself on [a] nihility [that] pursues its own desires unreservedly.[45]

In other words, Nishitani fears that the success of our mechanical technology will return us to a state of unreflective instinct. Our machines have made us so accustomed to the satisfaction of our desires that we have now come to presume that our desires ought to be satisfied as a part of the natural course of things. It is the unsatisfied desire that has become the anomaly, at least in our mentality. There is no need to weigh desires against each other so as to decide which is most worthy of pursuit. Supplies for desire satisfaction are seemingly unlimited because our machines, to use Heidegger's apt phrase, have rendered nature a "standing reserve" for our consumption.[46] Thus, there is no need to reflect on the worthiness of any given desire, and our ability to engage in such ethical reflection is greatly diminished. Once "nature becomes a gigantic gasoline station," the notion of evaluating the worthiness of desire seems quite foreign to many of the denizens of technological society.[47] Sample and indulge freely, because our machines can always make more. Thus, with the rise of machine-based civilization there is an overwhelming tendency to think of the satisfaction of any desire as a self-justifying practical possibility. Once we come to expect that our desires can and will be sated in the ordinary run of things, there is then no expectation that one might need to live with unfulfilled desire (trivial or grave) as integral to the human condition, because our machines have promised us an unlimited stock for fulfillment. Moreover, where this unreflective indulgence of desire carries unwanted consequences, we have likewise grown to expect our machines to provide us with technological means of avoiding such fall out. Under the illusion of mechanical supremacy, we are apt to leave our distinctively human, practical rationality to atrophy. In other words, a complete dependence on machine technology absolves us of the responsibility for our reasons, and it grants us the illusion of a complete

45. Nishitani, "Nihility and Sunyata," 86.
46. Heidegger, "Question Concerning Technology," 17–19.
47. Heidegger, "Memorial Address," 50.

independence from other humans by fostering fantasies of infallibility and infinite satisfaction of our desires, i.e., it subverts the very notion of free agency. In the idiom I have introduced in these chapters, with the rise of the supremacy of the machine, we are threatened with the loss of our place in the logical space of reasons, our very status as participants in *Geist*, because the machine promises to absolve us of the need to accept ownership of the normativity of our sayings and doings. The machine absolves us of our involvement with and responsibility for the *Lebenswelt* in which our mindedness participates. In short, the ubiquity of the machine threatens to undermine our participation in the world and instead give us the impression that it is here for us as consumers. This leaves us with the Weberian question we raised at the onset: Consumption to what end?

The worry is not only that the unchecked machine will rob us of responsibility for ourselves, but that it may also undermine the pre-reflective conditions necessary for our rising to responsibility in the first place. In chapter 2 we discussed the emotional, cultural, and skillful preconditions for normative standing in the logical space of reasons. *Geist* emerges only in a pre-given world of attachment to particular persons, places, histories, and institutions, which ground us in the nitty-gritty skills of getting around in a world that we care about. Rationality, both practical and theoretical, whatever its transcendent possibilities, is framed by these emotional and cultural ties. Human access to the universal is always grounded in the particularities of bodily, cultural, and emotional life. As Merleau-Ponty argues, distinctively human behaviors (including our technological innovations and manipulations), "create significations that are transcendent in relation to anatomical structure and yet immanent to behaviors," but we "cannot do without this irrational power that creates and communicates significations."[48] In other words, if our technologies undermine or replace the formation of our pre-rational emotional attachments and practical wherewithal, our distinctively human status as rational beings, which is grounded in these living embodiments, will likewise erode as participants in *Geist*.

Mark Wrathall outlines the technological threat to the pre-rational conditions of human mindedness:

> But as Technology begins to increase the range of our activities, it by the same token undermines the nearness and farness of our world, thus undercutting our belonging to a place and,

---

48. Merleau-Ponty, *Phenomenology of Perception*, 195.

by the same token, the sense that anything genuinely matters. Thanks to technological devices like the internet, I, in fact, can act at the greatest possible distances. The subsequent extension of reach leads to a homogenization of objects, which need to be placed on call for exploitation in the widest imaginable set of contexts. The result we are driving toward is that no particular thing or location will matter at all to our ability to live our lives, because an indistinguishable alternative is readily available. The perfectly technological world will be one in which we can be completely indifferent to particular places, people, and things.[49]

To the degree that our technologies have begun to untether us from these pre-rational and worldly ties by absolving us from the necessity of developing bodily epistemic skills, replacing emotional attachment with the mere simulacrum of bonds (children raised by screens), and distracting us with generally ephemeral and superficial aesthetic experience, we should thereby expect that our standing as free and responsible participants in *Geist* will be undermined. Before we can justify our sayings and doings, we must first care about them in their particularities and the world in which they are embedded. The problem, however, is that our technological success has reached such a high degree that our sayings and doings are losing their embedding and embodiment in the world, and subsequently the grounds for our concern are slipping away.

It was our ability reflectively and rationally to appropriate nature to our human ends that marked the great human advance, but now there is a tendency to obscure this source of our dignity. Thus, Nishitani claims that our unreflective, *carte blanche* expectation of satisfaction is essentially to render *homo sapiens* to a sub-personal existence:

> man shows the counterdependency to forfeit his human nature and to mechanize it. At the extreme of the wholesale controls that the laws of nature exercise through human work, these laws come under the control of man as a subject in pursuit of desires, one who behaves as if he stood outside of all law and control. The emergence of the mechanization of human life and the transformation of man into a completely non-rational subject in pursuit of its desires are fundamentally bound up with one another.[50]

Hubert Dreyfus makes much the same point:

49. Wrathall, "Between the Earth and Sky," 75.
50. Nishitani, "Nihility and Sunyata," 87.

> People have begun to think of themselves as objects able to fit into the inflexible calculations of disembodied machines: machines for which the human form-of-life must be analyzed into meaningless facts, rather than a field of concern organized by sensory-motor skills. Our risk is not the advent of superintelligent computers, but of subintelligent human beings.[51]

Our mechanical control of nature, along with its associated illusion of supremacy, is what ultimately submerges us in a new sub-humanity; we are dominated by nature through our enslavement to our own desires and our mechanical power to satisfy them. Moreover, since we mostly experience nature as a standing-reserve, inasmuch as we can still think of ourselves as a part of nature, we will likewise take ourselves (at least in our bodily existence) as grist for our own desirous mill. We see ourselves as material to be plied for the satisfaction of our wants, just like any other non-rational being. As the sociologist M. A. Casey puts it, following the mechanization of life, the human individual finds himself "([l]iving in a social and cultural context marked by complexity, fragmentation, and dispersion that means that even as he exploits the limitlessness of possibilities the individual finds himself its victim."[52] Thus, humanity "is being dragged along by the machines" into a sort of self-consumption.[53]

Heidegger makes much the same point when he claims that once we have entered the machine age and man sees himself as primarily the "orderer of the standing-reserve, then he comes to the very brink of a precipitous fall; that is, he comes to the point where he himself will have to be taken as a 'standing reserve.'"[54] That is, humanity no longer finds a dignity in its self-binding to world-disclosing norms, but instead sees itself as just more fodder for manipulation and consumption. For Nishitani, this situation cannot but lead to a sort of mass nihilism: "the mechanization of man and his transformation into a subject in pursuit of desires . . . has opened up . . . a sense of the meaninglessness of the whole business."[55] The greatest danger threatening us, then, is not physical destruction at the hands of our own machines (though that too is a threat), but a slow slip toward a final obliviousness to our dignity, like a sublime landscape slowly becoming obscured as the sun sets. As our desires become

51. Dreyfus, *What Computers Still Can't Do*, 280.
52. Casey, *Meaninglessness*, 3.
53. Nishitani, "Nihility and Sunyata," 87.
54. Heidegger, "Question Concerning Technology," 27.
55. Nishitani, "Nihility and Sunyata," 88.

automatically satisfied, we will lose the impetus that forced us originally to distance ourselves from our desires. It was that critical distancing of ourselves from what we *happen to be*, that let us look to what *we ought to be*; and the achievement of that normative horizon is the dignity of being in the logical space of reasons. The self-consumptive consequence of our technologically driven consumptive attitude is not merely that we will increasingly become the literal grist for our mechanical mill (though that is a worry), but the fact that we will undermine the conditions of our self-conscious sense of ourselves as free and rational. That sense only came from our interaction with a world that refuses to be consumed.

Notice, that as a self-imposed twilight falls on humanity, so too will nature fade back into the meaningless obscurity that reigned before it was raised to a higher, ideal plane in our practical and theoretical achievements. As Nishitani and Aquinas both see it, it is the light of the distinctively human space of reasons that illuminates the natural world explicitly in its normative structure; our self-consciousness is the place where the perfection of nature can show up. Carl Jung makes much the same point:

> man is indispensable for the completion of creation; that, in fact, he himself is the second creator of the world, who alone has given to the world its objective existence—without which, unheard, unseen, silently eating, giving birth, dying, heads nodding through hundreds of millions of years, it would have gone on in the profoundest night of non-being down to its unknown end. Human consciousness created objective existence and meaning, and man found his indispensable place in the great process of being.[56]

With the emergence of distinctively human mindedness, nature becomes conscious of itself, i.e., the normative structure of its being is made self-reflectively explicit. Our *Geist* is a perfection or completion of nature (however fallible and incomplete). This is not a bold humanism or anthropocentrism that gives human consciousness a "status as an all-important, pampered dimension of the universe."[57] Nature is not here

56. Jung, *Memories, Dreams, Reflections*, 256. For a very helpful treatment of Jung on these issues, see Kastrup, *Decoding Jung's Metaphysics*.

57. Harman, "Plastic Surgery for the *Monadology*," 224. Harman is correct to levy this complaint against the humanistic and idealist pretensions ("overmining") of much philosophizing. We do typically overestimate the importance of *Geist* in the ontological structure of Being and the standing of the objects we encounter (the beings we

for us, either for our sake to consume or as merely an appearance we concoct. In fact, that humanist or idealist attitude is part of the delusion we are enticed into by our technological progress. Rather, the idea is that *we are here for the Being;* we provide the place it can show itself. Our task is not to make nature *be* by our cognitive invention nor *to grind it up* by our unbridled consumption, but to prepare a suitable theater and attentive audience for its virtuoso performance. The problem is that there is a paradox written into our being: our distinctively rational powers are given to undermine themselves as we become more advanced in their exercise. The irony obscures us from ourselves and thereby returns nature to its original obscurity. Thus, as we forget our own mindedness, nature's being will likewise dim with the loss of its reflecting pane. Once we displace ourselves from the space of reasons, the lights go out on the universe as we descend into sub-human oblivion. In Heidegger's words: "The world's night is spreading its darkness."[58]

---

encounter have the greater vote than we do in determining our world), and Harman's staunch rejection of reductive materialism ("undermining") and permission of vast hybrid objects is also akin to much of what I have argued in this book. I too want to defend the reality of the middle. That, however, does not preclude a novel vocation for *Geist* as that to which Being can show itself. Though I am compelled by much of Harman's overall reading and critique of Heidegger (see Harman, *Tool Being*) and I am not yet able to defend this point in depth, I fear it is one place where he short-changes Heidegger and misses an important philosophical point. For the view to the contrary, see Harman, *Object Oriented Ontology* and *The Quadruple Object*. These remarks are provisional, and my criticism may be too quick, as Harman does admit a privilege of human-mindedness with respect to the revelation of some objects, e.g., he denies that there can be art without humans, and he argues that aesthetic (primarily theatrical) notions should be explored as providing a better understanding of our access to objects than use or knowledge (see Harman, *Art and Objects*). The latter claim is at least *prima facie* resonant with the case I am making now. I am planning further inquiry into Object Oriented Ontology, which I believe holds great promise as an ontological counterpart, though maybe with some substantial revision, to the philosophy of mind I have developed in this book.

58. Heidegger, "What Are Poets For?," 89. The senses in which the world is darkened by the loss of the relation of *Geist* to nature are quite different between Heidegger on the one side and Nishitani and Aquinas on the other. To the latter, the world is perfected by its being rendered actually (as opposed to merely potentially) intelligible by the activity of the intellect, whereas for the former we simply occasion a space in which Being can reveal itself. Heidegger would say that *Dasein* illuminates the world or nature because of its truth-bearing relationship to being, but he does not mean this as a correspondence, conformity, or exemplification. Rather, for Heidegger, *Dasein* bears truth by being a place (a "*da*" or "there") where Being can show or disclose itself. *Geist* (definitely not Heidegger's word) illuminates the world by providing a dwelling place where it can show itself, as opposed to capturing it in some sort of conceptual grasp

3. Nietzsche and Techno-Nihilism

Not everyone will see the dimming of the light cast by our *Geist* as an unwelcome consequence. Carrying the torch that illuminates nature may well be our greatest glory, but it is likewise our most dire burden. Might there not be something to gain from being relieved of this responsibility, and all the anxieties and occasions for tragedy I have dwelled on above? If the sense of dignity that came with our supposed status as the light of nature was a sham because there really is no distinctive space of reasons that we occupy, it would then seem that the very mandate for authenticity would require us to move beyond this fiction. We thereby free ourselves from a ponderous weight, while at the same time achieving spiritual maturity, an honest and calm nihilism. If the technologization of humanity promises this two-fold liberation, we ought not resist the mechanical demise of *Geist*. Indeed, we should do all we can to speed along the final technological overcoming of the illusion of a distinctive human nature.

Friedrich Nietzsche is well-known for his diagnosis of humanity as suffering from an "ascetic ideal," which did us the great service of providing meaning for our inevitable suffering, while also causing acute pains and maladies of its own. For Nietzsche, humanity is a "*diseased* animal: but suffering was not his problem, rather the answer was missing to the scream of his question: '*to what end* suffering?'"[59] Human beings inevitably suffer, just like every other animal. There is no physical difference between us and all living things regarding the hard facts of finite existence: we face mortality, inevitable decline, all order of injury and disease (plaguing both mind and body), etc., whatever our merits and efforts. Our lot, however, is worse than all other animals, because we are plagued to question *why* we should suffer. Not only do we suffer, but we know we suffer, we reflect on our suffering, and we demand some account for this seemingly absurd arrangement. Our self-conscious suffering is problematic, but that is not the whole of the difficulty for Nietzsche. Indeed, he claims that humanity is "the bravest animal" who even "wants" suffering and "seeks it out provided one shows him a

---

or snare. In fact, Heidegger sees something like the understanding of truth we find in the Aristotelian-Thomistic tradition as one of the originary germs that eventually grows into the modern technological attitude. For a classic and extensive treatment of the uneasy relationship between Heidegger and Aquinas, see Caputo, *Heidegger and Aquinas*

59. Nietzsche, *On the Genealogy of Morality*, 117. Author's emphasis.

meaning for it."[60] Humans, more than any other animal, willingly endure pain and even personal extinction, if we can see some point to it. When we believe suffering serves some good reason, we will consciously decide to endure it. The original human problem is then not the *fact* of suffering, nor just our awareness of our suffering, but the absence of any available reason justifying our suffering. As Nietzsche puts it, "the meaningless of suffering, not the suffering itself, was the curse thus far stretched out over humanity."[61]

The "ascetic ideal" is a reinterpretation of our situation providing us the illusion that our suffering does serve some ultimate end, i.e., there are reasons to be given for our suffering:

> *and the ascetic ideal offered a meaning. . . . The interpretation—*
> there is no doubt—brought new suffering with it, deeper, more
> inward, more poisonous, gnawing more at life: it brought all
> suffering under the perspective of *guilt. . . .* But in spite of all
> this—man was rescued by it, he had a *meaning*, he was hence-
> forth no longer like a leaf in the wind, a plaything of nonsense,
> "without sense," now he could *will* something—no matter for
> the moment in what direction, to what end, with what he willed:
> *the will itself was saved.*[62]

Humanity, while unable to stand the higher-order suffering of self-conscious awareness of meaningless first-order suffering, subconsciously concocted a dream world, and called it the real world. This illusion is purported to be inhabited by The True, The Good, and The Beautiful as ends that can justify our striving in this nightmare of the natural world. Morality and science (in the sense of *episteme* for the Greeks or *Wissenschaften* for the Germans) are the pursuits of this illusion of normativity, i.e., a projection of absolute standards in practical and theoretical matters by which we can measure ourselves. These projected standards, the space of reasons, imbue our lives with useful illusions of meaning or purpose, which would otherwise be wrought with unredeemable suffering. For the sake of these ideals, we can make some sense of our otherwise pointless striving, since we can interpret our sayings and doings as aimed to and justified by (even when they cost us terrible pains) these ends. Nietzsche does not deny that our projection of this dream world has made us great,

---

60. Friedrich Nietzsche, *On the Genealogy of Morality*, 117.

61. Friedrich Nietzsche, *On the Genealogy of Morality*, 117.

62. Friedrich Nietzsche, *On the Genealogy of Morality*, 117–18. Author's emphasis.

or greater than the diseased animals that we would otherwise have been. Indeed, the great achievements of civilization are paid for by the suffering humanity willingly shouldered for the sake of the ascetic ideal. The ascetic ideal is a lie, but a falsehood that did shut the door "to all suicidal nihilism."[63] All of this is to say that, for Nietzsche, the space of reasons is a useful fiction. There is only a space of causes, which we find so insufferable that we need to indulge the, albeit evolutionarily indispensable, fantasy of *Geist*.

The problem, however, is that the remedy is as bad as the ailment: we cannot measure up to these standards, and we are thereby bewildered apes wrought with self-loathing, haunted by puzzles forever beyond our meager cognitive pay grade.[64] As Nietzsche puts it, the ascetic ideal is finally "a will to nothingness, an aversion to life, a rebellion against the most fundamental presuppositions of life."[65] The attempt to redeem our suffering by holding ourselves to standards of justification is a fool's errand, because we can never live up to those ideals. These supposed justifications for human life have nothing to do with the real conditions of human existence; they are conjuring tricks, and not live possibilities. The reasons we give to justify our lives are not, argues Nietzsche, human reasons. Though the ascetic ideal moves us to see beyond the physical suffering of natural existence, it dooms us to ever greater pain in dealing with the sense of failure and guilt subsequent to our perennial failure to satisfy our illusions about what we ought to be. In fact, for Nietzsche, it is the pain caused by our invented sense of guilt that keeps the whole project moving. What I have been calling *Geist* is the commitment to living a life that can be rationally justified, and, for Nietzsche, that notion is an ingenious, though ultimately backfiring, attempt to concoct a dream of meaning for an otherwise pointless existence. There is no rational justification for life. Thus, Nietzsche sees the human lot as a tragic tension between two poles: on the one hand we are tormented by an awareness of the meaningless of our suffering, and on the other hand we are tormented by the frustrations that come from the fantasies that are supposed to

63. Nietzsche, *On the Genealogy of Morality*, 118.

64. For Nietzsche's all too often ignored application of his genealogy critique to science, broadly construed, and not just morality and religion, see Nietzsche, *On the Genealogy of Morality*, 108–15; *The Gay Science*, 144–86; and *The Birth of Tragedy*, 102–12.

65. Nietzsche, *On the Genealogy of Morals*, 118.

remedy this sense of futility. The cure is as bad as the malady it is supposed to relieve; we trade futility for anxious and torturous frustration.

Neither horn of the dilemma is palpable, but for Nietzsche this conundrum is an inevitable consequence of our *consciousness*: "In all becoming-conscious there is expressed a discomfiture of the organism; it has to try something new, nothing is sufficiently adapted for it, there is toil, tension, strain—all this constitutes becoming-conscious."[66] Nietzsche has in mind here all consciousness (even the simplest of awareness is fundamentally an irritation), but his main aim is self-consciousness or explicit/articulable consciousness. The former, on his view, only arises as a *post hoc* realization that the organism is somehow ill-fitted to its circumstances. Consciousness, for Nietzsche, is just a sense of nuisance, and self-consciousness is second-order reflection on such discomfiture. It is always a mere epiphenomenon that saddles its subjects with questions we cannot answer (Why must we suffer? What is Truth?) and causes unending anxiety. Consciousness is the least important part of us, but it causes the most pain.[67] In fact, for Nietzsche, what we have been taking as distinctively human consciousness (mindedness) is nothing more than a reflection of the gap between our aspirations (how we think things *ought* to be) and our real situation (how thing *actually* are). Consciousness for animals as intelligent as us inevitably carries with it a desire for a sort of normative participation, which can only lead us into torment, because we can never satisfy illusory norms. Nietzsche's solution is not to find a more solid ground for normativity (that show is over now that God is dead), but to overcome consciousness, at least in its distinctively human manifestation, *Geist*: "In the long run, it is not a question of man at all: he is to be overcome."[68] Our only way out of the human dilemma is to go, once again, beneath consciousness; move beyond the human by going under our all-too-human illusions raised by our self-consciousness.

Nietzsche calls the being who will move beyond (or below) the human predicament the *overman*, and he suggests how this next stage of evolution to a "higher form of being" might be played out:

> Once we possess that common economic management of the earth that will soon be inevitable, mankind will be able to find

66. Nietzsche, *The Will to Power*, 243.

67. See Nietzsche, *Will to Power*, 163–65, 238–39; *The Gay Science*, 297–33; and *Birth of Tragedy*, 76–86.

68. Nietzsche, *Will to Power*, 358. See also Nietzsche, *Thus Spoke Zarathustra*, 124–28.

its best meaning as a machine in the service of this economy—as a tremendous clockwork, composed of ever smaller, ever more subtly "adapted" gears; as an ever-growing superfluity of all dominating and commanding elements; as a whole of tremendous force, whose individual factors represent minimal forces, minimal values.[69]

The task is to make man as useful as possible and to approximate him, as far as possible, to an infallible machine: to this end he must be equipped with the virtues of the machine (—he must learn to experience states in which he works in a mechanically useful way as the supremely valuable states; hence it is necessary to spoil other states for him as much as possible, as highly dangerous and disreputable.)[70]

Nietzsche does not share Heidegger and Nishitani's horror at that reduction of humanity to a mechanized standing-reserved for production and consumption. In fact, the "transformation of mankind into a machine is a precondition, as a base on which he can construct his *higher form of being.*"[71] In other words, humanity needs a goal to avert the natural state of suicidal nihilism, and ours is to be the construction of a being that is not subject to crises of meaning, i.e., a machine. By becoming as machine-like as possible, or even raw materials for machine consumption, Nietzsche believes we (or at least the great being that arises through this process) can finally be free of both the unredeemable suffering of our cognizance of the meaninglessness of existence and the burden of *Geist* that is supposed to be its remedy.[72] Machines do not suffer, so they are not tempted to indulge fantasies that give *faux* justifications for their

69. Nietzsche, *Will to Power*, 464.

70. Nietzsche, *Will to Power*, 473–74.

71. Nietzsche, *Will to Power*, 464.

72. Given the tenuous status of the text as reflecting Nietzsche's fully honed views, any interpretation of Nietzsche centering on the *Will to Power* is itself tenuous; and, of course, Nietzsche says many different things about the overman in disparate places throughout his writings. The interpretation of Nietzsche as the ultimate technological thinker, however, is familiar territory, most famously as one of the main themes of Heidegger's post–*Being and Time* thought. Heidegger, "The Word of Nietzsche 'God is Dead'" and *Nietzsche Vol. IV*. The entire first part of Heidegger's *What Is Called Thinking?* is a very clear statement of his admiration for and ultimate departure from Nietzsche. Ernst Junger likewise found a philosophical inspiration for his vision of a mechanized humanity as the overman in Nietzsche's *Will to Power*. See Junger, *The Worker*. On the complicated relationship between Heidegger's and Junger's thinking about technology, see Zimmerman, *Heidegger's Confrontation with Modernity*, 46–93.

commitments to endure certain types of suffering. As Haugeland aptly puts it, machines don't give a damn, and Nietzsche takes giving-a-damn as the central human problem. As I suggested in the previous chapter, there is an anxiety that comes with not being a machine. We are not machines, primarily because we are concerned, and giving a damn about ourselves and our shared world comes at a cost in consternation. Nietzsche, at least as he expresses his vision in the passages I have cited immediately above, sees the mechanization of humanity at its own hands as the beginning of an evolutionary stage that will culminate in a being who is liberated from the burden of caring, who can operate with complete mechanical efficiency in an endless assertion of power; all of the domination of nature that came with human evolution without the pangs of conscience and worry associated with the ascetic ideal. By becoming cogs in a great machine, Nietzsche does not see a descent to the subhuman, but an ascent to the super-human; a being that transcends the demands of normativity. The machine is the unconstrained and unconscious expression of power, and beings that don't give a damn are beyond the bothers of good and evil, truth and falsity. The overman is then a fully mechanized humanity, *below* but *beyond* mindedness, that is prepared for the complete "technological transformation of the earth and human activity."[73] For Nietzsche, the overcoming of *Geist* by a transhumanist mechanization of humanity is not to be rued but welcomed as the resolution of the problem of suffering itself.[74]

4. Shall We "Go Gentle into That Good Night"?

Suppose Heidegger and Nishitani are correct, i.e., we are entering into a new dark age, because we have succumbed to the technological will to power. Should this be resisted? Nietzsche, as we have seen, seems to counsel a negative answer to that question. Our going under distinctively human *Geist* is ultimately our going over to an unconscious, superhuman being not burdened with the demands of life in the space of reasons; a being beyond the obligation to justify its sayings and doings (not giving a damn is to go beyond good and evil). There is much romantic bravado associated with these Nietzschean prescriptions; notions of being liberated

73. Heidegger, *What Is Called Thinking?*, 59.
74. For a stark vision of a post-human overcoming through a technological singularity, see Jorjani, *Prometheism*.

from illusions of meaning, morality, comforting superstition, and the
like, which have supposedly served sickly types to inoculate themselves
against the cold realities of existence while revenging themselves on their
natural and primordial superiors who originally flourished without these
lies. One might see something laudable in the courage to be finally done
with *Geist* and all its attending delusions. There is, however, a less flattering interpretation of all that.[75] One can see the techno-overman as a
fantasy concocted to justify a certain *cowardice*. Because the burden of
Geist is too much, the Nietzschean has simply abdicated responsibility
for herself and the world she inherits. The cost of life in the logical space
of reasons is anxiety; the worry that one has not measured up to her form
of life, the world, and herself. To participate in *Geist* is to live the examined life, but honest examination does not foreclose against any possible
results. Thus, denizens of the logical space of reasons demand justifications from themselves and their shared traditions, and thereby suffer the
worry that their reasons will be found wanting. Our willingness to go to
battle over our forms of life, most significantly to battle against ourselves
and our possible delusions, is why we can see *Geist* as a noble status that
places us in a realm above "merely natural creatures."[76] On this interpretation, the mechanization of humanity is to be resisted at all costs.

So which interpretation is correct? Which of these opposed ac-
cusations of cowardice is to be preferred? Well, the problem with *in-
terpretations* is that those sorts of questions are notoriously difficult to
sort out, but I do believe there is something to be said that favors the
anti-mechanization stance. At this point you have engaged in a discourse
with me that has played out over many dozen pages. We have exchanged
reasons. Maybe you have agreed with what I have argued, and maybe
you have refuted me at every step of the way. That is all well and good,
but either way you have spent a good bit of time thinking about thinking, and you are, like it or not, doing it right now. Maybe these exercises
in attempting to make our thinking explicit have given you comfort or
maybe they have caused discomfort. I welcome both consequences, and

75. For a recent and very influential packaging of the Nietzschean view (which I
am convinced is unfair to Nietzsche in some of his more insightful moments) wrapped
in masculinist fantasy, see Bronze Age Pervert, *Bronze Age Mindset*. In the rest of this
chapter, much of my effort is aimed to expose this sort of thinking as a self-referentially
incoherent and cowardly evasion of humane responsibility.

76. Brandom, *Reason in Philosophy*, 62. For an excellent discussion of the role of
risk and courage in the Hegelian account of self-conscious rationality, see Pippen,
Hegel on Self-Consciousness.

either way you have taken up the very practice that I have argued is one of the distinctive marks of human freedom and rationality, i.e., the ability to take a second-order critical stance regarding our sayings and doings. If you claim that such a distinctive type of rationality is a fantasy our ancestors conjured to absolve themselves of the meaninglessness of suffering, then I wonder what you would make of the time you spent in the discourse we shared in this book?[77] Have you not entered the space of reasons? Have you not asked me for justifications of what I have written (hopefully which I have provided)? Have you not put your own stances on these issues into question? I find it hard to believe that one could follow this (or any) philosophical discourse to this point while rejecting the normative status of the space of reasons.[78] Moreover, if you reject that there is such a normative stance, you have made a claim. Can you justify that claim? It seems almost inevitable that you will enter the arena of giving and taking reasons. It is far from clear that one can make *intelligible sense* of entering that arena when the issue is whether the space of giving and taking reasons is legitimate. It seems the only motive for taking-up philosophical discourse is a desire to take responsibility for one's sayings and doings. Thus, I claim, that your very act of taking seriously our conversation strongly suggests that you are committed to the normativity of your sayings and doings; you implicitly think of yourself as a participant in *Geist*. Roger Scruton puts it well:

> I know with certainty . . . that I can give and receive reasons for action, judgment, and belief. The question "why?" makes sense to me, and when asked of my own beliefs, intentions or acts I can respond with the same authority with which I know my own state of mind.[79]

---

77. Of course, there is a genetic fallacy in this vicinity too: one could grant that our practices of normative justification have their origin in non-normative, pragmatic fictions, and yet these practices could nevertheless be legitimately normative. In other words, Nietzsche's genealogical, just-so stories could be correct, though *Geist* has come to serve purposes that transcend its unflattering origins.

78. The status of arguments made based on such performative inconsistency is certainly controversial. Notice, however, that I am not claiming to have a proof, or even a particularly strong argument, but a way of motivating a certain interpretation of what we have been doing, a phenomenology of the exercise we have enacted throughout our conversation. For a discussion of these arguments, with particular relevance to how they bear on Nietzsche's position, see Armitage, *Heidegger and the Death of God*.

79. Scruton, *The Face of God*, 34.

The dignity and responsibility of *Geist* is inescapable. To raise the question of *Geist* is to answer it affirmatively, even if one has yet to recollect her status as a minded being in full explicitness.[80] Nietzsche himself conjectures that the origin of the "ascetic ideal" is humanity's primordial *demand for reasons* from the universe that causes us to suffer. To deny the legitimacy of that questioning, the wondering that puts us in the space of reasons, is itself to enter the space of reasons. Living things are *sense-making* beings, and we rational animals, one way or another, try to make explicit sense of things.

My hope is that this conversation has made that dignified status explicit. If that is the case, then there are good reasons to resist technological mechanization. We have a higher dignity than a machine. We have a distinctively free and rational way of being in the world, and, if Aquinas is correct in the remarks I highlighted above, our cultivation and exercise of those powers for thought and action are perfections of the natural order, a rising sun that lets a landscape show itself. It would be cowardice indeed to abdicate such a solemn responsibility for ourselves and the world. With this talk of resistance to mechanization, I do not want to suggest a Luddite nostalgia as a remedy for what I agree is the incipient nihilism of the technological age. Such suggestions are far from feasible and performatively inconsistent to the point of being laughable. Certainly, there really is no putting the genie back in the bottle, and attempts to turn the clock back also ignore what I take to be one of Nishitani's insights: technology, especially machine technology, is an expression of what is both transcendent in the human being and our connection with the rest of nature. Those of us in the Aristotelian tradition will want to put purely contemplative pursuits on a higher pedestal, but as we have discussed, those pursuits are only possibilities once we have used the machine to tame nature, and we do well to celebrate our technological participation in the laws of nature as an expression of our embodiment and spirituality. The plausibility of the extended-mind thesis leaves us unable to disentangle our mindedness from our technological manipulations of our environment.[81] Like it or not, technology is our way of being in the world. A nostalgic refusal of this fact is the height of inauthenticity.[82]

80. Hegel, *The Phenomenology of Spirit*, 36–37.

81. For a fascinating study of how cultural and technological development is illuminated by the extended-mind thesis, see Pasulka, *American Cosmic*.

82. Rather than thinking of "modern technology" as something qualitatively new, one does better to see it as an increase in the scale of human hybridization with the

Technology, in some sense, is our destiny or fate, and there is very little we can do about that in any practically significant sense. With respect to the technological aspect of our being, we then find ourselves in another of the ironies of our *geistig* being: we cannot but "affirm the unavoidable use of technological devices," and at the same time we must "deny them the right to dominate us, and so to warp, confuse, and lay waste our nature."[83] We need to proceed knowing both that technology is unavoidable for us and that it also holds the seeds of our undoing; it is a necessary rudiment of our mindedness, and yet it threatens to undermine our mindedness. For Heidegger, however, the admission of that ironic destiny may hold the paradoxical beginnings of our liberation: "As destining, the coming to presence of technology gives man entry into that which of himself, he can neither invent nor in any way make. For there is no such thing as a man who, solely of himself, is only man," and "the coming to presence of technology harbors in itself what we least suspect, the possible arising of the saving power."[84] This line of thought is among the most obscure we find in Heidegger, but I see it is as something of a reiteration of *The truth will set you free!*: "Such ambiguity points to the mystery of all revealing, i.e., to truth."[85] That is, the danger of technology is the hubristic illusion that nature exists for us, at our beck and call. To realize that we are trapped in the technological attitude that is not ours to change by an act of will is to renounce that very technological mindset. It is the admission that we must begin by taking the world as it is given to us, even if the form it currently takes for us is a disenchanted standing reserve. By admitting that we are destined to encounter being as revealed through our truncated technological attitudes, even when we realize that doing so causes us despair, is precisely to admit that we are not lords and masters of the world. Being, by abandoning us to our technological reductions and the subsequent nihilism they bring, has shown us that it is not ultimately ours to have on our own terms. The grim realization that technology is our destiny disabuses us of the fantasy that we dictate to the

---

environment. As Latour puts it, though while addressing a different issue, "Modern knowledge and power are different not in that they would escape at last the tyranny of the social, but in that they add many more hybrids in order to recompose the social link and extend its scale," (Latour, *We Have Never Been Modern*, 109). Latour's pointed criticism about overly moody Heideggerian critiques of modern technology is an important cautionary note to anyone following the path I have attempted to lay down in this chapter. See Latour, *We have Never Been Modern*, 65–67.

83. Heidegger, "The Memorial Address," 55.

84. Heidegger, "The Question Concerning Technology," 31 and 32.

85. Heidegger, "The Question Concerning Technology," 33.

world according to our own provisos and turns us toward a realization that we are always in a conversation with Being. If we thought we could liberate ourselves from technology, this cardinal lesson would be lost on us; everything would still be up to *our agency*. Our liberation from our technological destiny begins with the admission of the truth of our technological destiny and our helplessness to stave it off.[86]

Though we could all do with a bit less screen time, throwing out our devices is then obviously not the point. Rather, we need to accept the anxiety of our human condition. We need to come to peace with the fact that the injunction to "know thy self" will likely always leave us with some dissatisfaction, and there is no way out of that spiritual suffering however far we advance technologically. Rather than allowing our technologies to give us the illusion that we can conquer our wantonness, we need to affirm desire, discomfort, and anxiety as the necessary by-products of the distinctive human dignity. This acceptance of our homelessness assures that we will never be too comfortable. We will not abjure our vocation to put ourselves and our institutions to critical questions, and thereby always act as evidence to ourselves that we are not mere machines, and the world is not our submissive plaything. This reorientation toward accepting the discomfort of desire will, hopefully, put us in a position in which we can listen to whatever may speak to us anew. In fact, we should see this desirous restlessness as a gift: our wanting sense of homelessness is what moves us to ever-higher planes of dissatisfaction with the hope that at some point we will come to rest.[87] As the Psalmist prays:

> As the deer longs for flowing streams, so longs my soul for you, my God.
> My soul thirsts for God, for the living God.
> When shall I come and behold the face of God?
> My tears have been my food, day and night, while men say to me continually "Where is your God?"[88]

Does the Psalmist lament his yearning? Maybe not, for the tears his wanting causes him are also his very food! It is our anxiety and restlessness that show us our dignity, and that "is, quite simply, the price we pay for consciousness."[89]

86. See Heidegger, "The Memorial Address," 53–56.

87. The reader might fruitfully compare Heidegger's treatment of *pain* and *stillness* in "Language," 187–208, with Nietzsche's confrontation with these themes in *Thus Spoke Zarathustra*.

88. Psalm 42:1–3.

89. Scruton, *The Face of God*, 39. Scruton connects these considerations to Schopenhauer's notion of "Schuld des Dasein," i.e., the fault of existence.

Epilogue
Thinking about Eternal Thinking

They camped, since evening was coming on, beside the river of forgetfulness, whose water no vessel can hold. All of them had to drink a certain measure of this water. But those not saved by wisdom drank more than the measure. And as each of them drank, he forgot everything.

—PLATO, *REPUBLIC*[1]

For me, philosophy consists in giving another name to what has long been crystalized under the name of God.

—MAURICE MERLEAU-PONTY, "MAN AND ADVERSITY"[2]

I SEEMINGLY LEAVE YOU with the dignity of *Geist*, though wrought with occasions for self-scrutiny and likely ripe for subsequent revision, entailing all the troubles and anxieties therein. As I claimed earlier, *Geist*, as far as we know it, is a historical being, and therefore a moving target. Is there ever anything final, eternal, or transcendental in our thinking? Can we ever come to rest? Our thinking can make itself explicit, but I have conceded throughout the prior chapters that it is always seemingly tied to our bodily, worldly engagements, which do not appear to be on their way to a terminus, a point of rest. Does our thinking ever push away the ladder of becoming? Is there something immortal in us in virtue of our participation in mindedness? This whole drama of dignity and rationality,

1. Plato, *Republic*, 325–26.
2. Merleau-Ponty, "Man and Adversity," 240.

with all its ironies and anxieties, has the air of a Sisyphusian struggle: more dignified than the tragic oblivion of Oedipus, though no less absurd for its self-awareness of ultimate futility. Though the march of *Geist* may be a rich and meaningful journey, we are left to wonder, as the Greeks standardly posed these sorts of questions, whether we are forever on the way of becoming without ever reaching Being. It was Nietzsche's claim that settling for the former is the only non-delusional course open for a newly matured humanity awakened from the spell of a promised ultimate Being.[3] Even if I have shown in the last chapter that a sort of anxious hope for the latter is the only courageous and consistent stance (the space of reasons cannot be reasonably eschewed), we might despair rather than go in for an unreasonable hope. For all the dignity of Qoheleth's questioning, he nevertheless concludes that "For in much wisdom is much vexation and he who increases wisdom increases sorrow."[4]

Aristotle, though he is certainly not alone in this claim, argued that something existing in the fullest sense, *to be unconditionally* rather than just to be in the process of *becoming something*, would have to be a complete actuality (activity), devoid of further potency: "Activity, then, is the existence of the thing not in the way in which we say that it exists potentially."[5] Unconditional being, on this rendering, is to be in a sort of active rest, an engagement that is not going anywhere else. Worldly creatures are in constant activity, but most of our activities are on the way somewhere else (potentially where they are going, but not there yet), and they cease as they reach their terminus. Consider the act of shopping for a gallon of milk: the entire time one is engaged in such an action it is incomplete, and simultaneously with its completion it ceases. At no point is one in a state of unmixed activity in his or her shopping for a gallon of milk; the duration of the activity is a state of potency, and its fulfilment is also its cessation. There is a certain absurdity to incomplete activities: even though they might cause their ends, their completion is tantamount to their demise.

3. For a compelling suggestion of how one might philosophize in perpetual becoming without succumbing to the temptations of Nietzschean techno-nihilism, see Merleau-Ponty, "The Primacy of Perception," "Man and Adversity," and the innovative fourth chapter of *The Visible and the Invisible*. For commentary on these texts, see Sallis, *Phenomenology and the Return to the Beginnings*.

4. Ecclesiastes 1:18.

5. Aristotle, *Metaphysics*, 149 (1048a30).

Certain other activities, Aristotle notices, such as "what sees and or walks or is seen," are importantly different, as they can be "truly said to be unconditionally."[6] For example, while *seeing a painting* one is not actually on the way to something else inasmuch as she is in the *act of seeing*. The act of seeing the painting needs nothing more added to it to make it fully actual. Internal to the act of seeing is its end, *the seeing*. One does not need to cease *seeing* in order to *see*; the activity and the end of the activity are inextricable. The activity and the end of the activity are simultaneously present, so seeing a painting is not a potency for an end, but the actuality of its end. As Aristotle puts it, these cases are such that the end "belongs in" the activity, it "really *is* an action."[7] *Seeing* understood in this way is a completed activity whenever it occurs; it is not on its way, but *is* already there. Aristotle elaborates with some further examples: "at the same time one is . . . thinking [something] and has thought [it], is understanding [something] and has understood [it], whereas it is not the case that [at the same time] one is learning [something] and has learned [it], nor that one is being made healthy and has been made healthy."[8] Thus, maybe we can come to an engaged rest by pursing complete activities, among which Aristotle counts thinking.

Notice, however, that a creature could engage in all order of these complete activities and yet come to no actual rest or completion itself. A series of intrinsically complete, but nonetheless temporary, activities is itself no guarantee of Being. Aristotle adds one more example of a complete activity that seems to be intended to address this worry: "Someone who is living well, at the same time has lived well, and is happy and has been happy."[9] The point here is that a good life or a happy life is something that is present throughout the entire activity of living. Our life is not made good, according to Aristotle, by an end that is only actual at the cessation of our living.[10] The good life is an end in itself. A life can only be deemed good retrospectively (as we discussed in chapter 3), but, if that is how it turns out, it was a life well-lived throughout the entire process. In

6. Aristotle, *Metaphysics*, 149 (1048b12–13).

7. Aristotle, *Metaphysics*, 149 (1048b23). Author's emphasis.

8. Aristotle, *Metaphysics*, 149 (1048b21–23).

9. Aristotle, *Metaphysics*, 149–50 (1048b23–25).

10. Though he limits the terms "death" to human mortality (as opposed to the "demise" of any living thing), this is how I understand Heidegger's claim that death is our "uttermost possibility." See Heidegger, *Being and Time*, 296–311. See also Rojcewicz, *Heidegger, Plato, Philosophy, Death*, 53–82.

other words, all the while one is engaged in such a process of living well, one is also at its completion or fulfilment. We cannot know that such a life was a complete activity until it can be seen retrospectively, but a well-lived life will have been complete from its inception.

Of course, even creatures living good and happy lives do eventually come to their demise. My pet chameleon may exist through a process of magnificent tail growing, proud crest flaring, bold displays of colors, deft insect hunting, and rapturous acts of lizard reproduction, which together amount to the chameleon version of the good life, but even that completed activity is ultimately fleeting. We might say that the chameleon form of life is good in itself, aiming at nothing beyond itself because of its intrinsic worthiness, but, nevertheless, Bob the chameleon, despite his lizardly grandeur, will succumb to final becoming and go the way of his forefathers. Thus, even the grandest chameleon is still a mixed being, a tension between act and potency. Bob's completion is coincident with this death. His being immediately comes to nothing. Maybe we could say that chameleon-kind, the species, enjoys an eternal grandeur through its completeness in an endless process of generations of chameleons engaged in their distinctive activities. Though Aristotle thought something like that was the case, we can no longer take the eternity of the species seriously, and we therefore cannot see Bob's fulfilment in the infinite completeness of chameleon-kind. Chameleons, as individuals and a species, will all succumb to becoming in the end.

Is there a form of life that is itself complete and unmixed in this strictest sense? Interestingly, Aristotle sees the "primary god" as living a kind of life:

> And life too certainly belongs to him. For the activity of under-
> standing is life, and he is that activity; and his intrinsic activity
> is life that is best and eternal. We say, indeed, that the god is a
> living being who is eternal and best, so that living and continu-
> ous and everlasting eternity belong to the god, since this is the
> god.[11]

The primary god not only lives, by Aristotle's accounting, but possesses a life of understanding, a contemplative life. Aristotle arrives at this conclusion through a line of reasoning we should expect in light of the foregoing: the primary god's activity, because it exists unconditionally, must be a complete activity (its end is intrinsic to its performance); moreover,

11. Aristotle, *Metaphysics*, 206 (1072b25–29).

the object of this activity must itself be permanent and unvarying, or else some mixture with potency will infect the unconditional divine being; and the only activity that has this unmixed object is the contemplation of the ultimate normative or rational structure of universal being, what Aristotle calls *understanding*. Thus, the primary god's essential activity, indeed its only activity—its *form of life*—is the eternal making explicit of the normative structure of all possible judgments. Once again, this primary god cannot be mixed with potency of any sort, and if the object of its understanding were distinct from itself, Aristotle worries that the supposedly unconditional being would be moved to something else, i.e., the god's being would be incomplete. Thus, the object of the primary god's understanding can be nothing other than the primary god: "It is itself, therefore, that it understands, if indeed it is the most excellent thing, and the active understanding is active understanding of active understanding."[12] That is, *the primary god is thinking about thinking*, not in the sense that thinking is what it happens to be doing, but in the sense that is what the primary god *is*. In other words, the primary god, according to Aristotle, is an eternal, explicit act of thought about the normative grounds of all possible judgments, and the primary god must itself be those rational grounds of all possible judgments. The primary god is an act of rational self-consciousness, an eternal *Geist*. We might say that the form of life of the primary god is The Form of Life as such, i.e., it is the essentially complete way of being. Indeed, Plato seems to make just this association: "the god, and the Form of life itself, and anything else deathless, are never destroyed."[13]

We finite participants in *Geist* likewise think about thinking. We too make explicit the normative structures of judgment, and, just like the god's understanding, Aristotle claims that our active understanding "is separable, unaffectable, and unmixed" and "it alone is immortal and eternal," because in bringing things into their actual intelligibility our understanding participates in that divine nature.[14] In other words, inasmuch as we are thinking about thinking (making explicit the normative structures of judgment, which are the norms of the world) our activity is the same as the primary god's eternal act. Supposing we can make explicit the truly universal normative structure of being, then our making explicit of our

12. Aristotle, *Metaphysics*, 210–211 (1075a15–35).

13. Plato, *Phaedo*, 91 (106d).

14. Aristotle, *De Anima*, 55 (430b17–25).

reasons is a participation in the very life of divinity, The Form of Life. The space of reasons would then be the space of the eternal, the divine. Thus, Aristotle comes to see the contemplative life as the completion of our life, our coming to rest in being beyond becoming:

> But such a life would be more excellent than one in accord with the human element, since it is not insofar as he is a human being that someone will live a life like that but insofar as he has some divine element in him. . . . We should not, however, in accord with the makers of proverbs, "think human things, since you are human" or "think mortal things, since you are mortal" but, rather, we should as far as possible *immortalize*, and do everything to live in accord with the element in us that is most excellent. For even if it is small in bulk, in its power and esteem it far exceeds everything.[15]

Aristotle is the last to deny that our participation in *Geist* is a worldly and embodied involvement, which is always to some degree embedded and engaged with nature and culture. He nevertheless argues that animals like us can reach from those earthly foundations to achieve immortality inasmuch as our lives are guided by the fruits of contemplation, i.e., we live by, judge by, and ponder over the normative principles revealed by our *thinking about thinking*. Inasmuch as such contemplation is "the controlling and better element" in us, The Form of Life will be our form of life, and therein lies the possibility of Being beyond all becoming.[16] These speculations, no doubt, assume that there is an eternal thinking about thinking, and further that we can indeed contemplate the same ultimate normative structure as such a primary god. I make no claim to have done anything to motivate such heavy premises here, and for now I can only say, with Alasdair MacIntyre, "here natural theology begins."[17] Our self-understanding will not be settled until that project has come to fruition, and until such time we are at least left to wonder. Maybe, as Aristotle's teacher suggests, in the meantime our attempts to think about thinking will, however flawed by our finite perspective, occasion our recollection of an Eternal Understanding. Recollection, however, is beyond our control.

15. Aristotle, *Nicomachean Ethics*, 187 (1177a26–1178a1). My emphasis.
16. Aristotle, *Nicomachean Ethics*, 186 (1177a2).
17. MacIntyre, *Ethics in Conflict with Modernity*, 315.

Bibliography

Aeschylus. *Prometheus Bound.* Translated by Deborah H. Roberts. Indianapolis: Hackett, 2012.

Anscombe, Elizabeth. "Immortality of the Soul." In *Faith in a Hard Ground: Essays on Religion, Philosophy, and Ethics by Elizabeth Anscombe,* edited by Mary Geach and Luke Gormally, 69–83. Exeter, UK: Imprint Academic, 2008.

Aquinas, Thomas. *Truth.* Translated by Robert W. Mulligan. Chicago: Henry Regnery, 1952.

Aristotle. *De Anima.* Translated C. D. C. Reeve. Indianapolis: Hackett, 2017.

———. *Metaphysics.* Translated by C. D. C. Reeve. Indianapolis: Hackett, 2016.

———. *Nicomachean Ethics.* Translated by C. D. C. Reeve. Indianapolis: Hackett, 2014.

———. *Politics.* Translated by C .D .C. Reeve. Indianapolis: Hackett, 2017.

Armitage, Duane. *Heidegger and The Death of God: Between Plato and Nietzsche.* New York: Springer, 2017.

Beiner, Ronald. *Dangerous Minds: Heidegger, Nietzsche, and the Return of the Far Right.* Philadelphia: The University of Pennsylvania Press, 2018.

Benardete, Seth. *Sacred Transgressions: A Reading of Sophocles' Antigone.* South Bend, IN: St. Augustine's, 1999.

Bennett, Maxwell, and Peter Hacker. *Philosophical Foundations of Neuroscience.* Oxford: Blackwell, 2003.

Bouche, Bouche. *Reading Brandom: On a Spirit of Trust.* New York: Routledge, 2020.

Braine, David. *Person: Animal and Spirit.* Notre Dame, IN: University of Notre Dame Press, 1992.

Brandom, Robert. *Articulating Reasons.* Cambridge: Harvard University Press, 2001.

———. *Between Saying and Doing: Toward an Analytic Pragmatism.* New York: Oxford University Press, 2008.

———. *Heroism and Magnanimity: The Aquinas Lecture 2019.* Milwaukee: Marquette University Press, 2019.

———. *Making It Explicit: Reasoning, Representing, and Discursive Commitment.* Cambridge: Harvard University Press, 1994.

———. "Never Mind: Thinking of Subjectivity in the Dreyfus–McDowell Debate." In *Mind, Reason, and Being-In-the-World: The McDowell-Dreyfus Debate,* edited by Joseph K. Schear, 143–62. New York: Routledge, 2013.

———. "Reason, Genealogy, and the Hermeneutics of Magnanimity." University of Pittsburgh Web site, 2012. https://sites.pitt.edu/~rbrandom/Texts/Reason_Genealogy_and_the_Hermeneutics_of.pdf.

————. *Reason in Philosophy: Animating Ideas.* Cambridge: Harvard university Press, 2009.

————. *A Spirit of Trust: A Reading of Hegel's Phenomenology.* New York: Oxford University Press, 2019.

Braver, Lee. *Groundless Grounds: A Study of Wittgenstein and Heidegger.* Cambridge: MIT Press, 2014.

Bronze Age Pervert. *Bronze Age Mindset.* Independently published, 2018.

Cahill, Kevin M. *The Fate of Wonder: Wittgenstein's Critique of Metaphysics.* New York: Columbia University Press, 2011.

Caputo, John D. *Heidegger and Aquinas: An Essay Overcoming Metaphysics.* New York: Fordham University Press, 1982.

Carey, Jonathan. *24/7: Late Capitalism and the Ends of Sleep.* London: Verso, 2014.

Casey, M. A. *Meaninglessness: The Solutions of Nietzsche, Freud, and Rorty.* Lanham, MD: Lexington, 2002.

Catholic Biblical Association of Great Britain, ed. and trans. *The Holy Bible.* Revised Standard Version, Second Catholic Edition. San Francisco: Ignatius, 2006.

Chalmers, David. *Reality+: Virtual Worlds and the Problems of Philosophy.* New York: Oxford University Press, 2022

Clark, Andy. *Being There: Putting Brain, Body, and World Together.* Cambridge: Bradford, 1997.

Clark, Andy, and David Chalmers. "The Extended Mind." *Analysis* 58.1 (1998) 7–19.

Clark, Peter, and Bob Hales. *Reading Putnam.* Oxford: Blackwell, 1994.

Copeland, Jack. *Artificial Intelligence: A Philosophical* Introduction. Cambridge: Blackwell, 1993.

Crawford, Matthew. *The World Beyond Your Head: On Becoming an Individual in an Age of Distraction.* New York: Farrar, Straus, and Giroux, 2015.

Critchley, Simon. *Tragedy, The Greeks, and Us.* New York: Random House, 2020.

Critchley, Simon, and Reiner Schurmann. *On Heidegger's Being and Time.* Edited by Steven Levine. New York: Routledge, 2008.

Cunningham, Connor. *Darwin's Pius Idea: Why Ultra-Darwinists and Creationists Get it* Wrong. Grand Rapids: Eerdmans, 2010.

Darby, Ryan, et al. "Lesion Network Localization of Free Will." *Proceedings of the National Academy of Sciences* 115.42 (2018) 10792–10797.

Davidson, Donald. "Mental Events." In *Essays on Actions and Events,* 2nd ed., 207–24. New York: Oxford University Press, 2001.

Debord, Guy. *Society of Spectacle.* London: Rebel Press, 2002.

Dennett, Daniel C. "Consciousness in Human and Robot Minds" In *Cognition, Computation, and Consciousness,* edited by Ito, Yashushi Miyashita, and Edmund T. Rolls, 13–30. New York: Oxford University Press, 1997.

Dreyfus, Hubert. *Being-in-the-World: A Commentary on Heidegger's Being and Time, Division I.* Cambridge: MIT Press, 1991.

————. *What Computers Still Can't Do: A Critique of Artificial Reason.* Cambridge: MIT Press, 1992.

————. "Why Heideggarian AI Failed and How Fixing It Would Require Making It More Heideggarian." *Philosophical Psychology* 20.2 (2007) 247–68.

Dreyfus, Hubert, and Charles Taylor. *Retrieving Realism.* Cambridge: Harvard University Press, 2015.

Elliot, T. S. "Dry Salvages." In *Collected Poems 1909–1962*, 192–200. London: Faber and Faber, 2002.

Esposito, Robert. *Persons and Things*. London: Polity, 2015.

Ferguson, Michael, et al. "Fluid and Flexible Minds: Intelligence Reflects Synchrony in the Brain's Intrinsic Network Architecture." *Network Neuroscience* 1.2 (2017) 192–207.

Ferraris, Maurizio. "Total Mobilization." *The Monist* 97.2 (2014) 200–221.

Fischer, John Martin, and Mark Ravizza. *Responsibility and Control: A Theory of Moral Responsibility*. New York: Cambridge University Press, 1998.

Fletcher, Logan, and Peter Carruthers. "Metacognition and Reasoning." *Philosophical Transactions: Biological Sciences* 367. 1594 (2012) 1366–78.

Frankfurt, Harry. *On Bullshit*. Princeton: Princeton University Press, 2005.

Fukayama, Francis. *The End of History and the Last Man*. New York: Free Press, 2006.

———. *Identity: The Demand for Dignity and the Politics of Resentment*. New York: Farrar, Strauss, and Giroux, 2018.

Gabriel, Markus. *I Am Not a Brain*. Malden, MA: Polity, 2017.

———. *The Meaning of Thought*. Malden, MA: Polity, 2020.

———. *Neo-Existentialism*. Medford, MA: Polity, 2018.

———. *Why the World Does Not Exist*. Malden, MA: Polity, 2015.

Gallagher, Shaun, and Dan Zahavi. *The Phenomenological Mind*. 3rd ed. New York: Routledge, 2021.

Geach, Peter. *God and the Soul*. South Bend, IN: St. Augustine Press, 1969.

Gholipour, Bahar. "Does Free Will Exist? Science Can't Disprove It Yet . . . " *The Atlantic*, September 10 2019. https://www.theatlantic.com/health/archive/2019/09/free-will-bereitschaftspotential/597736/.

Gidon, Albert, et al. "Does Brain Activity Cause Consciousness: A Thought Experiment." *PLOS Biology* June 10, 2022. https://journals.plos.org/plosbiology/article?id=10.1371/journal.pbio.3001651.

Goff, Phillip. *Galileo's Error: Foundations for a New Science of Consciousness*. New York: Vintage, 2019.

Hacker, P. M. S. *Human Nature: The Categorical Framework*. New York: Wiley-Blackwell, 2010.

Harman, Graham. *Art and Objects*. Medford, MA: Polity, 2019.

———. *Heidegger Explained: From Phenomenon to Thing*. La Salle, IL: Open Court, 2007.

———. *Object Oriented Ontology: A New Theory of Everything*. London: Pelican, 2016.

———. "Plastic Surgery for the *Monadology*." *Cultural Studies Review* 17.1 (2011) 211–19.

———. *The Quadruple Object*. Winchester, UK: Zero, 2011.

———. *Tool Being: Heidegger and the Metaphysics of Objects*. La Salle, IL: Open Court, 2002.

Harris, Sam. *Free Will*. New York: Free Press, 2012.

Hasker, William. *The Emergent Self*. Ithaca, NY: Cornell University Press, 1998.

Haugeland, John. *Artificial Intelligence: The Very Idea*. Cambridge: MIT Press, 1993.

———. *Dasein Disclosed: John Haugeland's Heidegger*. Edited by Joseph Rouse. Cambridge: Harvard University Press, 2013.

———. *Having Thought: Essays in the Metaphysics of Mind*. Cambridge: Harvard University Press, 1998.

————. "What Is Mind Design?" In *Mind Design II: Philosophy, Psychology, and Artificial Intelligence*, edited by John Haugeland, 1–29. Cambridge: MIT Press, 1997.

Hedges, Chris. *Empire of Illusion: The End of Literacy and the Triumph of Spectacle*. New York: Nation, 2009.

Hegel, G. W. F. *The Phenomenology of Spirit*. Translated by A. V. Miller. New York: Oxford University Press, 1977.

Heidegger, Martin. *Being and Time*. Translated by John Macquarrie and Edward Robinson. New York: Harper Collins, 1962.

————. *Introduction to Metaphysics*. Translated G. Fried and R. Polt. New Haven: Yale University Press, 2000.

————. "Language." In *Poetry, Language, Thought*, translated by Albert Hofstadter, 187–208. New York: Harper & Row, 1971.

————. "The Memorial Address." In *Discourse on Thinking*, translated by J. Anderson and E. Freund, 43–57. New York: Harper, 1966.

————. *Nietzsche Vol. IV: Nihilism*. Translated by Frank A. Capuzzi. New York: Harper Collins, 1982.

————. "The Question Concerning Technology." In *The Question Concerning Technology and Other Essays*, translated by William Levitt, 3–35. New York: Harper, 1977.

————. "The Thing." In *Poetry, Language, Thought*, translated by Albert Hofstadter, 161–84. New York: Harper & Row, 1971.

————. "What Are Poets For?" In *Poetry, Language, Thought*, translated by A. Hobstadter, 87–140. New York: Harper, 1971.

————. *What Is Called Thinking?* Translated by Glenn Gray. New York: Harper, 1976.

————. "The Word of Nietzsche 'God is Dead.'" In *The Question Concerning Technology and Other Essays*, translated by William Levitt, 53–114. New York: Harper 1977.

Henry, Michele. *Barbarism*. Translated by Scott Davidson. London: Continuum, 2012.

Hobson, Peter. *The Cradle of Thought*. New York: Oxford University Press, 2004.

Holland, Nancy. *Heidegger and the Problem of Consciousness*. Bloomington: University of Indiana Press, 2018.

Husserl, Edmund. *The Crisis of European Sciences and Transcendental Phenomenology: An Introduction to Phenomenological Philosophy*. Translated by David Carr. Evanston, IL: Northwestern University Press, 1970.

————. *The Phenomenology of Time Consciousness*. Translated by James S. Churchill. Bloomington: University of Indiana Press, 1964.

Ito, Masao, et al., eds. *Cognition, Computation, and Consciousness*. New York: Oxford University Press, 1997.

Johnston, Mark. *Saving God*. Princeton: Princeton University Press, 2009.

————. *Surviving Death*. Princeton: Princeton University Press, 2010.

Jonas, Hans. "The Burden and the Blessing of Morality." In *Mortality and Morality: The Search for God after Auschwitz*, edited by Lawrence Vogel, 87–98. Evanston, IL: Northwestern University Press, 1996.

————. "Cybernetics and Purpose: A Critique." In *The Phenomenon of Life: Toward a Philosophical Biology*, 99–134. Evanston, IL: Northwestern University Press, 2001.

————. "To Move and to Feel: On the Animal Soul." In *The Phenomenon of Life: Toward a Philosophical Biology*, 99–107. Evanston, IL: Northwestern University Press, 2001.

Jorjani, Jason Reza. *Prometheism*. London: Arktos, 2020.

Jung, C. G. *Flying Saucers: A Modern Myth of Things Seen in the Sky*. Translated by R. F. C. Hull. Princeton: Princeton University Press, 1978.

———. *Memories, Dreams, Reflections*. Translated by Richard and Clara Winston. New York: Vintage, 1961.

Junger, *The Worker: Dominion and Form*. Translated by Bogdan Costea and Laurence Paul Hemming. Evanston, IL: Northwestern University Press, 2017.

Kalkavage, Peter. *The Logic of Desire: An Introduction to Hegel's Phenomenology of Spirit*. Philadelphia: Paul Dry, 2007.

Kant, Immanuel. *The Critique of Judgment*. Translated by Werner Pluhar. Indianapolis: Hackett, 1987.

———. *Critique of Pure Reason*. Translated by Werner Pluhar. Indianapolis: Hackett, 1996.

———. *Groundwork for the Metaphysics of Morals*. Translated by Lewis White Beck. New York: Bobbs-Merrell, 1969.

———. "What Is It to Orient Oneself in Thinking?" In *Religion within the Boundaries of Mere Reason: And Other Writings*, translated by Allen Wood and George di Giovanni, 3–14. Cambridge: Cambridge University Press, 2018.

Kastrup, Bernardo. *Decoding Jung's Metaphysics: The Archetypal Semantics of an Experiential Universe*. Winchester, UK: IFF, 2021.

Kerr, Gavin. "McDowell and Aquinas: Philosophical Concurrences." *The Thomist* 77.2 (2013) 261–97.

Kisiel, Theodor. "How Heidegger Resolved the Tension between Technological Globalization and Indigenous Localization: A Twenty-First Century Retrieval." In *Heidegger's Question of Being: Dasein, Truth, and History*, edited by Holger Zaborowski, 184–206. Washington, DC: The Catholic University of America Press, 2017.

Kojeve, Alexandre. *Introduction to the Reading of Hegel: Lectures on the Phenomenology of Spirit*. Translated by James S. Nichols. Ithaca: Cornell University Press, 1980.

Kording, Konrad, and Timothy Lillicrap. "What Does It Mean to Understand a Neural Network?" Cornell University, arXiv, July 15, 2019. https://arxiv.org/abs/1907.06374.

Kornhuber, Hans H., and Lüder Deecke. "Brain Potential Changes in Voluntary and Passive Movements in Humans: Readiness Potential and Reafferent Potentials." *European Journal of Physiology* 468.7 (2016) 1115–24.

Lakoff, George, and Mark Johnson. *Metaphors We Live By*. Chicago: University of Chicago Press, 1980.

Latour, Bruno. *We Have Never Been Modern*. Translated by Catherine Porter. Cambridge: Harvard University Press, 1993.

Lear, Jonathan. *Radical Hope: Ethics in the Face of Cultural Devastation*. Cambridge: Harvard University Press, 2006.

Libet, Benjamin. *Mind and Time*. Cambridge: Harvard University Press, 2004.

———. "Unconscious Cerebral Initiative and the Role of Conscious Will in Voluntary Action." *Behavior and Brain Science* 8 (1985) 529–66.

MacIntyre, Alasdair. *After Virtue: A Study in Moral Theory*. 2nd ed. South Bend: University of Notre Dame Press, 1984.

———. *Dependent Rational Animals: Why Humans Need the Virtues*. La Salle, IL: Open Court, 1996.

———. *Ethics in the Conflicts of Modernity: An Essay on Desire, Practical Reasoning, and Narrative.* Cambridge: Cambridge University Press, 2016.

———. "Hegel on Faces and Skulls." In vol. 1 of *The Tasks of Philosophy: Selected Essays,* 74–85. New York: Cambridge University Press, 2006.

———. *Three Rival Versions of Moral Inquiry: Encyclopedia, Genealogy, and Tradition.* Notre Dame, IN: University of Notre Dame Press, 1994.

Madden, James D. *Mind, Matter, and Nature: A Thomistic Proposal for the Philosophy of Mind.* Washington, DC: The Catholic University of America Press, 2013.

———. "Thomistic Theories of Intentionality and Physicalism." *American Catholic Philosophical Quarterly* 91.1 (2017) 1–28.

Maher, Chauncy. *The Pittsburg School of Philosophy: Sellars, McDowell, Brandom.* New York: Routledge, 2012.

Marcuse, Herbert. *One Dimension Man.* New York: Beacon, 1991.

Markham, Ian. *Truth and the Reality of God: An Essay in Natural Theology.* Edinburgh, UK: T. and T. Clark, 1998.

McDowell, John. "Avoiding the Myth of the Given." In *Having the World in View: Essays on Kant, Hegel, and Sellars,* 256–24. Cambridge: Harvard University Press, 2009.

———. *Mind and World.* Cambridge: Harvard University Press, 1994.

———. *Perception as a Capacity for Knowledge.* Milwaukee: Marquette University Press, 2011.

———. "Putnam on Meaning." *Philosophical Topics* (1992) 35–48.

———. "Sellars's Thomism." In *Having the World in View: Essays on Kant, Hegel, and Sellars,* 239–359. Cambridge: Harvard University Press, 1994.

McGinn, Colin. *The Problem of Consciousness.* Oxford: Blackwell, 1991.

McGrath, S. J. *Heidegger: A (Very) Critical Introduction.* Grand Rapids: Eerdmans, 2008.

Merleau-Ponty, Maurice. "Man and Adversity." In *The Merleau-Ponty Reader,* translated and edited by Ted Toadvine and Leonard Lawlor, 189–240. Evanston, IL: Northwestern University Press, 2007.

———. *Phenomenology of Perception.* Translated by Donald A. Landes. New York, Routledge, 2012.

———. "The Primacy of Perception." In *The Primacy of Perception and Other Essays on Phenomenological Psychology, the Philosophy of Art, History and Politics,* edited by James M. Edie, 12–42. Evanston, IL: Northwestern University Press, 1964.

———. *The Visible and the Invisible.* Translated by Alphonso Lingus. Evanston, IL: Northwestern University Press, 1968.

Millerman, Michael. *Beginning with Heidegger: Strauss, Rorty, Derrida, Dugin and the Philosophical Constitution of the Political.* London: Arktos, 2020.

Nagel, Thomas. *Mind and Cosmos: Why the Materialist Neo-Darwinian Conception of Nature Is Almost Certainly False.* New York: Oxford University Press, 2012.

Newman, John Henry. *An Essay on the Development of Christian Doctrine.* Notre Dame, IN: University of Notre Dame Press, 1988.

Nietzsche, Friedrich. *The Birth of Tragedy.* Translated by Francis Golffling. New York: Random House, 1956.

———. *The Gay Science.* Translated by Walter Kaufmann. New York: Random House, 1974.

———. *On the Genealogy of Morality.* Translated by Maudemariie Clark and Alan J. Swensen. Indianapolis: Hackett, 1998.

———. *Thus Spoke Zarathustra*. In *The Portable Nietzsche*, translated and edited by Walter Kaufmann, 103–439. New York: Penguin, 1954.

———. *The Will to Power*. Translated by Walter Kaufmann and R. J. Hollingdale. New York: Random House, 1967.

Nishitani, Keiji. "Nihility and Sunyata." In *Religion and Nothingness*, translated by Jan van Bragt, 77–118. Berkeley: University of California Press, 1982.

———. *Self-Overcoming Nihilism*. Translated by Graham Parks and Setsuko Aihara. New York: SUNY Press, 1990.

O'Callaghan, John. "The Identity of the Knower and the Known: Sellars's and McDowell's Thomisms." *Proceeding of the American Catholic Philosophical Association* 87 (2013) 1–30.

O'Hear, Anthony. *Beyond Evolution: Human Nature and the Limits of Evolutionary Explanation*. New York: Oxford University Press, 1997.

Pasulka, D. W. *American Cosmic: UFOs, Religion, Technology*. New York: Oxford University Press, 2019.

Pigliucci, Massimo. *Answers for Aristotle: How Science and Philosophy Can Lead Us to a More Meaningful Life*. New York: Basic, 2012.

Pippin, Robert. "Brandom on Hegel on Negation." In *Reading Brandom: On a Spirit of Trust*, edited by Gilles Bouche, 11–28. New York: Routledge, 2020.

———. *Hegel on Self-Consciousness: Desire and Death in the Phenomenology of Spirit*. Princeton: Princeton University Press, 2014.

———. *Hegel's Practical Philosophy: Rational Agency as Ethical Life*. New York: Cambridge University Press, 2008.

———. *Modernity as a Philosophical Problem*. 2nd ed. Malden, MA: Blackwell, 1999.

Plantinga, Alvin. *Where the Conflict Really Lies: Science, Religion, and Naturalism*. New York: Oxford University Press, 2011.

Plato. *Phaedo*. Translated by G. M. A. Grube. In *Plato: Complete Works*, edited by John Cooper, 49–100. Indianapolis: Hackett, 1987.

———. *Republic*. Translated by C. D. C. Reeve. Indianapolis: Hackett, 2004.

Putnam, Hilary. *The Many Faces of Realism*. La Salle, IL: Open Court, 1988.

———. "The Meaning of Meaning." In *Language, Mind, and Knowledge*, edited by K. Gunderson, 131–93. Minnesota Studies in the Philosophy of Science 7. Minneapolis: University of Minnesota Press, 1975.

———. *Reason, Truth, and History*. Cambridge: Cambridge University Press, 1982.

———. "Reply to Wright." In *Reading Putnam*, edited by Bob Hale and Peter Clark, 242–95. Oxford: Blackwell, 1994.

———. *The Threefold Cord: Mind, Body, and World*. New York: Columbia University Press, 1999.

Quine, W. V. O. *Word and Object*. Cambridge: MIT Press, 2013.

Rassano, Matthew J. *Supernatural Selection: How Religion Evolved*. New York: Oxford University Press, 2012.

Ricoeur, Paul. *What Makes Us Think: A Neuroscientist and a Philosopher Argue about Ethics, Human Nature, and the Brain*. Princeton: Princeton University Press, 2000.

Rojcewicz, Richard. *The Gods and Technology: A Reading of Heidegger*. Albany: SUNY Press, 2006.

———. *Heidegger, Plato, Philosophy, Death: An Atmosphere of Mortality*. Lanham, MD: Lexington, 2021.

Roskies, Adina L. "How Does Neuroscience Affect Our Conception of Volition?" *Annual Review of Neuroscience* 33 (2010) 109–30.

Rowlands, Mark. *The New Science of the Mind: From Extended Mind to Embodied Cognition*. Cambridge: MIT Press, 2010.

Rudde, Anthony. *Expressing the World: Skepticism, Wittgenstein, and Heidegger*. LaSalle, IL: Open Court, 2003.

———. "What It's Like and What's Really Wrong with Physicalism: A Wittgensteinian Perspective." *Journal of Consciousness Studies* 5.4 (1998) 454–63.

Ryle, Gilbert. *The Concept of Mind*. Chicago: The University of Chicago Press, 1949.

Sallis, John. *The Logos of the Sensible World: Merleau-Ponty's Phenomenological Philosophy*. Bloomington: Indiana University Press, 2019.

———. *Phenomenology and the Return to Beginnings*. Pittsburg: Duquesne University Press, 2003.

Schear, Joseph K., ed. *Mind, Reason, and Being-In-the-World: The McDowell-Dreyfus Debate*. New York: Routledge, 2013.

Scruton, Roger. *Art and Imagination: A Study of the Philosophy of Mind*. South Bend, IN: St. Augustine Press, 1998.

———. *The Face of God*. London: Bloomsbury, 2012.

———. *The Soul of the World*. Princeton: Princeton University Press, 2014.

Searle, John. *Intentionality: An Essay in the Philosophy of Mind*. Cambridge: Cambridge University Press, 1983.

———. *Mind: A Brief Introduction*. New York: Oxford University Press, 2005.

———. "Minds, Brains, and Programs." *Behavioral and Brain Sciences* 1 (1980) 417–24.

———. *Minds, Brains, and Science*. Cambridge: Harvard University Press, 1984.

———. *The Rediscovery of Mind*. Cambridge: MIT Press, 1992.

Sellars, Wilfrid. "Being and Being Known." In *Science, Perception, and Reality*, 41–59. Atascadero, CA: Ridgeview, 1991.

———. "Empiricism and the Philosophy of Mind." In *Science, Perception, and Reality*, 129–94. Atascadero, CA: Ridgeview, 1991.

———. "Philosophy and the Scientific Image of Man." In *Science, Perception, and Reality*, 7–43. Atascadero, CA: Ridgeview, 1991.

Senior, Carl, et al. "Organizational Cognitive Science." *Organization Science* 22.3 (2011) 804–15.

Smith, James K. A. *Who's Afraid of Relativism*. Grand Rapids: Baker Academic, 2014.

Soames, Scott. *Reference and Description: The Case Against Two-Dimensionalism*. Princeton: Princeton University Press, 2016.

Solzhenitzyn, Aleksandr. "We Have Ceased to See the Purpose." In *The Solzhenitzyn Reader: New and Essential Writings*, edited by E. Ericson and D. Mahoney, 591–601. Wilmington, DE: ISI, 2005.

Soon, C. S., M. Brass, H. J. Heinze, and J. D. Haynes. "Unconscious Determinants of Free Decisions in the Human Brain." *Nature Neuroscience* 11 (2008) 543–45.

Sophocles. *Oedipus Rex*. In *The Three Theban Plays: Antigone; Oedipus the King; Oedipus at Colonus*, translated by Robert Fagles, 155–52. New York: Penguin, 1982.

Strawson, Peter. *Individuals*. London: Routledge, 1956.

Swinburne, Richard. *The Evolution of Soul*. Rev. ed. New York: Oxford University Press, 1997.

———. *Mind, Brain, and Free Will*. New York: Oxford University Press, 2013.

Tartaglia, James. *Philosophy in a Technological World: Gods and Titans.* London, Bloomsbury Academic: 2020.

Taylor, Charles. "Brandom's Hegel." In *Reading Brandom: On a Spirit of Trust,* edited by Gilles Bouche, 198–207. New York: Routledge, 2020.

————. *The Ethics of Authenticity.* Cambridge: Harvard University Press, 2018.

————. *Hegel.* New York: Cambridge University Press, 1975.

————. *The Language Animal: The Full Shape of the Human Linguistic Capacity.* Cambridge: Harvard University Press, 2016.

Thompson, Evan. *Mind in Life: Biology, Phenomenology, and the Sciences of Mind.* Cambridge: Harvard University Press, 2007.

Tomasello, Michael. *A Natural History of Human Thinking.* Cambridge: Harvard University Press, 2014.

Tomasello, M., M. Carpenter, J. Call, T. Behne, and H. Moll. "Understanding and Sharing Intentions: The Origins of Cultural Cognition." *Behavioral and Brain Sciences* 28 675–35.

Turing, Alan. "Computer Machinery and Intelligence." In *Mind Design II: Philosophy, Psychology, and Artificial Intelligence,* edited by John Haugeland, 29–56. Cambridge: MIT Press, 1997.

Vallee, Jacques. *Messengers of Deception: UFO Contact and Cults.* Brisbane: Daily Grail, 2008.

van Ingwagen, Perer. *The Problem of Evil.* New York: Oxford University Press, 2008.

Verdi, John. *Fat Wednesday: Wittgenstein on Aspects.* Philadelphia: Paul Dry, 2010.

Von Hipple, William. *The Social Leap: The New Evolutionary Science of Who We Are, Where We Come From, and What Makes Us Happy.* New York: Harper Collins, 2018.

Weber, Max. "Science as Vocation." In *The Vocation Lectures,* edited by D. Owen and translated by R. Livingston, 1–32. Indianapolis: Hackett, 2004.

Wegner, Daniel. *The Illusion of Free Will.* Cambridge: MIT Press, 2002.

Wittgenstein, Ludwig. *The Blue and Brown Books: Preliminary Studies for the "Philosophical Investigations."* New York: Harper and Row, 1958.

————. *On Certainty.* Translated by D. Paul and G. E. M. Anscombe. New York: Harper & Row, 1969.

————. *Culture and Value.* Translated by Peter Winch. Oxford: Blackwell, 1998.

————. *Philosophical Investigations.* Translated by G. E. M. Anscombe, P. M. S. Hacker, and J. Schulte. Oxford: Blackwell, 2009.

————. *Tractatus Logico-Philosophicus.* Translated by C. K. Ogden. New York: Routledge, 1995.

————. *The Wittgenstein Reader.* 2nd ed. Edited by Anthony Kenny. Malden, MA: Blackwell, 2006.

————. *Zettle.* Translated by G. E. M. Anscombe and G. H. von Wright. Berkeley: University of California Press, 2007.

Wrathall, Mark. "Between the Earth and the Sky: Heidegger on Life after the Death of God." In *Religion after Metaphysics,* edited by Mark Wrathall, 69–87. Cambridge: Cambridge University press, 2004.

Wright, Crispin. "On Putnam's Proof that We Cannot Be Brains in a Vat." In *Reading Putnam,* edited by Bob Hale and Peter Clark, 216–41. Oxford: Blackwell, 1994.

Yang, Tianming, and Michael N. Shadlen. "Probabilistic Reasoning by Neurons." *Nature* 447 (2007) 1075–80.

Zaborowski, Holger, ed. *Heidegger's Question of Being: Dasein, Truth, and History.* Washington, DC: The Catholic University of American Press, 2017.

Zimbardo, Philip, et al. *Psychology: Core Concepts.* 7th ed. London: Pearson, 2016.

Zimmerman, Michael E. *Heidegger's Confrontation with Modernity: Technology, Politics, and Art.* Bloomington: University of Indiana Press, 1990.

Index

Aeschylus, 1
Anscombe, Elizabeth, 29, 42–43
anxiety, 115–16, 128, 155–56. *See also* authenticity
Aquinas, Thomas, 165, 167, 169–70, 178–80, 188
Aristotle, 12, 20, 44, 97, 102, 105–10, 115, 164, 167, 171, 192–96
attachment
 as condition for thinking, 74–80
authenticity, 16, 108, 149–56, 161, 180. *See also* anxiety

Brains in Vats Argument, 37–40. *See also* Simulation Hypothesis
Brandom, Robert, 11, 14, 16, 48, 52, 58–59, 61–63, 66–67, 70–71, 80, 103, 108, 113, 115–16, 121–22, 138–39, 145, 172, 186

Chalmers, David, 11, 55–56, 57
Chinese Room Objection, 139–42. *See also* "Turing test"
Clark, Andy, 11, 21, 54–58
community (see also "tradition/inheritance" and "attachment")
 as condition of thinking 62–63, 67–68, 72–75
concern
 as condition of human cognition, 71–80, 147–49
Crawford, Matthew, 55, 80

Critchley, Simon, 9, 113

Davidson, Donald, 48
Deboard, Guy, 6
Dennett, Daniel, 134
Dreyfus, Hubert, 9, 18, 58, 143–46, 148, 151, 176–77
dualism, 13, 43–47
 not entailed by arguments against materialism, 42–43
 cognitive dualism, 46–52
 dichotomy with materialism, 10, 84

emergence, 48, 57, 61. *See also* Scruton, Roger
emotion
 as underpinning of rational cognition, 74–80
 See also moods
ethical agency, 104–10. *See also* free will
evolutionary psychology, 116–24. *See also* genealogy
Extended Mind Hypothesis, 11–12, 55–57, 77, 155, 167, 172, 188

free will
 standard debate, 88–91
 neuroscientific challenge, 92–96
 tragic challenge, 110–14
 See also ethical agency
friendship, 104–5, 114–15. *See also* community
Fukayama, Francis, 86

Grabriel, Markus, 11, 45–46, 48–49, 68, 70–71, 142
Geach, Peter, 29
genealogy, 116–24. *See also* evolutionary psychology
Goff, Phillip, 96

Hacker, P. M. S., 29, 42, 90, 101
Harman, Graham, 9, 151, 178–79
Harris, Sam, 91
Haugeland, John, 9, 18–19, 80, 84, 125, 130, 137–38, 147–49, 151, 156, 185
Hegel, G. W. F., 11–14, 48–52, 54, 67, 69–71, 73, 79–80, 85–86, 101, 103, 113, 115, 122, 186, 188
Heidegger, Martin, 7–10, 12, 15, 19, 44, 51, 79, 80, 115, 144, 148, 151, 154, 160–63, 174, 177, 179–80, 184–85, 187, 189–90, 193
identity theory, 22–27. *See also* supervenience
Michele, Henry, 47
Husserl, Edmund, 47, 82, 144

idealism, 38, 65, 84
immortality, 191–96
inferentialism, 58–66. *See also* Brandom, Robert

Johnson, Mark, 42
Jonas, Hans, 78, 80, 147, 164–65
Jung, C. G., 53, 178
Junger, Ernst, 184

Kant, Immanuel, 11, 14, 46, 48, 66–67, 80, 118–22
Kastrup, Bernardo, 178
Kojeve, Alexandre, 86

Latour, Bruno, 128–44, 157, 189
Lear, Johnathan, 155
Libet, Benjamin, 16, 94–100, 103
lifeworld/*Lebenswelt*, 47, 54

MacIntyre, Alasdair, 5, 11, 16, 50–51, 62, 71–72, 101, 103, 109, 113–15, 196
Marcuse, Herbert, 6
material commitment
   as condition for thinking, 65–67
materialism, 13, 33, 51, 179
   dichotomy with dualism, 10, 84
   See also identity theories; supervenience
moods. *See* emotions
McDowell, John, 11, 14, 61–63, 66–69, 71, 80, 84, 170
McDowell-Dreyfus Debate, 80–84
Merleau-Ponty, Maurice, 15, 21, 40, 53, 77–83, 85–86, 144, 167, 175, 191–92

Nagel, Thomas, 33, 51
Nietzsche, Friedrich, 20, 51, 87, 108–9, 119–22, 180–86, 188
nihilism, 1–10, 172–80, 191–96
Nishitani, Keji, 19, 162–64, 166–69, 171–74, 176–79, 185
normativity
   as condition for thinking 59–63

Object Oriented Ontology, 178–79

Pasulka, Diana, 188
Pippin, Robert, 11, 186
Pittsburg School, 14, 59, 62–63, 80. *See also* Brandom; McDowell; Sellars
Plantinga, Alvin, 51
Plato, 121, 122, 191, 193, 195
practical skill
   as condition for thinking, 80–86, 143–47
   See also McDowell-Dreyfus Debate; relevance sorting
Putnam, Hilary, 11, 38, 48, 84

qualia, 15, 77–78
   as necessary for semantic content, 78–79
Quine, W. V. O, 137

Rossano, Matt, 72–73, 75, 120, 168
relevance sorting
    as condition for thinking,
        143–47
    See also McDowell-Dreyfus
        Debate; practical skill
Responsibility/Commitment
    as condition for cognition,
        58–67
    as condition for ethical agency,
        104–10
Ricoeur, Paul, 45, 83–84

Schopenhauer, Arthur, 102, 190
Scruton, Roger, 46–48, 77, 96, 187,
    190
Searle, John, 18, 37, 139, 140–42
Sellars, Wilfrid, 14, 46, 48, 59,
    61–64, 80, 170
Simulation Hypothesis, 37–40.
    See also Brains in Vats
        Arguments
social cognition, 74–25. See also
    Tomasello, Michael
Solzhenitzyn, Aleksandr, 6
Space of Reasons vs. Space of
    Causes, 58–67, 116–24
Strawson, Peter, 48
supervenience, 12, 26–29, 31–32,
    41–42
Swinburn, Richard, 26, 95

Taylor, Charles, 5, 11, 72–73, 80–83
Technology, 3–10, 157–90
    connected to nihilism, 3–10,
        172–80

connected to human nature and
    evolution, 11–12, 54–58,
    163–72 (see also extended
    mind)
connected to the evolution of
    the universe, 13–172
possibility of resisting its
    advance, 185–91
theory of mind, 74
thinking, 24–41
    not identical or supervenient on
        brain states, 27–41
    not "inside" a mind, 41–43
    in the world, 83–86
Thompson, Evan, 12, 39–40, 79–80,
    82–83
Tomasello, Michael, 63, 73–75
tradition/inheritance,
    as condition for human
        cognition, 67–71
    as condition for ethical agency,
        104–10
Tragedy, 110–24
transhumanism, 180–85
Turing, Alan, 137
Turning Test, 137–42

Vallee, Jacques, 158

Weber, Max, 4–6, 8
Wittgenstein, Ludwig, 1–13, 15,
    29–33, 36, 38, 40–45, 47, 54,
    67, 70–71, 73, 77, 92, 115,
    133, 159–60